Thomas Osmond Summers

Sermons by Southern Methodist preachers

Thomas Osmond Summers

Sermons by Southern Methodist preachers

ISBN/EAN: 9783744744836

Printed in Europe, USA, Canada, Australia, Japan

Cover: Foto ©Lupo / pixelio.de

More available books at **www.hansebooks.com**

SERMONS

BY

SOUTHERN METHODIST PREACHERS.

EDITED BY

T. O. SUMMERS, D.D., LL.D.

Nashville, Tenn.:
SOUTHERN METHODIST PUBLISHING HOUSE.
1881.

Entered, according to Act of Congress, in the year 1881,
BY THE BOOK AGENT OF THE PUBLISHING HOUSE OF THE M. E. CHURCH, SOUTH,
in the Office of the Librarian of Congress, at Washington.

PREFACE.

This volume originated with the Book Agent and Business Manager of the Publishing House. There is a demand for homiletic literature, and they wish to do their part to supply it. They have accordingly secured contributions from several of the bishops and other ministers, whose discourses will be read with pleasure and with profit.

The Editor has not taken the liberty of making them quadrate with his views, in the few instances in which, on non-essential points, there may be a divergence; but, bating a few unimportant corrections, the Sermons appear in the printed page as in the manuscripts of the respective writers.

There is considerable diversity of style and method, as well as of topics; but the Sermons are all good to the use of edifying.

If this volume meet with a favorable reception, it may soon be followed by another series of a similar character.

THE EDITOR.

Publishing House of the M. E. Church, South,
Nashville, Tenn., Dec. 23, 1880.

CONTENTS.

I.

THE WORLD IN THE CHURCH. By Bishop Pierce...................... 9

II.

THE FIRST AND THE LAST. By Bishop Wightman...................... 24

III.

JOY IN HEAVEN OVER PENITENT SINNERS. By the Rev. Edward Wadsworth, A.M., D.D., Alabama Conference................... 38

IV.

ALL FOR GOD. By the Rev. W. T. Bolling, Western Virginia Conference........................ 55

V.

INQUIRY AND INVITATION; OR, PHILIP'S PHILOSOPHY. By the Rev. J. B. McGehee, A.M., South Georgia Conference.... 72

VI.

THE THINGS PREPARED FOR THEM THAT LOVE GOD. By the Rev. Linus Parker, D.D., Louisiana Conference......................... 89

VII.

PURE RELIGION. By the Rev. H. Pearce Walker, D.D., Kentucky Conference 101

VIII.

THE SUPREME AIM OF LIFE. By the Rev. J. D. Blackwell, Virginia Conference 126

IX.

THE LAST ENEMY. By the Rev. W. T. Harris, Memphis Conference 153

X.

THE SPREAD OF THE GOSPEL. By the Rev. S. A. Steel, North Mississippi Conference 165

XI.

THE HINDERANCES OF THE GOSPEL. By the Rev. A. W. Mangum, D.D., North Carolina Conference 185

XII.

CHRISTIAN COMMUNISM. By the Rev. M. Callaway, A.M., D.D., North Georgia Conference 209

XIII.

THE INEQUALITIES OF LIFE, AS ILLUSTRATING THE WISDOM AND GOODNESS OF GOD. By the Rev. Whitefoord Smith, D.D., South Carolina Conference 234

XIV.

THE INTELLIGENCE OF FAITH. By the Rev. T. J. Dodd, D.D., Vanderbilt University.. 258

XV.

FAITH IN CHRIST. By Bishop Paine......... 277

XVI.

LESSONS FROM THE BAPTISM OF JESUS BY JOHN THE BAPTIST. By the Rev. H. C. Settle, D.D., Louisville Conference...... 304

XVII.

FUTURE REWARDS AND PUNISHMENTS. By Bishop Kavanaugh............................ 318

XVIII.

CHRIST AND HIS WORK. By the Rev. A. A. Lipscomb, D.D., LL.D., Vanderbilt University.. 340

XIX.

THE GREAT AWAKENING. By the Rev. O. P. Fitzgerald, D.D., Editor of the "Christian Advocate"....................................... 371

XX.

LIFE LOST AND FOUND. By the Rev. John C. Granbery, D.D., Vanderbilt University.. 384

THE REV. BISHOP GEORGE F. PIERCE, D.D.,
Of the Methodist Episcopal Church, South.

I.

THE WORLD IN THE CHURCH.

BY BISHOP PIERCE.

"Ye adulterers and adulteresses, know ye not that the friendship of the world is enmity with God? whosoever therefore will be a friend of the world is the enemy of God." James iv. 4.

The Epistle of James is general, addressed to the twelve tribes scattered throughout the world. Among them was great diversity of moral character and condition. There were stout, inveterate unbelievers, full of prejudice, and active in their hostility to the gospel of Christ. Some were true Christians, poor and persecuted, needing the consolation which the apostle administers. Others were merely nominal believers, united with the Church, but corrupting it by their hypocrisy and worldliness. These are specially characterized and condemned in the language of the text.

The Church has never been entirely pure. The gospel net, when thrown, gathers in the good and the bad. The time of separation is not yet; indeed, the work is divine. It belongs to God to discern between the righteous and the wicked. The ministry sow the seed, the good seed, the seed of the kingdom. In unguarded hours and in covert ways an enemy, the great adversary of God and man, scatters tares. "Let both grow together till the harvest," is the Master's command. In the meanwhile, although despairing of universal success, the ministry must so address the judgment and the conscience of all and of each as if possible to increase the number of the pure and faithful. The state of the Church as a collective body is a subject full of interest and of vast importance as to power among men and as to final issues, but the question of our individual salvation is yet more vital and absorbing.

To form a safe judgment of the Church or ourselves, we must recur to first principles. The Bible makes a broad distinction between the Church and the world—the flesh and the spirit. These are contrary the one to the other. They cannot be reconciled. The antagonism is radical and immutable. Yet the vain, wicked, corrupting experiment of harmonizing the two goes on, perhaps in no age of the Church more broadly and with less disguise than now. Men and women, for the sake of interest and pleasure, and in the spirit of a cowardly conformity, are adopting the maxims and methods of the world, and so obliterating the lines of demarkation as to confirm the world in its follies, and to demoralize the Church in its principles and practice.

The "world" is a term of frequent occurrence in the New Testament, and always of significant import. We are not to understand by it the outward frame of things, the visible heavens and earth, but the inhabitants—what we call "society," with its imperious fashions, its giddy dissipations, its manifold follies. The Apostle John, while he warns us and sets up an infallible test of judgment, at the same time defines the word in the following passage: " Love not the world, neither the things that are in the world. If any man love the world, the love of the Father is not in him." These affections are unlike—stand opposed—they cannot dwell together! The expulsive power of either excludes the other: if the love of the world dominates, the love of the Father is cast out. "For all that is in the world —the lust of the flesh, and the lust of the eyes, and the pride of life—is not of the Father, but is of the world." In the same line our Saviour said to the disciples, " If the world hate you, ye know that it hated me before it hated you. If ye were of the world, the world would love his own; but because ye are not of the world, but I have chosen you out of the world, therefore the world hateth you." At another time he said to the Jews, "Ye are from beneath, I am from above; ye are of this world, I am not of this world"—not in sympathy with its tastes or principles, its aims or ends. Now all these are strong declarations. They are instructive and monitory. Their meaning cannot be mistaken. They discriminate sharply between the religion of Christ and the world with its things and its ways.

The text implies that the world—the vain, vicious, defiling world—is to be found in the pale of the Church. Some have made a treacherous, profane, unholy alliance with it. The epithets employed to characterize them sound harsh and revolting, but milder ones would utterly fail to intimate the enormity of the sin condemned. In the language of

Scripture, idolatry is adultery. The friendship of the world is in the same category. The relation of the Church to God is referred to under the idea of a marriage covenant. He is the husband, she the bride. So Paul, writing to the Corinthians, said: "For I am jealous over you with godly jealousy, for I have espoused you to one husband, that I may present you as a chaste virgin to Christ." If we comprehend and appreciate this image as the true exponent of the pure and delicate relations betwixt Christ and the Church, no professor of religion can fail to see in how many ways character may be compromised, and with what diligent circumspection he must avoid the appearance of evil.

It is a melancholy fact that there are many in the Church wholly oblivious of these great principles and relations. Let us briefly describe them. There are some vain, giddy people — thoughtless and impulsive — not vicious, perhaps, but carnal — not immoral, nevertheless irreligious. They have no fixed habits, or purposes, or principles. They float with the current, are carried about with every wind that blows — light, frivolous, unstable. They are of the earth, earthy.

There is another class, worldly, unspiritual, who "walk disorderly." These have low conceptions of duty, and large ideas of personal rights and liberties. They see no harm in many things against which the Church in every age has borne the strongest testimony. Their senses have not been exercised to discern good and evil. They walk in darkness and indifference. The truth is, they have never been converted, and, as natural men and women, they do not discern the things of the Spirit.

Then, too, there are formalists, who have vague notions about the Church and its ordinances, talk glibly of baptism and communion, strangers to self-denial as a rule of life, but pious enough for *forty* days to lay up a surplus and purchase unlimited indulgence for the rest of the year. These are they who tithe "mint, anise, and cummin, and neglect the weightier matters of the law, judgment, mercy, and faith." They lavish their sensibilities on the outward, the non-essentials, the fringe and the flowers, until they have no heart left for genuine self-denial or painstaking duty.

Besides all these are those who cherish a liberal theology, holding very accommodating doctrines; talk much of the age, its enlightenment and progress; rejoice in their freedom from old superstitions, and mold their morals not by the pattern shown us in the gospel, but by the conventional notions of the social life to which they belong. The sentiments of "our set" are of far higher authority than the deliverances of Sinai or Calvary. These poor *slaves of the ton*, in their servile drudgery under the behests of their idol, have neither time nor heart for the holy, purifying tasks of a sanctified and sanctifying godliness. Beguiled by the subtlety of sin, they seem to be the victims of a hopeless infatuation.

Now all these indicate their moral *status* in various ways, and at all times, by taking their stand against scriptural fidelity to conscience, and in favor of worldly conformity. If duty exposes to reproach, if difficulty makes obedience a tax upon the will, if Christian independence and faithfulness are to be maintained at a loss, why then adherence to right would be an unreasonable exaction. Thus they reason: God is not such a tyrant as to demand it. The Church that insists upon it is puritanical, superstitious, ultra, over-righteous. They do not believe in strait-jackets, arbitrary rules, or that unrelaxing rigor which drives a man along a given line in the face of a burning furnace or a den of lions. Their theory of religion is flexible, consults flesh and blood, and allows fleshly wisdom to legislate for them, legalizing every compliance which will shun a cross or gratify the desires of a carnal nature. What is fashionable is a more controlling question than what is right. The friendship of the world is not to be jeoparded by intruding the claims of a Christian profession. Martyrdom for truth and righteousness and a good conscience did very well in the dark ages — the old-fogy times — but would be a folly in our advanced civilization. At any rate, these people are courting the world—do not mean to forestall the marriage by magnifying the trifles of religion into consequence enough to disgust the liberal, the respectable, and the refined.

Of course, these people who live in the sunshine of the world's friendship never take rank among the witnesses of Jesus. If truth be derided, spiritual religion laughed at, they join with the mockers. If error grows presumptuous and defiant, assailing all that is pure and of good report, they lift no voice in rebuke. Whatever their private opinions or convictions may be, the circle of their chosen friends is not to be broken, or even disturbed, by thrusting the verities of Christianity upon their unwilling ears. They do not confess Christ before men. They would rather give up their place in the Church of God than to lose caste among the devotees of fashion. In the conflicts of conscience with inclination, pleasure, honor, and profit, carry the day. They are not dead to sin. They are not crucified unto the world, nor the world unto them. The flesh, with its affections and lusts, dominates taste, choice, and action. A mess of pottage will bribe their conscience. The excitements, sensations, and dissipations of society, interest and absorb them. They know more about amateur theatricals than about missions; enjoy festal concerts and suppers more than revivals; will pay more for an "excursion" than to build a chapel for the poor; wonderfully active in getting up a tableau, or rehearsing for a musical entertainment (working for the Church, they call it); but they never attend a Church Conference, or a prayer-meeting; never speak in love-feast, seldom commune, and never exhort a sinner to flee the wrath to come. Poor souls! they work upon the ark, but they never enter in; they are counted with the Church, but live in the world and for the world; they swell our census, but encumber our progress.

There is hardly a sin so gross, or an evil so corrupting, but that the world has something to say in defense. Plausible pleas are made for suicide, dueling, gambling, horse-racing, prostitution, the liquor traffic. If it were possible, they would deceive the very elect. The milder expressions of human depravity are not only defended, but advocated and highly commended, and to censure them is well-nigh a personal insult. Such is the sophistry of passion and the deceitfulness of sin that, through obsequiousness to the sentiments and maxims of the world, the Church is relaxing her discipline, and the card-table, the theater, and the dancing-saloon, find friends and advocates among the professed disciples of Jesus Christ.

The unfaithful wife is universally condemned. For her there is neither pity nor pardon. But the gay, fast, fashionable woman, who, forgetful of the proprieties of wedlock, flirts promiscuously with men, and parades her sensuous charms for public admiration, while she may be the subject of sharp criticism, nevertheless is tolerated, and holds her place in society! So in the Church scandalous sin will exclude from membership, yet the doubtful compliances with the follies and demands of the world, now so frequent, are allowed an ominous impunity. In Christian morals it must be remembered that to impinge upon principle to do a doubtful act is not merely an impropriety, but a sin. "He that doubteth is damned if he eat." "Whatsoever is not of faith is sin." He who sacrifices an honest doubt comes into condemnation for more reasons than one. He consents under a slight temptation to offend God to please himself, showing that under more powerful solicitation he would yield to unquestioned transgression. His eye is not single. He does not aim to please God. The divine will is no bar to self-gratification. His duty to God, his relation to others, the influence of example, are all subordinate to profession, to temptation, the impulse, the whim of the hour. Like the wanton wife, who trifles with her sacred obligations, these worldly people make light of their vows and covenant with the Church, and recklessly wound their Saviour in the house of his friends.

These friends of the world are corrupting the Church, mortifying their pastors, and giving occasion to the enemies of Christ to blaspheme. The process of amalgamation goes on almost without let or hinderance. This discourse is entered as a *caveat*. Having stated the principles of the text, and the distinctive features of those who are condemned by them, I propose to make an application of all to a single popular amusement.

I select *dancing* as the more common, most popular, the least defensible, and, in some respects, the most demoralizing. In the cities other expressions of the worldly spirit occur and abound. They are in the same condemnation. Dancing is common to town and country. The evil is ubiquitous, pervading all places and all grades of society. It identifies itself as an evil by its effects on mind, character, and social life. Whatever its form, from the reel to the waltz, round or square, private or public, my observation is that in spirit, tendency, and result, it is inimical to every element of genuine religion. It is death to spiritual life. It is a profane intruder upon the sanctity of the Church. A dancing community is not religious — will not be, cannot be. Bishop McIlvaine uttered a great truth when, being asked by a lady, "Is it any harm for a Christian to dance?" replied, "A Christian never wants to dance." He or she has no heart for it. It is a forbidden thing, unbecoming, incongruous, out of character. The *desire* for it is proof either that we never were "renewed in the spirit of our minds," or that we have forfeited the grace of God and are backslidden. To patronize it, to defend it, to advocate it, is to take sides with the world against Christ. Nobody ever knew a *very* religious person to engage in it. The fear and love of God, a life of prayer and holy communion, the joy of the Holy Spirit, rule out this vanity!

I confess I have no patience with it, no toleration of it. I think it is the silliest, the most nonsensical amusement, that rational beings, so called, ever engaged in. It is heathenish in its origin—a pastime of savages—is a part of idolatrous worship—lewd, sensual, obscene. This is its history. It appeals to the lowest instincts of humanity, and is the chosen sport of the vilest and most imbruted of our race. The slum of society everywhere revel in it. Rowdies and prostitutes — these are its patrons. It is wicked, vile in its origin, yet worse in its lower associations, and worst of all in its last analysis. It has been refined, polished, I grant, but it cannot be dignified nor elevated. The venom of the serpent is in it. The taint of its birth, the virus of its constitution, is ineradicable. It is evil, only evil, and that continually.

No one claims for it a place among the agencies for *promoting* piety. No one has ever been made better by it. It is not so designed or expected. It is a carnal enjoyment, simple and uncompounded. The public estimate of the moral character of all Church-members who indulge in it is lowered. Take any man noted for his piety, any saintly woman, introduce them on the dancing-floor, and let them "trip the light fantastic toe"—the sight would be a shock even to the bad. Everybody would feel there had been a fall, a sad eclipse of consistency, a disgraceful betrayal of the Church and Christianity. For some people to do this would excite no surprise —nothing better was expected of them; but for those of real Christian reputation to mingle in these follies would be, not only in the Church, but among decent sinners, a cause of sorrow, regret, and shame. The well-nigh universal feeling would be that religion had been discounted, and the world damaged by the Church.

There is nothing *intellectual* about it to redeem it. A dog, an elephant, a monkey, can learn it. The fact is, take away the glamour of fashion and the countenance which men and women of culture give it, the whole thing would be contemptible, and would fall into desuetude in all respectable society. It is humiliating that our weddings, dinners, suppers, picnics, levees, entertainments for friends and visitors, are all degraded by this pagan, idolatrous, barbarian pastime. It is a reflection upon the intelligence of our friends, as if they could not be interested without this childish accompaniment; and upon our own, as if we could not be polite and entertaining without a "*hop*." What a name for an adult amusement! Come, now, we have exhausted refreshments for the body, and the topics for thought and talk, let us be children, play the fool, and "*hop*." Angels of heaven, turn your eyes away! Alas, to think that the Church of Christ is represented on these occasions! *Inconsistency* is the softest word the truth allows in speaking of this shameful treatment of a holy profession.

It is to be admitted that there are differences as to time, place, and company. I am told there is a difference (as the names imply) between square and round dances. The proprieties are comparative. So also between the simple cotillon and the intricate and voluptuous waltz, between parlor-dancing and the masquerade-ball. But the truth is, they are all related—blood-kin. The family is one. Private dancing is the prelude and preparation for public dancing. The simple leads to the complex, and the delicate to the gross. The passion grows by indulgence. For this reason I include those Christian parents who teach their children to dance in the same condemnation with the more open transgressors who misrepresent their Master, outrage the moral sentiment of the Church, and herd promiscuously with the world of the ungodly. The knowledge of the art involves the temptation to practice it. Indeed, this schooling is a preparation for it—"a provision for the flesh to fulfill the lusts thereof." The girl whose agility and grace is admired in the circle of private friends will long to display her *charming* accomplishment on a more public arena. Would a thoughtful parent commit the manners and the morals of his children to some strolling, transient master of mazes and positions, if he did not desire and intend them to shine with eclat in the giddy throng of the vain, the frivolous, and the worldly? Expecting them to love the world, they insure this morally disastrous result by training, physical endowment, and mental association. The friendship of the world is too precious a boon to be foregone, although the price of it be the loss of divine favor, and the end of it enmity to God. "For whosoever will be the friend of the world is the enemy of God."

Now, bearing in mind that the Church stands related to Christ as the spouse to her husband, what shall we say of the license and freedom with which so many members fondle the world? How indelicate! How suspicious! What occasion for sneer, and criticism, and damaging rumor! As the wife, by the wantonness of her behavior, reproaches her husband, and smirks herself even when she has not descended to positive infidelity, so these loose members discount religion, and mar Christian fellowship. When they joined the Church, they promised "to renounce the devil and all his works, the vain pomp and glory of the world, so that they would not follow or be led by them." Into this solemn covenant they entered voluntarily, understandingly. It was an oath in substance, binding the conscience. They accepted the pledge and promise, and enrolled themselves as disciples. In the sight of God and in the presence of witnesses the betrothal was made, the formula having sacramental force and sanctity. "O foolish Galatians, who hath bewitched you, that ye should not obey the truth," fulfill your obligations, redeem your promise? These world-courting, pleasure-seeking professors of religion, who esteem the favor, friendship, and praise of men above fidelity to Christ, are in a fearful dilemma. If, when they took these holy vows before God and his people, they were insincere, then they deceived the Church, played the hypocrite, lied to the Holy Ghost. Their sin is aggravated—their very profession is a falsehood. If they were honest—meant what they said—then their friendship with the world is perfidy to Christ. They have denied their Lord and Master, and gone into indiscreet, unchaste alliance with his enemies.

The moral character of all the compliances and associations which the text and the sermon condemn is determined by the fact that they who go into them intended to court the world, to gratify the flesh, to conform to fashionable society. They did not design to honor Christ, to glorify God, to promote their own salvation. These things were not in all their thoughts. Their motives were secular and selfish, their policy carnal. They consented to grieve the Spirit, sacrifice their honest doubts, break over the rules of the Church, to please ungodly friends, and to indulge "the lust of the flesh, and the lust of the eyes, and the pride of life." These things cannot be defended, and ought not to be tolerated. No use to argue or deny—they are inconsistent, unscriptural, and corrupting. No Christian society can long survive their allowance. In prophetic imagery, the earth will swallow the woman instead of the flood, and the tide of ungodliness will sweep on, burying the hopes of the good, and bearing the world farther from God and salvation.

O Church of the living God, "come out from among them—be separate," and singular—the children of God without rebuke, in the midst of a crooked and perverse generation!

II.
THE FIRST AND THE LAST.
BY BISHOP WIGHTMAN.

"And he said unto me, Fear not; I am the first and the last; he that liveth, and was dead, and behold, I am alive forevermore, Amen; and have the keys of hell and of death." Rev. i. 17, 18.

It is a wonderful thought how Jesus Christ is the supreme glory of the universe—"the first and the last;" how he is the ground and motive of all duty, in all relations, in all offices of life; the meritorious, procuring cause of every blessing; the bond of connection between the unseen, eternal Father, and the spirit of man; "made unto us wisdom, righteousness, sanctification, and redemption"—in a word, "all in all."

In the gospel which affirms all this there is no hesitation in the statement, at the same time of the fact, that He who came in the fullness of the time to his own nation was not received by his own people, was rejected as their Messiah, was condemned in the presence of the representative of the Roman power, and crucified as a malefactor. These wonderfully contrasted statements are both made with pronounced and equal distinctness. They involve in the person of Christ a dual nature—the divine and the human; they ground fundamentally in the

THE REV. BISHOP W. M. WIGHTMAN, D.D.,
Of the Methodist Episcopal Church, South.

unfathomable mystery of the threefold unity of the Godhead. The Father sends the Son; the Son, co-eternal with the Father, becomes incarnate, and is invested with the office of Mediator; the Spirit, proceeding from the Father and the Son, is the efficient cause of all gracious, spiritual changes, "the Lord, the giver of life."

Representations such as these had been made in verbal statement. They were illustrated in a Christophany—a glorious, transcendent manifestation to the beloved disciple John, in the Isle of Patmos. That disciple had often reclined on the bosom of his Master; was the one whom Jesus loved, by eminence, and had been for forty years an apostle. Now when that same Master speaks in person once more to John, and John beholds the glorified, divine-human, Lord Christ; sees him as Stephen saw him, as Paul saw him—not in visions of the night, or in day-dreams, but directly, distinctly, unmistakably; heard his voice speaking human words; recognized his identity—the occasion is as awful as it is glorious. He stands in the midst of a templar-scene. Symbolical investitures surround him. There are the seven golden candlesticks. He is clad with priestly and kingly garments of resplendent white, cinctured with a golden girdle. A dazzling brightness shines around his head; his eyes flame with the divine holiness; his feet are lustrous as molten brass; his voice is as the sound of many waters; his countenance is as the sun in its utmost power of light. When an appearance of this sort, the manifestation of Christ in his glory, broke upon the apostle's startled vision, he fell at his Master's feet as dead. That Master lays his right-hand on his prostrate servant, and utters the words of the text, the most sublime of all the words ever spoken by him—words that grasp eternities, solve the awful mystery of the divine government, so far as man's history and destiny are concerned, and claim authority paramount, unalterable, universal: "Fear not; I am the first and the last; he that liveth, and was dead, and behold, I am alive forevermore, Amen; and have the keys of hell and of death."

There are several instructive lessons here presented for our consideration:

1. It might be remarked that this is the only manifestation of the kind made to the beloved apostle. Before the crucifixion he, with Peter and James, had been permitted to see the transfiguration of their Lord and Master. On Hermon, in the night, the form of Christ shone in dazzling glory. Out of the radiance a voice said, "This is my beloved Son; hear him." This wonderful scene belonged to the time of the Saviour's sojourn on earth. In the manifestation before us it is the risen, glorified Lord, the Eternal, Living One, who breaks with majestic radiance from the dread secrecy of the world of spirits. Why, it might be asked, have appearances such as this been so rare? Why does the gospel satisfy itself with *sufficiency* of evidence, while its Author might, if he saw fit, shake the earth and cry aloud to the nations in a voice louder than ten thousand thunders?

We might safely reply, leaving out the grand consideration of man's responsibility, which is most carefully guarded in the administration of God's government in grace, that the momentous questions and concerns of spiritual religion connect themselves mainly with the conscience and the will, in the daily experiences of life—that is, with those elements of our nature which are moral, rather than with the mere æsthetical. The imagination holds a very subordinate part in the whole affair. On rare occasions the mind may be awed, excited, moved, by the grandeur of supernatural appearances; yet the great and absorbing interest we have in the gospel is of another kind. The supreme questions are, How can sin be pardoned? how can reconciliation with a holy God be secured? how may the mediation of Christ be made available, and peace of mind, rectitude, holiness of heart, and joyous obedience, become dominant and habitual? The fervors of a high-wrought imagination are one thing; quite another is the play of the genuinely devout affections. You may turn the worship of God into a magnificent dramatic exhibition, until the elements of scenic effect shall produce a spectacle transcending far the most splendid shows of the old Greek and Roman idol-worship. It is not difficult to conceive how the imagination would be excited to the damage of the moral sentiments and principles, had grand spectacular displays been the rule, instead of the rare exception, in that dispensation of grace which is to authenticate the maxims of eternal wisdom and vindicate the righteous government of God, while it offers salvation to penitent sinners believing on the Son of God. In the place of material images, producing impressions of beauty, terror, or sublimity, moral emotions, ideas of good and evil, of penitence and trust, of righteousness and true holiness, flow from the central facts of the Christian Revelation. Its voice is, "Say not in thine heart who shall ascend into heaven, that is to bring Christ down from above; or who shall descend into the deep, that is to bring Christ again from the dead. But what saith it? The word is nigh thee, even in thy mouth and in thy heart, that is the word of faith which we preach."

2. Behold in the words of Christ spoken on this occasion a summary of the gospel for all time and all men.

"I am the first and the last, and the living One." Here he asserts his supremacy and his eternal existence as the Son of God. In the days of his flesh he had said to the Jews, "Before Abraham was *I Am*." In his prayer to the Father he spoke of the glory he had with him "before the world was." Now the declaration in the text, "I am the living One," sets forth his claim to be the living God from all eternity. His eternal existence is the root and foundation of his power to save to the uttermost, to give life, to raise from the dead, to confer the boon of everlasting life in the world to come. Here we have the solid basis of redemption.

But this living One became incarnate in Jesus. He took not on him the nature of angels, but the substantial nature of humanity. He thus became the Second Adam. In this human personality he "tasted death for every man." The death was a real separation of soul and body—not an ideal or imaginary one. The lance of the Roman soldier pierced his heart. This death was sacrificial. "He gave himself a ransom for all." "He suffered, the Just for the unjust, that he might bring us to God." "Through the eternal Spirit he offered *himself* to God." This death was an atonement, an expiation for that essential element in sin, *guilt*. Remorse of conscience testifies to the vital relation of sin to law and justice, and the sacrificial expiation made by the death of the Mediator is the sole objective ground on which the subjective wants of a soul conscious of guilt can rest for satisfaction. A provision for spiritual and entire sanctification is necessary in its place, but, in the order of the plan of salvation, atonement for guilt is first provided for. Hence alone can come peace of conscience and reconciliation with God. It will remain eternally true that "when we were enemies we were reconciled to God by the *death* of his Son." "We have boldness to enter into the holiest by the *blood* of Jesus."

I "have the keys of hell and of death." In the tone of absolute authority Christ proclaims that he has obtained the government, and taken possession of earth, the under-world, and heaven. Of these he holds the keys, and maintains the dominion. So that, according to St. Paul's view in the Epistle to the Philippians, he receives the homage of "things in heaven, and things in earth, and things under the earth;" of disembodied spirits, departed, blessed saints, and of infernal spirits in the seats of destruction, after he had "spoiled principalities and powers, making a show of them openly," triumphing over them by their defeat and overthrow, and stripping them of their power of injuring those who believe in him, and bruising the head of Satan as the earnest of the world's final deliverance from the powers of darkness.

O Christian soul, is this thy Saviour? Canst thou fear the grave, or dread the state of separate spirits? When thy last moment comes, and thou must depart, is it true that thy Christ is Lord of every part of the universe? Then, if we are Christ's, all is ours! We are in the dominions of our Sovereign. The ensign of his authority waves over sea and shore, over planetary systems and solar universes. Take courage. He has closed the gates of the under-world paradise for his faithful followers, and to die now is to depart and be with him. At his ascension he "led captivity captive." Myriads of angels did homage to him, and in his triumphal train the spirits of the just, who in joy and felicity had long waited in the under-world paradise for their deliverance, formed in long procession and went up to the *upper* paradise, where they are ever present with the Lord.

3. "Behold, I am alive forevermore, Amen." The resurrection of Christ forms the central point of the world's history. Here is indeed the *palingenesia*.

This is the starting-point of the career of Christianity. Think you that such a religion as it was, whose purity was opposed by the shameless vice of that time, by the thousand deadly fascinations of false religions, whose very worship was abomination; a religion which pretended to no resources of learning, wealth, power, or influence; which had neither synagogue nor sword; claimed no philosopher, poet, or orator for its champion, no prince or potentate as its patron—could such a religion as this have made its way in an historic age of the world, in the face of the three great civilizations of that time, unless it had been able to proclaim with tongues of fire, in words that moved like the tread of armed battalions, that Christ Jesus, the Son of David and David's Lord, the Son of the living God, had died for man's redemption, was buried in Joseph's sepulcher, had risen from the dead the third day? For the firm, constant, and triumphant proclamation of the resurrection, of which they were witnesses, by the apostles, there was their own conviction grounded on the strongest, most indubitable evidence. In the case, for instance, of St. Paul, nothing short of absolute certainty that the Jesus whom he once persecuted was alive again, the Conqueror of death, the glorified Son of God, and the Lord of all, could have arrested the persecutor, and bound him over, with passionate devotion and triumphant confidence, to a life-long service. His letters are in our hands. They abound in indications of the honest, affectionate, intrepid, and virtuous mind of the writer. They show a fine vigor of style, a knowledge of affairs, a sincere piety without hypocrisy or extravagance, and a hearty goodwill toward men. Is the fact of Christ's resurrection ever referred to in these Epistles? The world has known for eighteen centuries in what terms, with what emphasis, how often directly, how constantly, indirectly taken for granted, this all-important fact is mentioned in these writings. While they are in existence, ample information, exact, trustworthy, "fraught with the very soul of history," is in our hands, both as to the nature and the original promulgation of Christianity. In respect to recorded matters of history, the lapse of time makes no abatement in the force of the evidence. It has been well and finely said that "pillars of marble decay, and monuments of brass decay; the Egyptian pyramids are crumbling into dust; the earth itself wanes, and the heavens wax old as doth a garment; but *written testimony* endures from age to age, and knows no change; and so long as reason is the guide of man, whatever is established by that testimony holds an undecaying authority over his belief." And in respect to this central, fundamental, vital fact of Christ's resurrection, no middle position can be maintained. No vague neutrality is admissible. The fact is absolutely true, and in accepting it we own the authority of Christ's mission and doctrine; or it is wholly false, and in denying it we take position with unbelievers, and may be classed with those who love their infatuations better than themselves. In denying Christ's resurrection we deny the personal union of the divine and human in him. Denying this, with the person of Christ would be abolished Christian testimony and truth, and the Christian Church altogether. "But now *is* Christ risen from the dead." The faith in this glorious fact, "old and ever young," has outlived all attacks, and is now stronger than ever, the only refuge of a sinful world.

4. In fine, we have in the text the assurance that as Christ is eternally linked to the fortunes of the race he died to redeem, so the august powers of an "endless life" are now and shall forever be engaged in the work of completing and eternally perpetuating the salvation of his people. "For if when we were enemies"—such is St. Paul's argument—"we were reconciled to God by the death of his Son, much more being reconciled we shall be saved *by his life*."

He is alive forevermore, to consummate his redeeming work through all the ages of the world's future.

See this in the fact that he is present as glorified Mediator, in all the assemblies of his people, according to his own promise, "Where two or three are gathered together in my name, there am I in the midst." How high the honor, how unspeakable the privilege, to have Christ's spiritual presence wherever his people meet for prayer or praise!

Besides, every true and faithful minister of the gospel has his coöperation—that of a present and almighty Saviour. "Lo, I am with you alway, even unto the end of the world." "So, then, neither is he that planteth any thing, nor he that watereth, but God that giveth the increase." All the ability employed in planting the seed, and in its after-culture, is from the Lord, on whose blessing depends all success. His is the gift of the Paraclete, the Comforter, who is to abide with the Church forever.

But specially is he "the merciful and faithful High-priest," "who ever liveth to make intercession for us." This intercession grounds on the propitiatory sacrifice which made atonement for the sins of the world, and opened a fountain for sin and uncleanness. Being both the Victim and the Offerer, the Mediator now in heaven holds forever the office of intercessor; and his ministry in heaven must be conceived of as embracing a clear and comprehensive view of the wants of his people; a perfect sympathy, tenderer and more influential as their necessities deepen and demand his help in time of need; and intercessions, "each a distinct and separate act of his pleading will in their behalf," before the Father. How ample, then, is the provision made in the plan of redemption to meet the full extent of human guilt, spiritual pollution, infirmities, and responsibilities! How profound the adaptations of this scheme of heavenly mercy to an immortal spirit longing after the attainment of perfect purity, universal holiness, and a blameless and useful life! Why, then, should we not have "boldness to enter into the holiest by the blood of Jesus?" Why should not our devotions rise to higher and holier ardor, and fill the soul with richer joys, and lead up our spirits to their perfection of purity and growth? These provisions and adaptations, so lofty and yet so lowly, so solid and so universal, sublime as the height of heaven, and yet suited to all our earthly needs—ought they not to warrant "the full assurance of faith?" that faith which brings the soul into the clear light shining from afar on the table-lands that rise into the cloudless azure—Pisgah-summits whence Hope sees the promised land, and hears the echoes of its angel-minstrelsy?

But not thus alone is the Mediator occupied in the hallowed courts of the heavenly sanctuary; he appears in the presence of God for us as Leader of his people. "Father, I will that those whom thou hast given me shall be with me to behold my glory." The Precursor has entered heaven before his followers, "the Forerunner" has gone home to make every thing ready for their glad reception. Ah! shall we not be able to cry, as the light of this mortal life fades from our darkening eyes, "Thou wilt show me the path of life!" Yes, light from the shining gates breaks in; on the air is heard the rustle of angel-wings; lo, the prison-walls are giving way— "rise, let us go!" Were this matter of speculation only, it would deserve to be pronounced the sublimest ever opened to the vision of the human imagination. But when we consider that the risen Jesus, the victorious Redeemer, the Captain of our salvation, was seen by his followers to pass through the skies in his human body glorified; when we are sure that he is in the heavenly places with the Father, and lives forevermore, in majesty divine, clothed with all power in heaven and earth, and from the summit of glory and bliss eternal calls us to follow him without fear, then we may confidently affirm that, not as a lofty speculation, but as a solid, stupendous fact, it has no rival in human experience. And in faith's grasp of this fact, that our Christ is the eternal, "living One," who holds the keys of all dominion, lies the power of the organized Christianity of our time to conquer the world.

You who feel the throb of immortal aspiration, and hold heirship in the "power of an endless life;" who sometimes tremble in the anticipation of possible events, now hidden in the abysses of an inconceivable infinite; who wonder if the "eternal life" shall never ebb in its divine course, never falter in its victorious power, never lose the virgin freshness of its opening morning, take courage. This life, which was originally manifested in Christ, and communicated by him, is irrevocably vested in him as the eternal Son. He says, "I am alive forevermore, Amen; and have the keys of hell and of death." The new, heavenly, immortal existence, on which you shall presently enter, has the guarantee of his own deathless life and power. And in that realm of eternal life and love "there shall be no more curse; but the throne of God and the Lamb shall be in it; and his servants shall serve him, and they shall see his face, and his name shall be in their foreheads." Amen! So it is; so let it be forever. Amen! Let the ages, as they roll on to join the congregations of the mighty past, do homage to Him whose years fail not, who is "alive forevermore." Let them send on the echoing Amen to

Time's last hour. Let "every creature which is in heaven and on earth, and under the earth, and such as are in the sea, and all that are in them, say, Blessing, and honor, and glory, and power, be unto him that sitteth on the throne, and unto the Lamb forever and ever." Amen and amen!

III.

JOY IN HEAVEN OVER PENITENT SINNERS.

BY THE REV. EDWARD WADSWORTH, A.M., D.D., Alabama Conference.

"I say unto you, that likewise joy shall be in heaven over one sinner that repenteth, more than over ninety and nine just persons, which need no repentance." Luke xv. 7.

The Bible depicts human character descriptively. When we find our own persons described by marks which we recognize, then we may apply to ourselves whatever is mentioned as pertaining to those described. This may consist of blessings or judgment. In these descriptions the inspired word is specific and clear.

In the text we have two characters described by terms which may be accurately interpreted, and then we have the two compared to each other, and an assertion of interest taken in one of them by the inhabitants of heaven which fills us with wonder

The two characters mentioned are, just persons who do not need repentance, and the sinner that repents. The former in this text consist of *ninety and nine;* and the latter consists of *one*, solitary and alone. The assertion is made that there is more joy in heaven over *this one* than there is over ninety and

THE REV. EDWARD WADSWORTH, D.D.,
Of the Alabama Conference.

nine who do not need repentance. This assertion is truthful. It is very encouraging to penitents.

We propose to consider: 1. The just persons who do not need repentance; 2. The sinner that repents; 3. The great joy in heaven over the penitent sinner.

I. *The just persons who do not need repentance.*

The text, as expressed by the infallible Teacher, uses an adjective with no noun; and the translator, according to usage which is approved by all learned critics, puts *persons* as the noun which the adjective requires. Thus we have *just persons*. They are very numerous — "ninety-nine just persons." In finding these, we have a very large field to search for them. Some are now in glory; others are on earth, on their way to glory.

1. In this class we put angels.

These are created beings, of whom we find much in the word of God. That they were all in a state of probation, when first created, we are well persuaded, because some of them fell from their high position; they "kept not their first estate, but left their own habitation," is recorded in Jude 6. Those who kept themselves pure during their probation were so numerous as to be "an innumerable company of angels," now in "the city of the living God." Heb. xii. 22. These were present when God "laid the foundations of the earth;" and as they looked on his handiwork "they shouted for joy." Job xxxviii. 4–7. We are informed that they constitute a hierarchy in God's realm, and of their employment we have one declaration, which is infallible. It is made very strong by the use of the figure of interrogation: "Are they not all ministering spirits, sent forth to minister for them who shall be heirs of salvation?" Heb. i. 14.

Instances of this wonderful ministration are very numerous in the word of God. Lot was honored by two guests, who accepted his invitation to the hospitalities of his house in Sodom the night before God rained fire and brimstone upon that city. These guests were angels in the forms, or bodies, of men. One of these messengers was employed to punish David for his sin in numbering Israel when he was warned of its offensiveness; and he was seen stopping by the threshing-place of Araunah, the Jebusite, and was turned back from his destructive mission by prayer and sacrifice. Daniel, in the lions' den, was saved from the ravenous beasts by the interposition of an angel, for he said, in answer to the king's anxious inquiry, "O king, live forever! my God hath sent his angel, and hath shut the lions' mouths, that they have not hurt me." Our blessed Lord, in the unutterable agony of the garden of Gethsemane, when he sweated great drops of blood, and said, "Father, if thou be willing, remove this cup from me; nevertheless, not my will, but thine be done," was visited by one of these messengers in his extremity, for Luke tells us, "There appeared an angel unto him from heaven, strengthening him."

These angels of God never sinned. They never had need for repentance. They are persons, "just persons." From their vast number, so great, that Daniel tells us, "Thousand thousands ministered unto the Ancient of days, and ten thousand times ten thousand stood before him." Dan. vii. 10. We select ninety and nine for our purpose, and put them in one company. We request you to look at them. They are very lovely persons. God loves them, and values them. His love for them is joyful.

2. In this same class we may put disembodied spirits who are now in glory.

In respect to these, we are not left in uncertainty as to their personality nor their habitation. Both are made sure by the word. Among the innumerable company of angels, or associated with them, who have entered into glory, and now enjoy the felicity of heaven, mention is made of "the spirits of just men made perfect, who are written in heaven." Heb. xii. 23. Therein we have not persons only, but men—men made perfect. They were inhabitants of this earth during their probation. This world was the scene of their labors, their trials, and their conquests. In this world they heard the gospel, and were awakened by it; and under this awakening they saw the light which shines in a dark place; and, guided by it, they found their way to the cross of Christ, and experienced salvation. These have been washed and made clean in the blood of Christ. Fitted for heaven while they were on earth, they advanced onward and upward, until their probation ended, and now they sit with Abraham, and Isaac, and Jacob, and the company of prophets and apostles in the realm of glory. They came into this kingdom by repentance. They remained in this kingdom by faithful obedience. They went out of the kingdom of grace into glory.

It is certain that, in their present glorified state, they are pure spirits, and do not need repentance. Of their number we have this statement in Rev. vii. 9: "After this I beheld, and, lo, a great multitude, which no man could number, of all nations, and kindreds, and people, and tongues, stood before the throne, and before the Lamb, clothed with white robes, and palms in their hands, crying, Salvation to our God which sitteth on the throne, and unto the Lamb." Being among the inhabitants of heaven, many of whom are called angels, God may employ them as messengers to minister to them who are heirs of salvation. Doubtless they are ready for, and they rejoice in, this employment.

3. In the same class we put righteous persons who are adopted into the family of God, and are now in the state of probation.

They are led by the Spirit of God, and are the sons (or children) of God. They have not received the spirit of bondage again to fear, but the Spirit of adoption, whereby they cry, Abba, Father. Rom. viii. 15. The population of the earth, from the time of Adam to the present age, has always consisted of two classes—the saved and the unsaved. The former were brought into salvation by the grace of God working in them regeneration, and when this is wrought in them the Spirit bears witness with their spirits to their adoption. Evidences of this are abundant in the Holy Scriptures. "Abel obtained witness that he was righteous, God testifying of his gifts." Enoch was translated to heaven, and "before his translation he had this testimony, that he pleased God." Noah showed his faith by preparing an "ark to the saving of his household, by which he became heir of the righteousness which is by faith." As we come down the ages, the number of sinners saved by grace increases enormously, and we are sure that very many now living are righteous persons, and on their way to heaven. Having obtained forgiveness through the atonement appropriated by faith, and having witness that they are righteous, they do not need repentance of the kind described or referred to in the text. They remember their sins, and the remembrance is grievous unto them. Being now children of light, and judging their sins by the light which is in them, the guilt of these sins is to their vision, and in their judgment, vastly increased—so vastly increased that they count themselves the chief of sinners, and contemplate with adoring wonder the grace which stooped so low as to reach them. But in the midst of this wonder there is in them the conviction that they have passed out of darkness into light, out of bondage into liberty, out of condemnation into salvation.

Out of this immense crowd of sinners saved by grace—sinners who came with broken hearts and contrite spirits to God—sinners who believed in Christ with hearts unto righteousness—sinners whom God honors by making them witnesses, his own witnesses—yea, out of this crowd we select ninety-nine for our purpose in explaining and enforcing the truth contained in the text. We need them, and shall use them in making the comparison embodied in the text as vivid and powerful as we can.

We invite you to turn your eyes to and consider,
II. *The sinner that repents.*

In speaking or writing on this person, we remind you that herein character is described, and our attention should be fixed on the points, or qualities, which constitute this character. Two are mentioned—the *sinner*, and the *sinner that repents.*

1. A sinner is one who has committed sin. This is an accurate definition. It requires transgression of the law of God to fix this characteristic on a person. "Sin is the transgression of the law." 1 John iii. 4.

The law is what is called the moral law. It is contained in the Ten Commandments. The duties we are to attend to, and the evils we are to shun, are all condensed so rigidly as to be put in the space on which Moses, by command of God, wrote the Ten Laws. Of these laws we have commentaries. They are written by inspired men, and we rightly judge them to be infallible. The Sermon on the Mount, delivered by the great Teacher, and recorded in Matthew v., vi., and vii., explains the Ten Commandments. By this sermon we learn that we may transgress in our hearts, by cherishing evil passions and wrong motives, as well as by overt acts. In this way the breadth or comprehension of law may be known.

That all are sinners can be shown by proofs. Memory acts by retrospection, and takes in all our actions. It acts independently of the will, though it may be quickened into activity by the will. We speak truthfully when we say we are forced to remember our actions. Conscience judges the quality of actions by their conformity or opposition to law. Conscience acts independently of the will. We are forced to judge our actions. By this process all men are convinced that they are sinners, because all know that they have transgressed law. Whether this is felt as a heavy burden or not, it is felt as a fact, and it is a fact whose reality is permanent.

It is terrible to any thoughtful man to know that he is a sinner, for every sinner must be punished or pardoned. And in God's government forgiveness is not arbitrary, but judicial. It is granted not above law, nor contrary to law, but consistently with law. The only relief to the sinner is found in this: "It is a faithful saying, and worthy of all acceptation, that Christ Jesus came into the world to save sinners." 1 Tim. i. 15. By this wonderful revelation the terror of being a sinner is much diminished by the fact that we are redeemed sinners. Redemption embodies provision for salvation. Appropriation of the provision requires repentance, and to enjoy this each one must be "the sinner that repents."

2. The sinner that repents may be recognized by all who know the nature of **repentance**. To this we address ourselves.

Repentance is used in the Scriptures sometimes comprehensively and sometimes accurately. It mingles with faith so constantly that faith is never genuine and saving unless it is preceded by repentance, and repentance never reaches its acme until it merges into faith. Many texts teach us that faith is essential to salvation, and many that repentance is essential to salvation. They are harmonized by the fact above stated. Genuine repentance always leads to the acknowledgment of truth. There is a distinction between knowing the truth and acknowledging the truth. The latter comprehends the former, but the former does not comprehend the latter. The former is the act of the intellect, the latter is the complex act of the intellect and the will. One embraces truth, the other uses it. All need the Holy Spirit to enable them to repent. In this essential work God and man must be co-workers. When the sinner submits, "God gives repentance to the acknowledging of the truth," and the poor sinner " recovers from the snare of the devil." 2 Tim. ii. 25, 26.

Many awakened sinners are perplexed and led astray by looking for repentance in the sensibilities chiefly, and judging their cases by their feelings. Repentance consists in conviction of sin and sorrow for sin. These mental states are perceptible and real. They are felt and acknowledged. At times they burden the mind and produce a copious flow of tears, but the tears relieve for a season, and the sinner relapses into quietness which he considers hardness. He tries to measure his sorrow as if it had dimension, or to weigh it as if it had gravity. All these efforts are fruitless and discouraging. So long as he confines himself to the region of the sensibilities, he wanders in shadows and darkness. If he will change the field of examination from the sensibilities to the will, he can make progress in repentance, or he can judge his case profitably. Let the question be, What am I willing to do? and not, How much do I feel? Every sinner who is perfectly willing to humble his heart, and confess his sins to God, has conviction enough; conviction has done in him all it can do—indeed, all it was sent to do. And every sinner who is perfectly willing to forsake all sin, and consecrate himself unreservedly to God, has sorrow enough; sorrow has done in him all it can do—indeed, all it was sent to do.

The contest between the flesh and the spirit is carried on in the region of the will, and it is sometimes fearful, yea, terribly severe. Strong men are seen writhing in agony. Dignified men sometimes bow themselves in congregations, and cry aloud in anguish. The scene is similar to that described in Mark ix. 20. The battle is between Satan and God. They fight for an immortal soul. The victory always turns on the side which man's will takes. The work of repentance is perfect when the sinner willingly humbles his heart, willingly renounces sin, willingly consecrates himself to God, willingly trusts in Jesus Christ his Saviour. When the will acts freely in trusting in Christ, committal is accomplished, and believing is so easy that the man wonders that he should have struggled so hard. Repentance ever leads us to trust in Jesus Christ, and trust is made perfect by the action of the will in committing ourselves, with all our precious interests, to Jesus Christ. If we know Christ in his true character we will commit all to him, and then our souls will rest in consciousness of safety. Of this kind of experience Paul is a witness, as we see in 2 Tim. i. 12.

III. The *wonderful assertion that over one sinner that repents there is in heaven more joy than there is over ninety and nine just persons who do not need repentance.*

1. This is so wonderful as to astonish us, but so truthful as to command our faith—it is a record of fact. Ninety and nine persons in the state of salvation are in one crowd. On them God lavishes his love in the twofold form of benevolence and complacency. They are righteous persons, and, as such, they are partakers of the divine nature; they are holy persons, and, as such, God has joy when he looks upon them; they are heirs of the inheritance in heaven, and, as such, they are now enjoying it, and going on to enjoy it forever. In the range of our vision there is one person, standing all alone, and not in the crowd of the ninety and nine. In his face there is no beauty, in his person there is no attractive dignity, in his moral character there is nothing but deformity. He has made himself loathsome by nourishing his depraved nature. He has made himself devilish by indulging in sin. But he has one thing in him by which he is well marked, one characteristic by which he is distinguished; this one thing is penitence—he is contrite; he is *the sinner that repents*. The astounding declaration of the text is true: on this one sinner, because he is penitent, God looks with *more joy* than on the ninety and nine who are righteous. The joy is not in God's heart only—angels, and the spirits of just

men in glory, and righteous people on earth, all rejoice. It is not joy alone we have here, but we wish all to see that it is a large measure of joy—"more joy."

2. One word in the text must be enunciated with emphasis when the text is read in the church or in public. This word is "*likewise.*" It occurs twice in the discourse reported in the chapter. The chapter contains three parables, all turning on, and intended to illustrate, this—"more joy." And the truth is brilliant when all three unite in shedding light on it. We will make free use of the parables to enable the reader of this sermon to see that *more joy* is felt over *one* sinner that repents than there is over *ninety and nine* just persons. We will take them in the order that suits our taste.

1. A woman had ten pieces of silver, and lost one piece. The loss was the cause of sorrow. It caused diligent search, by the help of a lighted candle and a broom, until the silver was found. When it was found, she called her friends and neighbors together, and said, "Rejoice with me, for I have found the piece which I had lost." And then the Saviour says, "Likewise, I say unto you, there is joy in the presence of the angels of God over one sinner that repents."

2. A shepherd had in his flock one hundred sheep, and lost one. He left the ninety and nine in the wilderness, and went after the lost until he found it. His joy is so great he takes it in his arms, puts it on his shoulders rejoicing, carries it to his home in safety. The sheep could not walk fast enough—the

shepherd carries it himself. All the way home he goes rejoicing. He calls together his friends and neighbors to share his joy. It was not joy over the ninety and nine that were safe, and had not been lost; over these the neighboring shepherds had never been called to rejoice. The lost one, when found, gives them joy—"more joy" than the ninety and nine. And then the text occurs with the impressive expression, "I say unto you," and the emphatic word of comparison, "likewise."

3. A certain man had two sons. This introduces a parable whose beauty has excited the world's admiration. We use it to illustrate the text; so the great Teacher invented and used it. And we use it to illustrate one thing in the text, the "more joy;" so the great Teacher used it. The younger of the two sons was profligate, very wicked, and licentious. He wasted his property. He reduced himself to beggary, and to the point of starvation. He hired himself out to feed hogs, and longed to partake of the food which he gave to the hogs. In his reduced condition and squalid poverty, "he came to himself," and said, "How many hired servants of my father have bread enough and to spare, and I am perishing with hunger! I will arise and go to my father, and will say unto him, Father, I have sinned against heaven, and before thee, and am no more worthy to be called thy son: make me as one of thy hired servants." That is what he said he would say. Immediately he set out for his father's house. Evidences of joy at his return must be noted. His father saw and ran to meet him before he got to the

house. He fell on his neck. He kissed him. In his overflowing joy he stopped him in his confession. The son did not say what he said he would say. He ordered the best robe to be put on him. He put a ring on his finger. He killed the fatted calf, and called his friends to share his joy. Had the narrative ended here, it would not have illustrated the text in the chief thing, the "more joy." Who could say that this had never been done to and. for the elder son if he had not charged his father with partiality? The great Teacher is a Master in narration! The elder son becomes angry, and gives as his defense the fact that his father never exhibited such joy over him as was lavished on the prodigal. The father defends himself with dignity. His words move our hearts. This anger of the son, and his reason for it, bring out clearly, very clearly, that there was "more joy" over the penitent prodigal than there ever was over the obedient son. The latter was not a sample of the righteous man. The Teacher does not use him as such, no more than he uses "nine pieces of silver," and "ninety-nine sheep," as samples of righteous men. The thing aimed at and accomplished was to illustrate the text, and encourage sinners to repent. It does this with wonderful force. The joy of the father over the elder son is strongly expressed in these words: "Son, thou art ever with me, and all that I have is thine." In them we have approval and commendation.

In all the words used in this parable there is not one that expressed approval of the conduct of the prodigal before he returned to his father. His conduct was very bad. The narrative exhibits this clearly, and his own words show his opinion in respect to himself. "Father, I have sinned against heaven, and in thy sight, and am no more worthy to be called thy son." His sense of guilt is shown very plainly. And his remorse is bitter. But remorse is not repentance. It must be accompanied by, and productive of, unreserved renunciation of sin and consecration to God. In these the will is active, and when the will consents to renounce all sin, and to return to God with honest confession, then we see "the sinner that repents." God helps us to do this, for without him we cannot repent. He helps when we seek his help by prayer. He works in the intellect to convict, and in the sensibilities to produce sorrow, and this is done by his word and Spirit. But man's will is never *forced* to submit to the will of God in repentance and faith. When the sinner yields, willingly yields, then "God works in him to will and to do of his good pleasure." Phil. ii. 13.

In some men God works with much power to produce repentance. Their conviction is deep and their sorrow is great, and the evidences of it are harrowing. And these are often used as samples, after whom we must fashion ourselves. Such are seen in Luke vii. 44–46, and xv. 17–21, and in Psalm li. But in others repentance is equally genuine and saving, without signs of harrowing grief and dreadful anguish; and it is so because they yield readily to conviction, and humble their hearts in confession of sins, and freely consent to forsake sin and consecrate themselves to God. The contest between the flesh and the spirit is soon ended by their invincible resolution to submit to the will of God. In this contest God looks on with much interest, and when the contest ends, then "there is joy in the presence of the angels of God."

In concluding this discourse, and representing the conflict between God and man, we will use *two* extracts. The *first* is taken from Hickok's Science of the Mind: "When the awakened sinner yields to his animal nature, and descends into degrading vices, the enslaved man knows, and sometimes keenly feels, the deep degradation of his soul. The rational has most absurdly bent in servitude to the animal; the spirit has most unnaturally fixed its end in nature; but the reason sees the absurdity, and the spirit feels the indignity, and hence the wretched man cowers in shame and guilt before the upbraidings of his own conscience. He knows the alternative is open; the perpetuation of his shame and guilt is avoidable; that if he persist in his baseness it will not be nature holding him down under any form of necessity, but that his spirit freely stays, as it voluntarily went down into the place of its degradation. Every hour's delay, every fresh act of sensuous gratification, brings down another stroke of the whip of scorpions, for he is choosing carnal happiness, when he might be, and ought to be, aspiring after, and reaping, the immortal dignities and honors of his spiritual birthright."

The *second* is taken from Watson's Institutes. In the process of pardon there are three parties. "God, as Sovereign: 'Who shall lay any thing to the charge of God's elect? it is God that justifieth, who is he that condemneth?' Christ, as Advocate: not defending the guilty, but interceding for them: 'It is Christ that died, yea, rather, that is risen again, who is even at the right-hand of God, who also maketh *intercession* for us.' Rom. viii. 33, 34. 'If any man sin, we have an *Advocate* with the Father.' 1 John ii. 1. The third party is man, who is, by his own confession, guilty, a sinner, ungodly; for repentance in all cases precedes remission, and it supposes and confesses offense and desert of punishment. God is Judge in this process; not, however, by the law of creation and of works, but by the law of redemption and grace; not as merely just, though just, but as merciful; not as merciful in general, and without any respect to satisfaction, but as propitiated by the blood of Christ, and having accepted the propitiation made by his blood; not merely propitiated by his blood, but moved by his intercession, which he makes as our Advocate in heaven; not only pleading the propitiation made and accepted, but the repentance and faith of the sinner, and the promise of the Judge before whom he pleads. Thus, as pardon does not take place but upon propitiation, the mediation and intercession of Jesus Christ, and on the condition, on the part of the guilty, of repentance and faith in Christ's blood, it is not an act of mere mercy, or of prerogative, but one which consists with a righteous government, and proceeds on grounds that secure the honors of the divine justice."

IV.

ALL FOR GOD.

BY THE REV. W. T. BOLLING,
Western Virginia Conference.

"And there came a certain poor widow, and she threw in two mites, which make a farthing. And he called unto him his disciples, and saith unto them, Verily I say unto you, That this poor widow hath cast more in than all they which have cast into the treasury." Mark xii. 42, 43.

THE Master had finished a most remarkable discourse in the temple, in which he had fully unmasked the shallow hypocrisy of the Pharisees, and had put to shame the skeptical Sadducees. With his disciples he sat in the court, a silent yet deeply-interested spectator, while the people deposited their offerings in the treasury. The Pharisees, yet smarting under the severe rebuke administered, were of their abundance now casting in much, hoping not only to gain the plaudits of the multitude, but to draw some word of approbation from the great Teacher. No word, however, escaped him as he sat reading deeper than the act, penetrating to and analyzing the motive which prompted each donor. At last there came forward one whose face-lines of sorrow betokened a child of suffering, and whose garb proclaimed her at once poor and a widow.

This woman deposited her gift, two mites, aggregating in value one farthing, the price of two sparrows. No gift yet deposited was so small, and yet the little pieces had scarcely left her fingers before the Master broke the silence in the words of our text. Nothing in the great gifts of the rich was worthy his approbation, yet two mites—despised of man—called forth the beautiful words and lesson from the Lord. To the thoughtless these are strange and meaningless words, while to the earnest and patient searcher after truth they come richly laden with instruction and comfort. The child of God, in studying them, feels as though he was passing from the shadows of night into the beautiful light of a cloudless morning. They reveal the scope of God's law—the basis of divine valuation—and light up the path of practical living, and have been the source of comfort to thousands, as they were to this woman and his disciples. We should not confine the teaching here to the mere matter of giving, for giving was not the cause, but the occasion merely, of the utterance of these words. The Master, in making the time of giving the occasion, has given it its true value, and proclaimed giving as an important part of worship and a divinely-appointed means of grace. He who gives not receives not, for it is true here that "with what measure ye mete, it shall be measured to you again." The tendency of man is to stop here, and hence our Lord leads us far beyond the mere occasion, and points to the deeper cause which called forth his gracious approbation of this woman's course, and directs us beyond the mere letter to the spirit of worship. Let us, therefore, humbly and prayerfully consider the deep meaning of these words, that we may profit by the gracious lesson they contain. From them we may find set forth the lesson:

1. *That the law of God demanding performance of duty extends to every intelligent being.*

No circumstances, no condition in this life, can release any subject from its demand. How prone is man to neglect duty and plead circumstances as an excuse to his protesting conscience! This lesson will, if we consider it, awake us from this dream. The law of duty is coëxtensive with the provision for man under grace. "Christ Jesus tasted death for every man," and hence every man is called upon to consecrate his being to Jesus Christ, and there can be no exception. In this instance we find the law as recognized and enforced by our Lord as extending from the greatest to the smallest, from the Pharisee to the poor widow, from millions to mites. If there could be an exception, certainly this poor woman would have been that exception. Think of her condition, consider her surroundings, and think of the insignificance of her possessions. A widow, alone, and dependent upon her own exertions for a living. How small her all was! two mites—a single farthing! Might she not have paused and asked, What good can these do? Human sense would suggest they can do nothing, and surely they can never become factors necessary to the solution of the sublime problem of human happiness and divine glory. Compare these mites under human valuation with the golden deposits of the rich, and how Pride, that spirit of Satan, would urge, If you go with such an offering, the rich will laugh you to scorn! Surely, if any could find a just excuse, she could. The law of God demanded, and well for us this noble woman's conscience answered to its demands, deposited her mites, and made an investment which has brought a sin-burdened world a fortune, and caused millions of human hearts to rejoice in the light of the law of God as the Master unfolds its scope—holding the great and wealthy in its grasp, and yet calling to the poorest and weakest in that vast throng of humanity. Thousands are kept back from the enjoyment of all good by a failure to recognize and live under the law demanding the use of all man's powers and possessions, much or little, to the glory of God. Law pervades the universe, and under it alone is a wise end to be worked out by the harmonious development of all forces. There is no waste in the physical universe, and we have as wise an end to be worked out through the *ephemera* as the eagle, through the mole as a mastodon. So in the sphere of spirit-forces there must be no waste. Every being is important—none can for a moment be excluded as a factor in the unfoldment of the sublime end in view, the elevation of humanity in the scale of holiness and happiness, and the glory of God. The mighty instrument of universal creation must be in tune, and its highest harmony produced only when the fingers of God sweep its keys, from atoms to angels. So the Master here recognized the rich and this poor widow as common subjects of the same inexorable law.

This law does not merely come to man as a family, but presses upon each and every individual of our race. Christ Jesus suffered and provided for every man as a separate being, and every individual may claim all the blessings, and must recognize all the responsibilities, provided for under the gracious plan of redemption. Every man is a sovereign, governing a most wonderful realm, and the manner of his individual living here must settle his individual destiny in the world to come. While we should never forget that "none of us liveth unto himself, and no man dieth unto himself," yet we should ever remember that we have individual powers, privileges, and responsibilities, and that "every one of us must give an account of himself unto God." This poor woman's success, and our profit arising from this lesson, was and is the result of a proper conception upon her part of her duty as an individual, separate and distinct from every other being in that temple-throng. Whatever others might or might not do was no question with her. Had she paused to consider this question, she would have failed. The neglect of duty upon your part, dear reader, may carry some one down to woe, but the neglect of duty by some one else will never justify you or lift you up to heaven. Every man must, in this sense, "bear his own burden." Such was the conception of the great leader of the people of God when he said, "As for me and my house, we will serve the Lord." Such was the conception of the iron-nerved man of God when he stood at Carmel face to face with false prophets, a wicked king, and the wavering thousands of Israel. The great Apostle to the Gentiles realized this individual responsibility to law when, facing false teachers and a misguided people, he exclaimed, "God forbid that I should glory save in the cross of our Lord Jesus Christ!" Whatever course others may pursue, every man must remember his own individual responsibilities growing out of his own powers and privileges. These responsibilities we can by no process rid ourselves of; they come with our coming, go with us along the path of life, go with us into the mists of the valley and shadow of death, and more, must accompany us along the path of destiny even to the judgment-seat of Christ. Man is prone to forget that he must hold a personal, individual, interview with God. Alone with God he must be — alone with his life-record, to stand or fall upon his personal course while on probation. No doubt these truths pressed home upon this good woman, and though every Pharisee laughed, though the littleness of her offering caused a blush to mantle her face, though all else was gone but a tender conscience answering to the demand of the law of God, she came forward to duty, and blessed the world through all the ages, and went home happy in the consciousness of the approval of the Master, and renewed in strength.

2. *The Master demands that we do all we can, and gauges our responsibilities by our ability and opportunities.*

None are neglected in the distribution of divine gifts, and none can be excused for the want of opportunity to do good. All in the temple on this occasion have something, and every one the same opportunity to perform duty. Many, however, failed then, as many fail now, not for want of ability and opportunity, but from a refusal to recognize the law of God, requiring us not to do merely what we will, but to do all we can. God measures our responsibilities by our possibilities, and in all that throng this poor woman was the only one who measured and met the possibilities of the hour and the surroundings. The rich of their abundance gave much, but after all it was only a part. The widow gave less than they, and yet she gave more, for it was her all. No half-hearted service is acceptable to God. Nicodemus never gained by coming at night, and Ananias was lost by keeping back a part. The world would willingly give a part, and, indeed, all men do; yet few, comparatively, enjoy, because few give all. The great day will reveal the fearful woe coming upon many, not because of what they have done, but rather of what they have not done. How clearly is this revealed in the parable of the talents! The demand was made upon each in accordance with his ability and opportunities for improvement. Those who received five and two talents respectively, traded to the full measure of their ability and opportunities, and doubled their lord's money. The servant with one talent proves utterly criminal, and is cast out, not because he had squandered his lord's money, but because he had done nothing. He was not required to improve more than he had ability to improve, and yet it would require all his ability exercised to improve it. Here, then, we see God's law measuring our responsibility by our ability and opportunities.

The Master here did not condemn the rich for giving much, and commend the widow for giving little, but condemned those who kept more for themselves while giving to God much, and commended the poor widow who met the measure of possibility, and gave all she had, and thus coming entirely to God, and placing herself in his keeping. The idea that we are to do only what is pleasant to do is a most fearful device of Satan, leading thousands down to woe. It was pleasant for the rich to give some to God, with no inconvenience to themselves, but it was hard for this woman to yield her last farthing, and turn her face away from the temple with nothing left—all given to God. This was a grand faith —giving all to God, and trusting him for every thing. The religion of Jesus is one of crosses, of constant crucifixion of human pride and power. The man who serves God and despises evil must have a religion which costs him something; and if it cost nothing, he will soon give it away. The disciple must make a deliberate choice between values. God and the world both claim man, and he must give up one or the other, for "ye cannot serve God and mammon," for such is the constitution of humanity that "no man can serve two masters." The world must be used as a means to a higher end. Moses must give up the pleasures of sin, turn his back upon the crown of Egypt, to become the leader of, and a sufferer with, the people of God. Matthew must resign his place at the receipt of customs, and leave all to become an acceptable disciple. Peter, James, and John, when the night of weary and fruitless toil was over, were ready for any change; but Jesus did not call them then. It was only when they, by his command, had pushed out into deep water, and casting their nets, had filled their boats with the coveted load of worldly value, that the call came to them, " Follow me." They now knew its deep import, and left all, and followed him. Let us rest assured we can never enjoy the approval of the Master by a half-hearted service, which will prompt us to give of abundance even much to him. He demands a consecration of all we have. Endowed as man is with all-sufficient ability, and surrounded by abundant opportunities to call all his possible capacities into play, God demands that he do so, and whatever we have, millions or mites, all must be yielded to his glory. Moses on Nebo, viewing the promised land, and contemplating the glorious coming and conquering of the King of kings; Elijah, driving the chariot of God along the celestial way, above the path of death, and going home to rest; St. Paul, rising on the tides of assurance and joy, and from the crest of the last wave shouting the song of triumph back to a sorrowing world —all who ever stood in the glorious light of God as it makes beautiful the valley of death—all have rejoiced by doing not what they would, but, in consecration to God, doing what they could in the sphere where God places them. The great want of the world to-day is not mere hearers of the word, but doers of the works as well. "Whoso looketh into the perfect law of liberty, and continueth therein, he being not a forgetful hearer, but a doer of the work, this man shall be blessed in his deeds." Right-thinking is very necessary, yet right-thinking, uncoupled with right-doing, is utterly valueless. The duty of every follower of Christ is to do all he or she can, and that, too, just when and where God in his wisdom has placed them. This woman's presence in the temple at this time was an all-sufficient evidence of her orthodoxy of belief; yet, without the actual doing of her duty under the demand of the law of labor, she would never have received the blessed commendation of the Master, and the world would have lost the rich legacy of his words, and the comforting lessons they contain. We should ever remember the lesson here, that we are to do as we have ability. God knows us and our capacities. We frequently remain idle because we can find no great thing to do. How frequently do men fail at this point! Let me do some great thing! is the cry of Pride. All this is sin. We must labor just in the field God has selected for us. If, with small capacity, we fail to labor in a small field, would we not fail, with large capacity, to labor in a large field? Remember, our capacity is the measure of our responsibility. Had this woman possessed three mites, and given two, she would never have been noticed more than others; but when she gave all, though that all was almost as nothing, she met the demand, and her gift measured her capacity, and met her responsibility.

Because God has not given us much, we will be none the less guilty if we fail to use our little for his glory. If God has given you five talents, he will be satisfied only with five talents more at his coming. If he has given you two talents, he will require two more. Few may do great works, yet all may do important work. "As ye have opportunity, do good unto all men." This world is very wide, and as a vast ocean is lashed by the storms, so is this poor world lashed by the storms of trial. Ah, how poor humanity is suffering all over the sin-cursed sphere! The field is very large — large enough for us all to work in. The minister and the layman alike can find plenty to do. The clouds of woe, which hang so loweringly over the people who know no gospel light, tell us where much may be done, and the sorrow-burdened millions all around us are calling us to a duty we owe them. How strange it is that professed Christians say, "I cannot do any thing!" God bless you, my brother, or sister, it is because you will not do something. God is not calling alone for the millions of the rich, but for your two mites. You can do something for him if you will, and woe unto you if you fail in this duty!

3. *The Master values our efforts not by their apparent magnitude, but by the spirit in which they are put forth.*

Neither the much cast in by the rich nor the mites of the widow were within themselves of any value in the eyes of our Lord. No system of calculation could make much mites, or mites much. They had their human value, and no process could alter them.

In the eyes of the Master they had no value in themselves.

Deeds, labors, however great, can never, in the eyes of God, be meritorious in themselves. God is cause—not effect. He searches the heart, and regards not the mere act. He demands all, and that we do all we can, and then tells us: "So likewise ye, when ye have done all these things which are commanded you, say we are unprofitable servants, we have done that which was our duty to do." To assume that the Master will reward us according to the magnitude of our works, from the stand-point of human valuation, would have excluded this poor woman, and would indeed give the rich rewards of heaven to the more favored few, and cut off the vast majority of our race. Happily for us, the blessed Lord does not so judge. This woman's mites were of more value than all the rich cast in, not merely because they were all she had, for deeper yet lies the reason. These two mites stood out as her heart's offering to God in contrast with the pride-offering of the rich — the basis of divine valuation being not the earthly value, but the deeper cause, the prompting motive. Seeing, then, that there must be something deeper than the mere act, and that a certain spirit lends value even to the smallest offering, and its absence makes the much valueless, we may inquire what this is. One simple word answers, *Love.* The smallest labor performed by my child from love is precious to me, while the day's toil for wages is utterly of no pleasure to me. So no labor is rendered acceptable to the Master unless it spring from love. No matter how much a man may do, yet he must fail if he have not love as its basis. "If any man love not the Lord Jesus Christ, let him be Anathema, Maran atha." No man was ever more deeply versed in the things of God than the great Apostle Paul. Religion with him was his daily life. He was ever calm, and yet moved profoundly; while his heart was always hot, his head was always cool. He sounded the depths and ascended the heights of personal religious experience. Neither the serpent of Miletus, beasts at Ephesus, jail at Philippi, nor death at Rome, could cause him to hesitate for a moment; but amid all these things he exclaimed, "None of these things move me!" What does he tell us? hear him: "Though I give all my goods to feed the poor; yea, though I give my body to be burned, and have not charity [love], it profiteth me nothing." The reason he gives us for his giving up all, and counting suffering pleasant, and loss gain, is, "The love of Christ constraineth us." And he made this the basis of all his religious life.

No; these two mites were but little, yet this woman's all. No process of human reasoning, no pride could get them. It was only when love came in, and she valued God and his law above all worldly things, that her little mites became as nothing to her, and valuable to the Master. Peter and John seem at first to be led by very different motives, though at last they were in perfect agreement. John, from the first, was "that disciple whom Jesus loved," because from the first John was that disciple who loved Jesus. Simon's profession was great, and his outward acts of devotion many, but never until the moment of his trial did he realize that love alone could make a true disciple. When afterward the Master asked him, "Simon, son of Jonas, lovest thou me?" did he feel the full import of the divine requirement, and his throbbing heart answered its demands when he said, "Lord, thou knowest all things; thou knowest that I love thee." St. John gives us the reason of this requirement when he tells us, "God is love." Pride, or even fear, may cause us to give God some of our abundance, but love alone can lead us to the cross, and induce us to leave there our all as a pure heart-offering to the blessed Saviour.

The words of the Master are beautiful words; the works of the Master were grand works, but the love of the Master for a lost world contains the sublime force of the gospel. No human power, no wisdom of man, no wealth, could save a world lost in the gloom of the sin-night. The love of God, as unfolded in the gift of his Son, has concentrated and flashed its life-giving light upon us, kindled the fires of love upon the altars of human hearts, and moving them to labor until the truths of God are hung upon the mystic thread of the ages, sparkling with renewed beauty beneath each successive century's sun, raising poor humanity from the dust of woe, and making it rich in precious hope of eternal life. How precious is the truth that millions and mites are of equal value in themselves in his sight! Dives cannot purchase a mansion, yet poor Lazarus can gain one without money and without price. Pride may come, laden with its costly gifts; Fear may come, staggering under its heavy burden of duty; but the mists of selfishness will shut out the light of hope, and fearful silence will be unbroken by any word of commendation by the Master. Love may come, clothed in garments of poverty, or bathed in tears of sorrow, and yet her precious gift will be received, and the rich benediction, "Well done, thou good and faithful servant; thou hast been faithful over a few things, I will make thee ruler over many things," be heard. These lessons should impress us with the fearfulness of human life, with its vast privileges and great responsibilities. The Master sits in the great temple to-day, and watches each one of us in our coming and going, viewing and analyzing our motives, penetrating to the inmost depths of our souls.

The law of duty, demanding that we do something for God, holds us in its iron grasp. In the great world-temple we stand with the Pharisees or the widow in spirit, and our course in time must settle our estate in eternity. No circumstances can release us from its demands. All can do something for the Master—casting in much or mites. Though all cannot do great things, we can all do important things; for nothing can be so small but that, if done through love, it will be received as of value by the Lord. Brother, sister, wait not for greater opportunities, but go out to-day in the field God has assigned you, and where in his grace he has placed you; glean it, and bring the results—much or little

—and consecrate it to his service. Remember, even if you can do no more than give a cup of cold water to one of his suffering, thirsty ones, he has promised you shall not be unrewarded. Go out and perform duty — succor the distressed, relieve the needy, pray for the oppressed, even suffer for God, and leave results with him. How little did this woman know of the final results of her course in its effects upon the world! The Master's blessing to her was the least of it. That was a grand hour for her when she went home conscious of having then performed duty and received the blessed Saviour's benediction of approval; yet how small a part was this of the result of his words of comfort, drawn forth by her spirit and walk! how they have come to the weary millions with the ages, making the souls of men glad, even when curtained by the shadows of sorrow's dreary night! Her poverty has become a fortune to humanity, and the results of her performance of duty a heritage precious to the world. Let us do as she did, and thus bless ourselves and the world about us.

Child of God, look around you. A gladsome universe in the sublimity of its harmony invites us to join it in its mighty and harmonious anthem of praise to God. The bending heavens of the future, unflecked by clouds, and jeweled with stars of promise, are just before us. The redeemed, washed in the blood of the Lamb, await us just beyond the river, while the angels — busy workers for God — stand ready to greet and hail us as fellow-laborers and citizens in the kingdom of our Father. You may be poor, very poor, and be scorned by the rich—so was this poor woman; you may be wrapped in sorrow—and so was she. Remember, dear reader, all times, places, and circumstances, reveal something to do, or to be suffered, for the Master. "Our labor is not in vain in the Lord." This poor woman has no mites now, and no sorrow. Her mites have grown into a crown, a robe, a home, "an inheritance incorruptible, undefiled, and that fadeth not away." All these await us if we do all we can where God in his wisdom places us, using our all—much or mites—for his glory. Bring your gifts to the Master, dear reader. Bring your mental powers, bring your heart, bring your life to Jesus, and consecrate them all to him—keeping back nothing from him—and then will you be happy here; and when the end shall come—as come it must—then, above the grand, solemn doxology of fading spheres, you may join the glad anthem of praise which, from his laborers, called to an eternal rest, shall swell in billowy tides of joyous harmony, "Unto Him that loved us and washed us in his own blood." God help us to be faithful in all things—much or little—so as to live and die to his glory!

V.

INQUIRY AND INVITATION; OR, PHILIP'S PHILOSOPHY.

BY THE REV. J. B. McGEHEE, A.M.,
South Georgia Conference.

"And Nathanael said unto him, Can there any good thing come out of Nazareth? Philip saith unto him, Come and see." John i. 46.

NATHANAEL was not a free-thinker, skeptic, or rationalist. Had he been either, or worse, he is entitled to the benefit of correct criticism—a hearing characterized by candor and charity. This is dignifying in itself, advances the cause of truth, and should be awarded all men and every measure. With thinking men, impromptu and indiscriminate censure or praise are little more than the ebullitions of a madman and the flattery of a fool.

To these tests we propose to subject the question and conduct of Nathanael. Let us see if that charity which "thinketh no evil" does not acquit him of doubt, or downright denial. More—let us ask if the inquiry of the one was not as practical and profound as the invitation of the other was wise and weighty.

Nazareth was situated in Lower Galilee. Here was the home of our Lord for thirty years. Though a small city, it was not destitute of attractions and

THE REV. J. B. McGEHEE.
Of the South Georgia Conference.

advantages. Beautiful in scenery, commanding in situation, its sublime surroundings fully atoned the presence of difficult ascent, rugged rocks, and hills made bald by dashing rains. If we may credit Geike's admirable "Life of Jesus," "in spring-time Nazareth was the prettiest place in Palestine." In school and synagogue it was not wanting, nor in inlet and outlet. The old Roman road ran near the foot of the hill, and was intersected by other highways. These blessed or cursed the mountain city with the civilization, commerce, and crimes of Rome, Phenicia, and Arabia. Thus opened to the world, Nazareth increased in corruption. Her citizens grew turbulent; her own hands led her Christ "to the brow of the hill whereon their city was built, that they might cast him down headlong; but he, passing through the midst of them, went his way."

Some have supposed that exhibitions like this spread a film of prejudice over the eyes of Nathanael, and thus caused him to suspect the merit of any thing emanating from such a source. We are not surprised. The judicious Hooker himself indulges the thought that "the subtilty of Satan, casting a mist before his eyes, putteth in his heart the commonly-conceived persuasion concerning Nazareth."

Sentiments like these merit regard and remark, because they accord with our knowledge of Satanic working, man's weakness, and the law-world in which he lives. Between cause and effect, parent and offspring, government and citizen, home and character, there are, and will be till the trump sounds, relation and likeness. Name and nativity adjudge us little or large. Nothing is more common than the association of high expectation with many and high-sounding titles. We pause—to see if we are in the presence of a human. Left to ourselves, we cannot see how that crying child, buried in the bulrushes, can ever be learned in the wisdom of Egypt, the leader of all Israel, the lawgiver of the world. Like the son of Socrates, we are ever saying, "If we would develop a perfect man, we must surround him with perfect circumstances."

Does nothing correct this? We answer, Yes. There is a day-dawn that chases away the mists of the morning. There is a "day-star that arises in our hearts." Was not Philip's message the dawn of day to the mind of Nathanael? Was it not followed by the day-star flooding his moral being with beauty and ineffable bliss? We shall see.

The short, simple story that brought him to Jesus was this: "We have found him of whom Moses in the law and the prophets did write, Jesus of Nazareth, the Son of Joseph." Conversant with the law and the prophets, having so often heard "And thou *Bethlehem* of Judea," it was both practical and pious for him to ask, "Can any good thing [that good thing] come out of *Nazareth?*" Far from profaning, he was in intent guarding the sacred Scriptures. Free from deceitfulness—a vice so common with Jews—he was "an Israelite indeed, in whom is no guile." Fixing his eye on Jesus, and firm in the faith, grander discoveries, graver duties, and a glorious destiny, were in prospect. The sincere inquirer becomes Bartholomew—one of the twelve—and a life initiated by honest inquiry exchanges the cross of a martyr for the crown of a king.

Turning from these thoughts, indulged largely for the help they bring to a proper analysis of the text, we submit the following propositions:

I. All inquiries into the great truths of the gospel, if successful, should be conducted in reverence and profound humility.

II. The greatest truths of our holy religion—the good emanating from Nazareth—are apprehended, not by logical process, but by personal approach and individual experience.

III. The benefits flowing from such an investigation justify all the expenditure involved in Christian life.

I. Inquiries into the great truths of the gospel.

1. Are they admissible? We readily answer, *They are.* God has implanted in man a disposition to inquire into the origin and nature of things, and this in part distinguishes him from beast and bird, and assimilates him to loftier and purer intelligences. Inquisitiveness is a valuable ally. The spirit of search lies at the foundation of all mental progress. Right education seeks to foster it. To stimulate it, books and maps, pictures and prizes, lectures and essays, address the eye, ear, and heart, of youth. To its altar the sons of science and song bring their daily oblations. Born in the nursery, developed in the school-room, common to all ranks, essential to every avocation, it was given for great mental and moral ends. Sanctified, it sends forth

waters for the healing of the nations, clear as crystal. Secularized, it is a fountain of unmixed evil. The abuse of it gave the world "The Age of Reason," a publication as shallow and slanderous as Paine's life was licentious. **Loosely reined**, it led the well-intentioned Kant to diverge, till the defender of the faith developed into the father of German infidelity. Our own Commonwealth furnishes a sad illustration of its abuse. Proud intellect and brilliant oratory associated with irreverence and absence of regard for the living and the dead! What a monster! Let his name remain unmentioned. This is one side, but splendid illustrations of the other are not wanting. The names of Moses and Paul, Newton, Hugh Miller, and Livingstone, are as household words. Benefactors of the ages, their memory is as ointment poured forth. For the beauty and benedictions of their lives the world acknowledges its obligations to a patient, well-disciplined spirit of investigation.

That this spirit may be introduced into the realm of religious thought none can deny. "All Scripture is given by inspiration of God, and is profitable for doctrine, for reproof, for correction, for instruction in righteousness." These things are to be in our hearts, and we are to teach them diligently to our children. The Bible belongs to the world, and should be studied, *and may be understood*. It does not shun, but seeks, investigation. The practice of it supposes search and a right understanding. He who discourages this search is unlike Jesus and the apostles. The priest or Church—though Rome herself should grow so arrogant—that locks up these sacred truths, and withholds their light from the masses, is an apostate from the faith, no friend to Jesus—*an enemy to all civil and religious liberty.*

2. How far may these inquiries be indulged? Lest our meaning be lost in words, we answer, As far as human intellect and things revealed will allow. Beyond the former we cannot go. Any effort, yea, even wish, to transcend the latter is impious and profane. The two were made for each other, and are in happy harmony. Taken together, they illustrate the unity of God, and the divine philosophy that pervades the world. To be loyal and normal, mind must respect revelation as revelation respected mind. Harmony must continue. Long ago the question was asked, "Canst thou by searching find out God?" "Canst thou find out the Almighty to perfection?" and there was but one response—"The world by wisdom knew not God." What is true of God is true of all the fundamental doctrines. Familiar as we are with the Apostles' Creed, what unscaled heights it contains! what fields yet unexplored! Where God leads and lights the way we can go—not beyond. In the nature of the case we know but in part. A unit cannot compass a million.

We speak of limitations. God's revelation everywhere regards man as man. Man's ability and *inability* receive equal and proper emphasis. Both are visible in the facts that God made revelation, and that this revelation proceeds as far as it does, and pauses at the proper place. Somewhat of its grand truths, so much as is said, I can comprehend;

but each truth can spring a thousand questions I cannot answer. Had it been possible, and had God revealed all the modes by which these truths exist; all the reasons affecting the existence of each; all their connections and dependencies, and all the philosophy of any thing the adorable Trinity has said or done for us, such a revelation would have bewildered the world.

But such is not the case. Heaven sees us as we are, not as we pretend or presume to be. What is needful, and admits of comprehension, God reveals. What is speculative, and beyond our capacity, he wisely withholds.

There may be other reasons for the restriction. In placing facts above philosophy, no doubt great moral ends were subserved. As a creature, man was under a government which supposed probation, and extended to all the powers that make up a free moral agent. To make this rule successful, to educate, purify, and save this subject, a revelation must needs appeal to more than his intellect. Faith has a function, and so have hope, humility, patience, and love. All these are to be trained and tried; and, in doing this, what better methods than those furnished by the callings and conflicts of this life? Do men complain that revelation does not declare all? that it does not compel faith, but leaves room for doubt? Do they reject it because they cannot solve every thing suggested by revealed facts? If so, they are in arms against probation, and all around them other books, systems, kingdoms, objects, atoms, have their fastnesses which human power cannot penetrate. As in this department we are exercised for our good, so in the other "tribulation worketh patience, and patience experience, and experience hope, and hope maketh not ashamed, because the love of God is shed abroad in our hearts by the Holy Ghost."

For one, we are sick of the senseless cry of "Mystery! mystery! nobody can understand the Bible." It is a reflection on its divine Author, and not honoring to man. The difficulty is not in the book, but in a want of proper study. Take it as it is—a publication of facts—and we have the plainest, best-established, most beautifully-illustrated book in the world. No doctrine is incomprehensible, no precept impracticable, no promise precarious. All may be seen, illustrated, and enjoyed.

3. With what spirit should these inquiries proceed? "If thine eye be single, thy whole body shall be full of light. But if thine eye be evil, thy whole body shall be full of darkness." In pursuing the truth, care should be taken to ascertain all that may cause us to stumble. Should indifference, vain conceit, prejudice, previous opinion, or evil intent, prove a hinderance, it should be put away. More: "If thine eye offend thee, pluck it out." As ancient Israel, consulting Urim and Thummim, put away uncleanness, and presented the required offerings, in like manner must we knock at the door of truth. The sacred awe and reverent posture that transfixed and transformed Moses, as the first beam from the burning bush fell on his astonished gaze, should be seen in all who would know more of the

deep things of God. These are his truths—from him, by him, for him. From such a source, conveyed to us through the flesh of the Only-begotten, waiting to be crystallized in the songs and hallelujahs of the saved, *no wonder* angels desire to look into these things. Ranged about the throne, they rejoice in the simplest edict that calls a human being to worship or work. If we would be like them, if we would grow in knowledge, we must imitate their reverence and humility.

But this is not all. So far no real step has been taken. The labor, though not lost, is chiefly preparatory. With the mind thus cleared, some one must be seen who can say, "We have found him"— some Philip who, taking the honest inquirer by the hand, will lead him to a loftier plane and larger enjoyment. And this introduces our second proposition.

II. The greatest truths of our holy religion— Nazareth's substantial good—are apprehended, not by logical process, **but by personal approach and individual experience.**

We say the greatest truths, without reflecting on any part of the inspired volume. The gospel contains *no unimportant fact*—all are edifying. By the greatest we mean fundamental doctrines.

Our reference to "logical process" should not be construed into an assault on real science, advanced education, high culture. The ability to pursue a train of thought, embellish and enforce it, has a price above rubies. Nor should it be confined to academics, Congress, and Parliament. The parent, man of business, Sunday-school teacher, and embassador of Jesus, cannot be too highly endowed. Exhortation may fire a field-piece, but it requires trained thought to forge, bring into position, and give aim to these weapons of war.

Important, however, as training is, it is not the great requisite. This is found in Philip's philosophy. How wise he was! When Nathanael would find the chief good, he engaged him in no controversy; nor did he remand him to a metaphysical treatise on the "isms and ologies" of the day; but, like a well-instructed scribe, he found in "come and see" a more excellent way. Concise, direct, sufficient, it recognized the fact that the hearer had no time to lose, and the preacher no vanity to indulge. It enthroned the idea that *motion toward Christ* is worth a *thousand dry discussions about the "absolute" and "infinite."* With Philip, *doing* was better than thinking. The one was a mere path that *might* find the highway, but the other was the royal road leading to real attainment and rich adornment. No wonder he said, "Come," enlist head and heart, hands, feet, *all*—nothing can substitute approach, contact, and consecration.

It is no arrogance to say this should be the practice of every minister and all Churches. At a time when infidel publications flood the world, and the cry of "mystery" falls on every ear, the little ones who cannot come to Christ should be carried in the arms of the Church, and adults, already perplexed, should be started into action toward him. "If the trumpet give an uncertain sound, who shall prepare himself to battle?" Can we do better than fill the world's ear with the stirring strains of Philip's philosophy? We cannot, if our proposition is true.

1. Let us test it by the Scriptures. The author of the seventy-third Psalm, speaking of his experience, says: "My steps had well-nigh slipped, for I was envious at the foolish, when I saw the prosperity of the wicked. When I thought to know this [the knowledge of God's purpose], it was too painful for me, until I *went* into the sanctuary of God; *then* understood I their end. Thou shalt guide me with thy counsel, and afterward receive me to glory. My flesh and my heart faileth; but God is the strength of my heart, and my portion forever." The congregations of the great Teacher were not unlike ours. Comprehend the deep spirituality of the law they did not, but rather made it void through their traditions. How the Master pitied them! How his heart was moved as he saw them bending under "burdens which neither they nor their fathers were able to bear!" Standing in their midst, stretching out his arms, the Prince of compassion cries, "*Come unto me,* all ye that labor and are heavy-laden. *Take my yoke upon you, and learn of me; and ye shall find rest unto your souls.*" Take another picture. The scene is laid in Jerusalem. It was the Feast of Tabernacles. "Now about the midst of the feast Jesus went up into the temple and taught. And the Jews marveled, saying, How knoweth this man letters, having never learned? Jesus answered them, My doctrine is not mine, but

his that sent me. If *any* man will *do* his will he shall *know* of the doctrine."

Turn we to Saul of Tarsus, sitting at the feet of Gamaliel. What opportunities for knowing the truth! Who can predict that this conscientious soul, consecrated to the study of the learned expositions around him, will ever count them "as loss for the excellency of the knowledge of Christ Jesus?" Alas! sitting at Gamaliel's feet left him far from truth—from Jesus—the same blind, bigoted, blood-thirsty Saul of Tarsus. St. Luke records the story of his progress. Somewhere between Jerusalem and Damascus he realizes the necessity of *learning himself*, and getting *to and into* Jesus Christ. By some means he recognizes the voice of that Christ, saying, "If *any* man will be my *disciple*, let him deny himself, and take up his cross." It is enough. He begins to do by praying, "Lord, what wilt thou have me to do?" The sequel we know. His after-life—a living epistle known and honored by all—we need not detail. Let Paul speak: "I neither received it of men, nor was I taught it but by the revelation of Jesus Christ—it pleased God to reveal his Son in me." His life accorded with his experience. Ever afterward he cautioned the Churches against philosophy, vain deceit, and the rudiments of this world. To him, as Neander, "the heart was the best theologian." With him, the great obstacle to the progress of the gospel was moral obliquity. Of the gospel he was not ashamed, for therein is the righteousness of God revealed. If hid, "it is hid to them that are lost, in whom the god of this world hath blinded the minds of them that believe not, lest the light of the glorious gospel of Christ, who is the image of God, should shine unto them." "To this man will I look—even to him that is poor, and of a contrite spirit, and trembleth at my word." "The secret of the Lord is with them that fear him; and he will show them his covenant."

2. Tried by the soundest philosophy—common sense — and Philip's philosophy holds good. A visit to a place modifies our opinion of that place. Reading men at a distance is a slow, uncertain process. Approach, spirit-communion, correct our prejudices and change our estimate. Merchandise ordered is not so satisfactory as stocks selected. Matrimonial alliances conducted by telegraph have a spice of novelty, and create a sensation, but seldom bring the glowing sunshine and unmixed sweetness of married life. These are most apt to flow from the lifted latch, quiet approach, gentle rap, and soft-sitting sofa, where eye speaks to eye, and each heart fancies it hears the throbbings of the other.

The praise of practice is on the lips of every profession. Great masters in science, poetry, diplomacy, and war, were men who *moved up*—doers, and not idle dreamers. The pen, chisel, plane, plow, sword —*grasped and in motion*—are more potent for the solution of difficulties, and more prolific of results, than those locked up or idle at our side. *Nothing is equal to taking hold of a thing.* Contact brings inspiration and strength. This is the philosophy of invitations to the altar. On this principle a sinner that will comply with some proposition—move in some direction, however slight the motion—may be called hopeful; but one that stands aloof, stands still—*excepts to every thing, and does nothing*—places himself where his personal salvation would violate the laws of common sense and revealed religion.

We cannot conclude this branch of the subject without emphatic reference to the world's folly. In matters trivial, compared with the interests of the soul, how many try every issue! Here they bring their batteries, collect crucible and chemical, and exhaust every energy; but in things that affect their souls—the great, green, fresh forever—how many occupy the seat of the scorner and skeptic, and decline Bible-reading, prayer, and every thing that might better them or confirm the truth of Christianity! To all such we would say, This system is true or false. If true, it is graciously yet fearfully true, and it becomes you to avail yourselves of all the blessings these truths impart; and you should do it at once, lest that come upon you which was spoken of Jerusalem: "If thou hadst known in this thy day the things which belong unto thy peace! but now they are hid from thine eyes." If false, it is harmless, and as such is unlike any other falsehood the world ever saw; if false, the mightiest intellects have failed to detect the sophistry; if false, no combination has been able to effect its overthrow. Down to this day no sincere Christian has regretted his allegiance; and not one has died exclaiming against his principles, and exhorting his son, as did the expiring Altamont, not to follow his footsteps. But we will not anticipate.

III. The benefits flowing from an investigation, as already foreshadowed, justify all the expenditures involved in Christian life.

Christianity brings with it gifts far surpassing those the wise men laid at the feet of the world's Redeemer. As a system of doctrines, it is instinct with authority, beauty, certainty, harmony, bespeaking its divine origin, and proclaiming it unique and unrivaled. In the light of this blazing constellation the world deciphers its high-born parentage, the source of evil, the remedy of the lapsed, the path of life, and the changeless destinies to come. Far removed from atheism, fate, materialism, it dignifies the soul, and would elevate it to associations and employments angelic and endless.

Its worship of denial and duty, prayer and praise—no mean exercise should hereafter prove a fable—is a fit acknowledgment of our dependence, and a nearer approach to those loftier intelligences who find ecstatic joy in tributes of thanksgiving to "the only wise God and our Saviour Jesus Christ."

Its incomparable morals command the admiration of the ages. Beneath their sheltering wings families repose in safety, society dwells secure, and nations find a bulwark unknown to bristling guns and frowning fleets.

But these benefits are not confined to homes, communities, and commonwealths. The kingdom of which we speak cometh not with observation; it is a kingdom within you. Its benefits are personal, spiritual, saving. To one properly testing these truths there arises a stability of sentiment, and a sweet serenity of soul, not unlike that which comes to him who, long tossed on some uncertain sea, sees the distant land. Long driven here and there, the sport of every wave, now he finds a footing on his native shore, and smiles adieu to ocean-fears. He who effects a landing on *credenda* of the Nazarene, finds "solid rock—and all is sea beside."

Did Christianity pause *here*, and do no more than afford an anchorage for the world's faith, *who does not see in that* ample remuneration for all the thought and effort expended? Improved self-respect, born of a consciousness that we have a faith, and are no longer "like a wave of the sea, driven with the wind and tossed," is worth thousands of gold and silver.

But creed and stability of soul are not all man needs, or Nazareth affords. He must have something to restore his relations, return forfeited estate, witness his enrichment, guide his goings, sanctify his labors, losses, and life, stand by his dying couch, and bid him "Go thou thy way till the end be; for thou shalt rest, and stand in thy lot at the end of the days." Vast as are these requirements, Jesus of Nazareth is equal to all. "In him dwelleth all the fullness of the Godhead bodily." He "by the grace of God tasted death for every man." "He that spared not his own Son, but delivered him up for us all, how shall he not with him also freely give us all things?" Already multitudes have been justified and adopted into the family of God. "And because ye are sons, God hath sent forth the Spirit of his Son into your hearts, crying, Abba, Father." Living, they desire to depart and be with Christ; dying, they sing,

> Jesus can make a dying-bed
> Feel soft as downy pillows are,
> While on his breast I lean my head,
> And breathe my life out sweetly there.

What a cloud of witnesses compass us about! They are from the north, south, east, and west. Among them are those who loved and prayed for us. Throned and harped, they speak to you and me. From every cliff of glory these voices come. There is no discord. There is but one message, and that is, "Come and see."

Gentle reader, accept the invitation; approach, and dismiss your doubts; see and live, and live forever!

VI.

THE THINGS PREPARED FOR THEM THAT LOVE GOD.

BY THE REV. LINUS PARKER, D.D.,
Louisiana Conference.

"But as it is written, Eye hath not seen, nor ear heard, neither have entered into the heart of man, the things which God hath prepared for them that love him. But God hath revealed them unto us by his Spirit." 1 Cor. ii. 9, 10.

This passage is quoted substantially from Isaiah, illustrating what the apostle means by "comparing spiritual things with spiritual." The product is a sort of double inspiration, and the authority irresistible. Through Isaiah and Paul a great truth is declared. In this case it has to do with something exceedingly momentous, and relates to that which is most vital in doctrine and experience.

I. *The things prepared of God.*

A clew to these may be obtained by reference to the words of the prophet: "For since the beginning of the world men have not heard, nor perceived by the ear, neither hath the eye seen, O God, besides thee, what he hath prepared for him that waiteth for him. Thou meetest him that rejoiceth and worketh righteousness, those that remember thee in thy ways." Manifestly the things in the prophet's mind were spiritual, such special blessings of grace and providence as are prepared for them that wait on God. The drift of the apostle's discourse, and the whole connection, limit the things prepared to the gospel and its privileges, the revelations of truth by it, and a spiritual and supernatural experience of its benefits. They are "the things of God," "the deep things of God," "the things of the Spirit of God," that "which none of the princes of this world knew." There is in all this no direct allusion to the marvels of the future life, none to the heavenly glory. Grace finally ripens into glory, and that glorified state is something wondrous fair, and beautiful beyond conception, transcending all we have seen, or heard, or imagined. But the language of the text describes the present experience of the child of God. They are things now felt, realized, possessed. It is a present salvation through faith, and what is revealed by the Spirit in the believing heart; for, what eye hath not seen, nor ear heard, neither have entered into the heart of man, God hath revealed unto us by his Spirit. These wonderful things, if anywhere, are in the heart, and manifested to the loving soul.

They are described as things "which God hath prepared." The gospel is of God. Neither angels, men, nor devils, could have been the authors of it. The moral evidences are sufficient. Whatever may be the weight of prophecy and miracles, to us the more direct and convincing proof is in the divine teaching, in the person and character of Christ, and in the power of the gospel to save, to change the heart, and to reform the conduct. The world, with all its wisdom, and learning, and philosophy, could never have produced the Bible or invented Christ. Salvation is of God—the plan is his—the execution of the plan, and all the doctrines connected with it, are of God. It is the wisdom of God, distasteful to the wisdom of men, and infinitely above the grasp of human reason.

The blessings of the gospel are "things prepared." In the most obvious sense of being arranged beforehand, "which God ordained before the world unto our glory," here is the foreknowing and the predestinating—the preparing of salvation for a race that, in the divine presence, had fallen into sin, and come short of the glory of God. The ideal of grace existed before the actual catastrophe. It goes back into the abyss of eternity, and into the depths of the preëxistence of the Son of God. It was "the wisdom of God in a mystery, even the hidden wisdom." It was long preparing; how long we cannot tell. But before the world it was ordained. The universe, in all its vast and remote economies, the divine government, and the work of creation, were all adjusted with reference to the plan of redemption, and the rescue of a ruined world. Noah prepared the ark for the saving of his house—a preparation extending through more than a century. David, with lavish expenditure and almost incredible industry, prepared for the building of the temple. On a grander scale, and with a sweep sublime in its vastness, God has prepared the blessings of salvation for them that love him, "even the mystery which hath been hid from ages and from generations, but now is made manifest to his saints."

The things were prepared in the kindred sense of being stored up and held in reservation. As Joseph prepared against the famine in Egypt by filling the granaries, and laying up for the time of dearth, so it may be said that God has prepared for human sin and woe. The store-house of grace is full. The means of meeting the terrible outburst of sin are at hand, and ready. As God in his providence has stored up coal and oil for our comfort, and all mineral treasure for the benefit of men, so has he prepared these spiritual things. They are things prepared, the remedy for the disease that preys upon us, the provisions which our desperate condition calls for. "Thou meetest him that rejoiceth, and worketh righteousness." A Saviour is ready for the lost, a sin-offering is at the door, the light of the Holy Spirit meets the soul at the dawn of consciousness.

Since before the world, and through all the ages and generations, God has been arranging for and providing the things of salvation. That they are thus prepared of God, ordained before the world unto our glory, indicates the surpassing excellence of them. God has been occupied about them, and bringing them to perfection. His power, wisdom, and love, are displayed in redemption as these attributes could never have been exhibited in material creations. In the fact of the divine preparation we see how wonderful these things must be, and how exalted the privilege of believers, "to whom God would make known what is the riches of the glory of this mystery among the Gentiles, which is Christ in you, the hope of glory." The feast, long in preparing, is ready; it is a royal spread of all that the heart hungers for, a munificent provision, and the invitation is, Come, for " all things are now ready."

II. *The things prepared revealed to the heart by the Holy Spirit.*

They are not revealed through the physical senses. "Eye hath not seen, nor ear heard." These and other senses connect us with the outer and material world, but they cannot of themselves put us in connection with the things of God. The eye cannot see God—it cannot take in spiritual forms. The ear cannot hear the divine voice.

Nor have these spiritual things entered into the heart of man. The world by wisdom knew not God. None of the princes of this world knew the hidden wisdom. Whether princes of the Jewish hierarchy, the princes of worldly power and dominion, or the princes of thought and learning, this was something beyond their grasp. Taken for the reasoning faculties, or for the sensibilities, for the imagination and the affections, it is still true that the things prepared have not entered into the heart of man.

Sense and reason, apart from the supernatural work of the Spirit in the heart, have never been able to comprehend spiritual things. They are beyond the reach of the senses, and above the unaided reason of men. No glimpse of them comes to the eye, no echo of them to the ear, no conception of them ever reaches the heart of the natural man.

He can take in the sublimities and beauties of landscape, enjoy the harmony and melody of music, and revel in the fields of poetry and science, but he knows nothing of spiritual things.

The things of the Spirit must be made plain to us by the direct operation of the Holy Spirit in the heart. "But God hath revealed them unto us by his Spirit." The word inspired is not sufficient in itself. There must also be a revealing Spirit, to open the blind eyes, and to unstop the deaf ears, and to shine into the dark and sinful soul. The gospel was not understood by the apostles till the Pentecostal baptism. Christ was to be glorified by the Spirit. "He shall glorify me; for he shall take of mine, and shall show it unto you." We are absolutely dependent upon the aid of the Spirit to apprehend Christ truly and savingly, and to grasp any spiritual truth whatever. The natural man is spiritually blind, and he "receiveth not the things of the Spirit of God; for they are foolishness unto him; neither can he know them, because they are spiritually discerned." The Bible is largely a sealed book until the Spirit comes to us with this inner revelation, until he shines upon the sacred page, and floods the heart with a divine light. The gospel is the wisdom of God in a mystery to every reader and hearer until the Spirit opens the eyes of the understanding. The Spirit must take of Christ, and show it unto us. No matter how plain the word may be, how clear the teaching, neither senses nor reason can comprehend without the aid of the Spirit. The divine Healer must touch the sightless eye, and utter the powerful "Ephphatha," before we can see, or hear, or comprehend.

We were once in a blind asylum on a visit. There were none but the blind there. But the inmates were moving about as if they could see. A lady was playing on the piano, and others were engaged in conversation. In the beautiful grounds without boys were at play, seemingly intent on their sports, running, leaping, and laughing. It was not easy to realize that the world of light, of color, of form, the bright flowers, the luxuriant shrubbery, the blue sky, and the green earth, were all a blank to them. There was the noonday sun, and all the brightness of a perfect day, but the world was dark to them. Thus, in a world of light, with the open Bible before us, with the gospel sounding in our ears, there is spiritual darkness because we are spiritually blind. The need of the Holy Spirit, the absolute need, is emphasized here. David's prayer must be ours: "Open thou mine eyes, that I may behold wondrous things out of thy law." "Lord, that I might receive my sight," should be the cry of the dark and benighted soul. Our prophesying must be in this felt dependence upon the Spirit: "Come from the four winds, O breath, and breathe upon these slain, that they may live."

The things prepared are revealed by the Spirit in Christian experience. "Now we have received, not the spirit of the world, but the Spirit which is of God, that we might know the things that are freely given to us of God." Nicodemus could know nothing of them; he could neither see nor enter the kingdom until born again. In conversion, the light breaks upon the soul. In penitence and prayer, and in humble trust, the riches of grace pour into the hungering and thirsting heart. The cross is illuminated, Christ is apprehended, and the great plan of mercy stands out in its symmetry and majesty, radiant with divine wisdom and love. It is out of darkness into God's "marvelous light." Even outward nature seems transfigured to the new-born soul. There is a new earth. The inward glory invests nature with a shining livery, and clothes the entire outer world with a new and peculiar beauty. Surely, eye hath not seen, nor ear heard, neither has entered into the heart of man, any thing that approaches the peace, the rest, the raptures of the soul that feels the unutterable blessedness of sins forgiven.

And the things prepared unfold more and more as experience advances. Peace at length passes understanding, there is "joy unspeakable and full of glory," and as the soul presses on to know the love of Christ which passeth knowledge, it is "filled with all the fullness of God." How inexplicable to human reason, to all ordinary human experience, is the grace that sustains the Christian in suffering, and that brings holy triumph in the hour of death! How utterly above all natural reason the death of Stephen, with his shining face, heavenly visions, and unconquerable love! There is in these experiences something abundantly supernatural, something transcending all that men have seen, heard, or thought.

Grace, as a conflict and a victory, as a period of suffering made joyous by spiritual consolation, as a nature weak and fallen made pure and holy, is something very wonderful. Can there be any thing surpassing this in heaven? The pure in heart see God in this world. Through this medium God is seen in his works, in his providence, and as spiritually manifested to the eye of faith. Save what heaven may be, there can be nothing greater. To be the sons of God, to have the witnessing Spirit, and to realize that we are heirs of God and joint-heirs with Christ, are among the privileges of every Christian. To unbelievers the preaching of the cross is foolishness, but to them which believe it is the power of God. What eye hath not seen, nor ear heard, nor have entered into the heart of man, God hath revealed to the humblest of his children. His experience exceeds all that men have seen or imagined.

III. *The things are prepared for them that love God.* We know that the provisions of salvation are for all. Christ, by the grace of God, tasted death for every man. "For God so loved the world, that he gave his only-begotten Son, that whosoever believeth in him should not perish, but have everlasting life." Salvation is freely offered to all. The invitation is to all that labor and are heavy-laden. "And the Spirit and the bride say, Come. And let him that heareth say, Come. And let him that is athirst come. And whosoever will, let him take the water of life freely." In the divine intent there is mercy for every sinner. God "will have all men to be saved, and to come unto the knowledge of the truth." This is beyond doubt, that the scope of redemption takes in the entire world of sinners. And yet the things prepared can be known and possessed only by loving hearts.

It is only to the eye of love that they are manifest. Love sees and hears, and receives into the heart, what no stretch of divine power can make the property of unbelief. Love itself is light, it is divine communion, it is peace and victory. It is the vital element in salvation, it is salvation realized in purity of heart, and in all the fruits of the Spirit. Love only can comprehend love. It alone can understand God. It is something so potent that "we know that all things work together for good to them that love God." It turns every thing into good. It extracts the good even from affliction, and compels tribute from every thing within the range of providence and grace. Such is its celestial armor, that nothing can hurt Love. It is the one safe, invincible, all-appropriating grace. It outstrips the senses, it moves easily and luminously in a plane higher than reason. The things are prepared for them that love God, because only love can receive and apprehend them.

And because love only has the capacity to enjoy them. They are foolishness to the natural man. They are offensive to him. Without love neither grace nor heaven could be enjoyed. God can make no soul happy without love. The things prepared are such as only loving hearts delight in; hence it could be no other way. This is the distinguishing privilege and blessedness of love. All the wealth of the divine love, all the riches of glory, all the products of the infinite wisdom and mercy, are laid at the feet of Love. So it is appointed a rapture, an insight, an inheritance that palls all other brightness with its surpassing splendors. What an amazing declaration, that the things prepared, things employing the hand and heart of God before the world, should all be poured into the soul opened in love to the light of God!

We have kept back from this exposition all direct reference to the future glory. We have been careful to direct the application rather to the present experience. Such we believe to be "the mind of the Spirit" in this scripture. We would, if possible, magnify this matter of experience, the supernatural character of it, and the greatness of the blessings in it. It is the miracle of miracles, as much above material miracles as soul and spirit are above the dust beneath our feet. The things prepared are in the believing heart. They are the present heritage of God's children. We are to look for them, and to find them, in conversion, in holiness of heart, in growth in grace, and in victory over the world. And yet the things prepared for them that love God, as felt and known here in the realm of grace, are things immortal. "It doth not yet appear what we shall be; but we know that when he shall appear, we shall be like him; for we shall see him as he is." In the breadth and enlargement of what love now enjoys we can begin to imagine what heaven will be. If eye hath not seen, nor ear heard, neither have entered into the heart of man the things that God hath prepared for them that love him here, what must not that world of perfect day be? We may stand upon this Nebo and look across Jordan, and obtain, at least, a distant view of the goodly land of promise. From this high place of grace experienced, of love, with its clear, far-sighted vision, we may see the New Jerusalem, and, standing in this grace, we may rejoice in hope of the glory of God. The present grace is the earnest and assurance that "thine eye shall see the King in his beauty; they shall behold the land that is very far off."

VII.

PURE RELIGION.

BY THE REV. H. PEARCE WALKER, D.D.,
Kentucky Conference.

"Pure religion and undefiled before God and the Father." James i. 27.

WHILE all professing Christians believe that religion is in some sense divine, yet both the thing itself and its psychological manifestations are variously understood. Upon both these, as also upon many doctrinal and ecclesiastical points, widely divergent, often contradictory views obtain. Of two or more contradictory theories some must be false, but not necessarily all. Something must be true, else the opposite could not exist. Wherefore, the effort to ascertain what is truth, as regards the essential nature and manifestations of religion, cannot be a work of supererogation.

When we survey the Christian world, notwithstanding the points of agreement, it presents a strange scene of clashing and confusion. That great body of Christian professors united in protesting against the corruption and tyranny of Romanism, and in giving the Bible to all the families of mankind in their native tongues, is itself split up into manifold, and in many instances antagonistic, sects and parties, each perhaps holding some grains of truth covered up in heaps of chaff. To determine the exact proportions of truth and error in each would be difficult, perhaps impossible; not, however, because truth is inscrutable, but because of our partly necessary, partly volitional, and partly adventitious, limitations.

Whether this Babel of tongues and this multiplication of sects be the better, or the best, state of things in the present condition of the race, judge ye; we shall not undertake to decide this question; still, may we not be allowed to say that it does not seem to be in accord with the genius of Christianity? nor does it favor the most faithful and efficient use of means for the conversion of mankind. From the first chapter of Genesis to the last sentence of the Apocalypse, the Almighty seems to have contemplated the most perfect unity of the body of Christ; nor shall we ever believe that Christianity is so imperfect, or the Holy One of Israel so poor in resources, as to make error a necessary factor in the success of the gospel scheme. I know the defendant's plea by which it is sought to reconcile the existence of some hundreds of separate, independent, and fragmentary bodies of Christians with the teaching of revelation; but the reasons assigned seem to be purely apologetical, rather than necessary and scriptural.

It is true that, between all these separate organic bodies of professed Christians, claiming to stand on the Bible, there are points of agreement as well as points of disagreement. Between some, more—between others, less. Some forms of Christianity have become quite exclusive, placing all, or nearly all, the other forms quite outside the pale of the Christian religion; while other bodies are latitudinarian, including all forms of professed Christianity as valid, however widely sundered in doctrinal, ecclesiastical, and practical teaching. At least one of these extremes must be wrong—possibly both. The truth may lie imbedded in the mean, with increasing degrees of error upon either side; or, it may be, and we believe, that there are Christians among them all—even where they belong to false forms of Christianity. Yet none, nor all, of these facts can ever pronounce a single one of these forms to be genuine, or justify its independent existence. Questions of this sort can be settled by the living oracles only.

However much we may be interested in knowing whether the points of agreement and the points of disagreement between the various organic bodies of Christianity are for the most part essential or nonessential to Christian experience and growth in grace; whether some or many of these bodies contain error that may be fatal; or, whether most or all of them are to be esteemed as having salt enough to preserve them, are questions of vital importance, which we can commend only now to the prayerful study of every soul. But when we approach questions which relate directly to truths essential to salvation, the order in which they stand related each to the other, and the manner of holding them, we are in the presence of vast, of momentous, concerns that ought not to be passed lightly over.

The tendency of this age is latitudinarian. A disposition prevails to ignore doctrinal differences as obstructive to improvement in practical godliness, or at least to hold them in private, and make an outward show of unity in spirit. This is due in part, perhaps, to the recoil from the strait-laced, hypercritical orthodoxy of the past, and partly to the republican doctrine that men are not to be proscribed for opinion's sake. The idea is already popular that one has the right to believe what he pleases—that it does not matter what principles are held, if the life be right. Nothing could be more false. Never was the faithful advocacy of sound doctrine a bar to progress or a hinderance to true unity. Never was the advocacy of principles, in the Christian spirit, the enemy of justice and harmony. Truth is foe to all that is false—the enemy of all unrighteousness. Error of the head leads often to wrong-doing. Men of bad principles are men of bad lives. Men without principles are variable, unreliable, the dupes of error, open to temptation, easily drawn into sinks of evil. It is false teaching that men are never to be proscribed for opinions. It is false doctrine of the worst sort to teach that men have the right to believe error—to believe all things or nothing. Things different must not be confounded. The human mind often rushes from one extreme to its opposite. Doubtless, when religion was a thing of mere forms and creeds, much wrong was committed in the name of orthodoxy, and harmless opinions were treated as crimes. Still, it does not follow that one extreme is right because the other is wrong; nor should error be commended because truth has been abused. Error must be refuted, denounced, proscribed. Wrong-doing must be condemned. Truth and righteousness must be maintained. While sedulously guarding the doors against the spirit of persecution, we must not throw them open to welcome error, nor close them against truth and justice. The apostle tells us to "contend earnestly for the faith once delivered to the saints;" and the history of the past shows that all our liberties have been achieved, under God's blessing, not by the sacrifice of truth, not by compromise with error, but by conflict with it.

I do not undervalue the honest efforts of Christians to establish unity; I rejoice in it; only I protest against all sham unity by the sacrifice of sound doctrines. I mean only to warn the American people against the false glare of a mere formal fraternity, an irresponsible evangelism, an apparent unity by the compromise of truth, the effect of which is, perhaps, to certify a dangerous heresy to public confidence, and give a passport to error to corrupt the fountains and to eat away the core of vital godliness.

Are we in danger of forgetting the warning of Jesus against deceivers—"wolves in sheep's clothing?" or that of Paul and John against false teachers? Surely we cannot fail to know that not all who bear the name Christian are entitled to the distinction. What revolting scenes have been enacted in the name of Christianity! How cunning has error ever been to lift itself into public favor, either under the garb of religion, or on the ground of religious tolerance! These are the same old tricks which deceivers have "played off before high heaven" upon mankind from the beginning of the temptation in paradise down to the present day; and they are none the less successful because so old and so well known. "By their fruits ye shall know them." Always ready, then, to recognize a disciple of Christ where differences of opinion exist on many points, we must be careful, nevertheless, not to indorse and encourage a "form of godliness without the power thereof," from which the apostle commands us to "turn away."

But viewing this subject in its personal relations, we enter the Christian world with questions like these trembling on our lips, viz.: What is religion? how shall I obtain it? and how know that I am religious? I find myself in the presence of three massive systems, viz.: Catholicism, Calvinism, and Arminianism. The first is founded on the papacy, the second on the eternal decrees, the third on the universality of the provisions of the atonement and the free moral agency of man. The answers they give to my questions are in substantial agreement with the foundations on which they rest. Whatever their views may be as to what religion as a principle is, the following is patent: with the Romanist there is no salvation for me, unless I am united to the papacy; with the Calvinist there is no salvation for me, unless I am included in the eternal decrees predestinating me to everlasting life; with the Arminian there is no salvation for me without the exercise of my free moral agency in coöperation with God's grace to appropriate to myself by faith the special benefits of the atonement of Christ. Here are wide divergences. But I continue to propound the inquiry throughout all the societies of Protestant Christendom, What must I do to be saved? One tells me to repent; another to confess; another to believe; and another to be immersed. Here I am told that repentance and faith are fruits of regeneration; there I am informed that they are precedent, indispensable conditions. One tells me religion is a gift, and I must seek it; another assures me it is a work, and I must do it; a third declares it to be a state, and I must enter into it by an act of obedience. Finding myself at the intersection of so many cross-roads and sign-boards, each purporting to be the way, and to point the way, what confusion, and fears, and doubts, must result! Fortunate for me if, instead of hesitating, doubting, fearing, and lingering in the midst of the confusion of this moral mist, which covers me like the dense fog thrown over the shoulders of the mountain, or drawn like a thick covering over the sleeping form of the valley, I betake myself prayerfully to the written word, and there search with "trembling awe" for the light that shineth in darkness. While I believe that there is saving truth held by many of the Churches of this day, yet am I satisfied that, in the midst of these opposing views, many earnest, anxious souls are at a loss to know which way to turn, or what to do. Their doubts and reasonings are aptly expressed in these lines:

> So many people, in these latter days,
> Have taught religion in so many ways,
> That few can tell which system is the best;
> For every party contradicts the rest.

Let us endeavor to ascertain, in the light of the divine word, what pure and undefiled religion is, and what its essential manifestations are. Webster derives it from *religare*, to bind anew or back, to bind fast. He defines it: 1. The recognition of God as an object of worship, love, and obedience; right feelings toward God as rightly apprehended; piety. A high sense of moral obligation and spirit of reverence and worship, which affect the heart of man with reference to the Deity. 2. A system of faith and worship. 3. The rites or services of religion. The Greek word *threeskeia* signifies worship, piety, service.

By accommodation it is used to denote a system of rules and doctrines, a creed, acts of worship, but properly it signifies more than these. It signifies a certain state of mind and heart in relation to God. Religion is a word expressive of all that is comprehended in piety, devoutness, righteousness, godliness, reverence, holiness. Hence, we may say that, in the true sense of the word, it is a *life in* God, and a life of union and communion *with* God. As a principle, or essence, it is the divine life in the soul: "That by these ye might be partakers of the divine nature." "He that believeth on the Son hath everlasting life." "He that hath the Son hath life, and he that hath not the Son of God hath not life." This life of God in the soul is religion in essence, or principle, and as such it is the gift of God through Jesus Christ. This life cannot be considered as an abstract principle wholly separate from God himself. In fact, it is God with us and in us, imparting to us his own life and likeness. It is an immediate conjunction of the Holy Spirit with our spirit. Hence the Holy Spirit is given unto the believer, not to endow him with the miraculous gift of tongues and the power of working miracles, as with the apostles, but to give him the life and the likeness of God. By the impartation of this spiritual life by the Holy Ghost we are begotten of God, have given us a new nature, become a new creation, or a new creature. The result of the gift of spiritual life is the new birth of the Spirit into the kingdom of God, and all the experiences and activities of the soul flow from it — such as love, joy, peace, long-suffering, meekness, temperance, and brotherly kindness. This divine life in the soul is a life of growth and development manifesting itself on all sides of our being in acts of worship, such as prayer and praise; in deeds of benevolence and kindness, such as visiting the sick, feeding the hungry, clothing the naked, instructing the ignorant, comforting the distressed; in the practice of self-denial and cross-bearing, keeping one's self "unspotted from the world;" and in an obedient, consecrated disposition of mind and heart, conforming the whole life to the will of God in Christ. This principle of the divine life in the soul by which it is begotten of God, and born of the Spirit, is religion, and all these soul-experiences of love, joy, peace, etc., and the activities of the daily life in self-denial, deeds of benevolence, and acts of worship, are the results, the effects, the croppings out, the manifestations, of the indwelling principle and power of the life received from God. Hence we read, "Of his own will begat he us with the word of truth." "Being born [begotten] again, not of corruptible seed, but of incorruptible, by the word of God, which liveth and abideth forever." Every act of Christian obedience, all the Christian virtues, all the pure, holy, beatifying emotions, desires, and affections of the soul, all the fruits of the Spirit, are referred by the Holy Scriptures to the Spirit of God, which is the principle and power of the life imparted to the soul by God through Christ, and the efficient cause of all our spiritual life and godliness. The Holy Ghost is the agent and power by which the soul is begotten of God and born again, by which it is quickened, raised from a state of death, and fructified with virtue and holiness. By him we receive the essence and power of religion. In him is found the fact and philosophy, the origin and power, of all spiritual life, its experiences and its activities. Hence we read again, "Whosoever believeth that Jesus is the Christ is born [begotten] of God; and every one that loveth him that begat, loveth him also that is begotten of him." "For whatsoever is born of God [begotten] overcometh the world; and this is the victory that overcometh the world, *even* our faith." "If ye know that he is righteous, ye know that every one that doeth righteousness is born of him." "Whosoever is born of God [begotten] doth not commit sin, for his seed remaineth in him; and he cannot sin, because he is born of God." "For love is of God; and every one that loveth is born of God, and knoweth God." "Except a man be born again he cannot see the kingdom of God." Whatever else any of these passages may teach, one thing is undeniable, is certain, that is this, that love, entering into and enjoying the kingdom of God, righteousness, doing righteousness, the faith itself that overcometh the world, in fact, all spiritual life in us, all truly religious experience, and all works of righteousness that are pleasing and acceptable to God, have their origin in an indwelling principle of divine life, and spring from it. The spiritual begetting and birth, by the presence and power of the Holy Ghost, giving us a new nature and a new source of life in God, is the prime cause of all the good that exists in us. To the same effect are the teachings of John on the holy anointing, or the ointment from the Holy One, which abides in believers, and so effectually teaches them that they have no need that another should teach them. What is this chrism but the Holy Ghost? Thus Christ was anointed with the Holy Ghost, and thus Christians are anointed. Dr. Braune says, "The chrism, or ointment, will have to be understood as the Holy Spirit, and *humeis ekete chrisma"—you have an ointment, or an anointing*— " reminds the readers of the great gift which makes them priests, kings, and prophets, the *genos eklekton, basileion hierateuma, ethnos hagion*, of 1 Pet. ii. 9"—a chosen race, a royal priesthood, a holy nation. The same author says, "Christians are anointed, and their name should daily remind them of what they owe to God and their neighbor, as spiritual kings, priests, and prophets." "As is a king without a kingdom, a ruler without subjects, a general without soldiers, so is a Christian without the anointing"—only in name. "None but those who have the Holy Spirit and the anointing can be sufficiently on their guard against the lies of antichrist. All other knowledge is too weak by far to be able to withstand temptation and spiritual conflicts." Dr. Mombert, translator of Dr. Braune's Commentary of John's Epistles, sums up the benefits of the Holy Spirit, or holy anointing, to all believers thus: "1. The chrism (Holy Spirit) is a general gift, vouchsafed to all Christians; 2. Not transient, but permanent; 3. Leads them into all truth; 4. Moves them to the practice of all the precepts of Christ; 5. Assures them of their Christian privileges (children of God, members of Christ, and inheritors of the kingdom of heaven); 6. Teaches them in all things— they are therefore disciples and learners all the days of their life; 7. Preserves their fellowship with the Father and with the Son; 8. Makes them temples of God." Again we read, "There is a divine seed in those who are born of (out of) God; they have not become God, deified, or absorbed, in God, or God in them, but only partakers of the divine nature, germ-like, like new-born babes, so that a beginning has been made, but only a beginning, although the beginning of a life, divine, coming from and leading to God. This birth out of God is a translation of man from death to life, brings him to the

Light of the world, and gives him eternal life, and effects the blessed result that God is in us and we in him, as the children of God out of God." "The cause of regeneration is the righteous God, and an ethical *status* is its *mark* and *sign*. God gives, and man not only *has* but *becomes* (comes into existence). God rules over thee, and has his work in thee, that thou mayest become and remain his child. God's attribute of righteousness is not only energetically active, but also communicative. The import of regeneration should be laid hold of by its indispensable consequence, viz.: *Poiein teen dikaiosuneen* [*doing the righteousness*], and even its nature defined as a beginning of a new, divine life."

I have been thus particular to define and set forth what religion is, in the true scriptural sense, whence its origin as a controlling principle of life in the soul, and what are its effects, because we so often hear it taught now that religion consists in doing something—that is, in keeping the commandments; or, that the observance of certain preceptive requirements constitutes religion, and makes one religious. The idea is being extensively circulated, that a religion of inward life and power, effectuated by the personal power of the Holy Spirit, operating directly on the soul, regenerating it, and giving it life and purity, is absurd, a dream of the imagination, and groundless in reason and Scripture. The doctrine that seeks to displace this regards religion as wholly educational and practical. We are told that religion is obedience to the law, and that this is secured by instruction. So that religion, according to this view, consists of two parts, viz., theory and practice. One learns the theoretical part as a child learns the multiplication table, and he practices the precepts as a man practices medicine, or farming, or mechanics. Even the scriptural doctrine of the vicarious atonement of Christ is set aside as repugnant to reason, and opposed to justice, and in its place is set up the poor, puny offspring of a rationalistic philosophy, which teaches that God had no need to be reconciled to man, because he was already reconciled, but that the simple design of the death of Christ was to afford to man a display of the love of God, and furnish him with an example of self-denial and submission to the Father's will, thus seeking, in a purely educational and moral way, to reconcile man to God by the influence of ideas. According to this view, no satisfaction was made to divine justice, and no benefits were procured by the death of Christ. Hence man is redeemed and regenerated by the influence of ideas, and his own deeds of righteousness which result from them. Alas, for mankind, when religion falls into the hands of professional hucksters, who dilute it into thin gruel, consisting of a few emasculated ideas and perfunctory services; or reduce it to an unsubstantial wafer, and then peddle it out at cheap cost to men's worldly wisdom!

How unscriptural these views are will readily appear from all those scriptures which represent our recovery from sin, and death, and misery, to God, and life, and holiness, as effected by himself: "You hath he quickened who were dead in trespasses and sins." "By grace are ye saved through faith, and that not of yourselves, it is the gift of God." "Who hath saved us and called us with a holy calling, not according to our works, but according to his own purpose and grace." "Not by works of righteousness which we have done, but according to his mercy he saved us, by the washing of regeneration and renewing of the Holy Ghost, which he shed on us abundantly through Jesus Christ our Saviour." "In whom after that ye believed ye were sealed with the Holy Spirit of promise." "But ye are washed, but ye are sanctified, but ye are justified, in the name of the Lord Jesus, and by the Spirit of our God." Whatever be the term used to express our moral recovery, whether delivered, redeemed, quickened, reconciled, begotten, born, raised up, justified, sealed, created anew, or saved, the Scriptures uniformly refer the work to God as the doer, the author of it. Paul shows conclusively that something more than motives, arguments, ideas, is required to convert and save, for he declares that "his speech and preaching" "was not with enticing words of man's wisdom, but in demonstration of the Spirit and of power; that your faith should not stand in the wisdom of men, but in the power of God." Spiritual conversion, according to the sacred teachings, is effected by a personal power, the power of God, or of the Holy Spirit, and not by arguments, or works of obedience to law. The intellectual relation to God is of a secondary character, because it is mediated by ideas, thoughts, and images; but the religious relation is one of real existence, of personal life and being. Scientists, philosophers, artists, and moralists, together with all religious formalists, "have God only in the reflected images of thought and fancy, while the devout Christian has him in his very being. The reality of this difference forces itself upon us when we set prophets and apostles over against poets and philosophers."

The religious relation to God must be one of personal holiness. The voice of the unrenewed conscience is a continuous demand for it. It is equally true that man cannot make himself holy by any act or series of acts of any kind whatever, for then he would have no need of a vicarious offering, or a Holy Spirit. He might make his own atonement, and be his own saviour. But the Bible, recognizing man as utterly lost, and unable to save himself, teaches that "without shedding of blood there is no remission" of sins; that "it behooved Christ to suffer" and to die, in order "that repentance and remission of sins might be preached in his name among all nations;" that man is "elect" only "through sanctification of the Spirit unto obedience, and sprinkling of the blood of Jesus Christ."

This demand for holiness to fit man for fellowship with God is the grand characteristic of the Christian religion. It belongs to no false religion, but it runs all through the word of God, from its Alpha to its Omega. Every essential fact of revelation looks to it. To raise up a holy seed, to make man a holy being, a vessel and abode of Deity, and an organ for the revelation of the Holy God, is the grand aim of the whole gospel scheme. This is the teleological design of Holy Love, both in creation and in redemption, and the reason for its marvelous manifestation on the theater of time. This is the meaning of Bethlehem and Gethsemane, of Calvary and Pentecost. "Without holiness no man shall see the Lord."

The source of this holiness is in God, not in us. It is an essential attribute of Deity. He is the God of holiness, and his is the Spirit of holiness. And it is not till the human-created will, in its relative freedom, influenced by grace, meets with and merges into the absolutely free and uncreated will of God, that a spiritual transfusion of the divine nature into ours takes place, and we become partakers of the divine holiness. The entrance of the holy personality of God in all his communicable fullness into the human personality, without the loss of either, thus making the human nature a partaker of the divine nature of holiness, was the miracle of the incarnation; and it is precisely this miracle that is repeated, or rather continued, throughout the new creation, throughout the whole body of which Christ is the head. "I in them, and thou in me." There is an organic, vital, essential unity between the vine and its branches, the same life in all, running from the vine into the branches, as the cause of all their vigor and fruitfulness. Holiness of heart and life is the fruit of an indwelling personal Christ. This is the essential relation, without which the intellectual, the natural, the moral, and the formal relations to God are miserable abortions; and the soul that is not brought into this relation to God of personal holiness is fit only to be cut off from the true source of life, as a diseased limb is amputated from its trunk, and cast into the abyss of things that might have been, but never were.

The very fact that genuine religion requires holiness demonstrates it to be the religion of conscience. Conscience is the co-, or concordant, knowledge of man with God, of the relation of his personal being to God. For I am what in conscience I know myself to be. Conscience puts us into the most direct personal relation to God. It relates not directly to the moral law, but to the holy personality of God. No one can be said to have a conscience for law, for abstract truth, or for an impersonal power. It is the perception and feeling of the moral relation between two personalities, in whom there exists, on the side of conscience, obligation and freedom, and on the side of the Holy Being, to whom we are bound, power, goodness, and justice. The moral law, a divine revelation, does not create conscience, but enlightens it as to the way by which the human personality is to be reconciled to the divine; and it is the office of conscience to bring our moral relation to God into the light of self-consciousness. This it does by means of its two great constituents, perception and feeling. Hence it is the culminating point of thought, of desire, of emotion, and of volition. The soul's telegraph-office, all its moral activities, meet and break into the light of self-consciousness here. For this reason it is the very seat, the *sanctum sanctorum*, of pure and undefiled religion, which can never be personal, holy, and regnant, until it is the religion of conscience. Seated here, religion becomes a personal possession, a controlling power, dominating the will, the desires, and the affections, in the light of the knowledge of our obligations to the Holy God. As all the juices of the tree run up into the fruit and make it, so all the sap of the soul, all its sweetness and vigor, run up into conscience and nourish religion, the life of the soul; and from this the soul's inmost *adytum* go forth in conscious approval or disapproval of all its sustaining or depressing power. Hence, the " relations between God and ourselves acquire religious significance only as they spring from, or are received into, this fundamental relation; and certainty about divine and human things of a religious cast becomes religious certainty only when it is the certainty of conscience."

Here, then, we discover the fact that one of the profoundest psychological manifestations of religion is that of feeling. Not that feeling is the sole exclusive form of its manifestation, but one which is inclusive of perception and volition. The Bishop of Holland, while admitting that feeling denotes the most immediate contact of consciousness with its object, and therefore denotes the foundation, though not the completion, of religious character, nevertheless says, " We are to treat the question [of religious manifestation] no longer as one of an *either, or,* but as one of a *both, and.*" Schleiermacher makes the feelings the exclusive seat of religion, and the form of feeling in which religion manifests itself that of absolute dependence. Another tells us it is the feeling of unbounded reverence; while the mystics describe piety as a *theo-*

pathic state in which one feels his inmost soul touched by the power divine — a holy pathos in which man feels himself to be a vessel and an abode of the Deity. Certainly all these views, which do not differ essentially, are scriptural, when not exclusive but inclusive of all the possible forms of religious feeling, such as love, joy, and peace. I cannot conceive religion as a principle in the soul, as a divine power, creating it anew in Christ, quickening it into spiritual life, and raising it up from a state of death, and translating it into the kingdom of light, without at the same time effecting a radical change in thought, feeling, and volition; and I cannot conceive of such a change taking place without the corresponding idea of the soul's consciousness of it. And I apprehend that the first, most reliable, and satisfactory evidence to the personal *Ego* of the work of the Holy Spirit in regenerating and sanctifying the soul, is to be found in its consciousness of the feelings of love, joy, peace, and unbounded reverence.

According to the word of God, one of the divinest and most sensible experiences of the converted soul is *love*. So much is this emphasized in Scripture, that we are told plainly, "Love is of God, and whosoever loveth is born of God, and knoweth God;" and Paul tells us that we come into the possession of *love* by the Holy Ghost, who sheds it abroad in our hearts. Along with the feeling of love comes the knowledge of what God has done for us and in us, for the soul is immediately conscious of its own experience, and the Holy Spirit comes and dwells in it, and bears testimony with it that it is a child of God. Speaking of the Holy Spirit, Jesus said, "But ye know him, for he dwelleth with you, and shall be in you. At that day ye shall know that I am in my Father, and ye in me, and I in you." John is equally clear on this point in his Epistles. Not only does he affirm that "he that believeth on the Son hath the witness in himself," but he gives several infallible proofs by which we know that we have passed from death unto life, are born of God, are the children of God, and have him abiding in us. Such are, 1. The anointing; 2. The love of God and of the brethren; 3. The indwelling Spirit of God; 4. Obedience; 5. Faith. Four of these proofs are objects of conscious knowledge, and one relates to our external duties, which are also objects of consciousness in the volitions whence they spring. First, then, we have the Holy Spirit regenerating the soul; from this, feeling; from this, conscious knowledge of what has taken place in us, and of our saved relation to God; from this, volition, resulting in acts of worship, deeds of kindness and love, and resistance to all evil, keeping ourselves "unspotted from the world." Thus we see that, in perfect keeping with the teaching of the Master, religion begins with a principle and power of life in the soul, and works from within out. It has its origin in the mysterious depths of our spiritual being, its visible manifestation in the outward life. It has its Gethsemane and Calvary, but they lead to a triumphant resurrection and a glorious Pentecost. It has its sowing-time, its growing-time, and its harvest-time; but there is hope in the first, and joy in the second, and glory in the last. What a divine fullness in religion! It has truth for the mind, love for the soul, joy for the heart, and God for its object.

A danger to which men are ever exposed, more particularly in an age like this, when so many minds are occupied with the study of material facts and forces, with money-making and pleasure-seeking, is that of holding religion at second-hand. This is the case when religion is sundered from its vital source in the affections, when religious views are held in a merely intellectual, or æsthetic, or formal way, because these persons know nothing of the personal feelings and determinations of conscience. However correct in theory, or refined and beautiful in its forms, a religion which does not originate in conscience, and is not sustained by a personal, experimental knowledge of God's saving power, is nothing more than second-hand, because it is wholly mediated by ideas, and not by the soul's personal contact with God's holy love. The holding of a comprehensive system of religious truth is no proof that one is religious. Thousands have represented religious ideas with great plastic power without any personal possession of it in themselves. Paul shows us that tongues, and knowledge, and self-sacrifice, and miracles, even faith itself, were it possible to separate it from love—all these, however great and powerful in themselves, are insufficient, nay, worthless, without love. And a religion in which the Holy Spirit of life and love is an unknown quantity is second-hand, a mere sham, a disgustingly useless and puerile thing with the Almighty.

Let us make ours the religion of conscience and personal holiness—a religion of character, of "perfect love that casteth out fear." Then we shall find every noble purpose that breathes across the laws of life refreshing, and every effort to walk in the broad daylight of duty invigorating, and down every channel furrowed out by prayer in its flight to heaven will rills of joy descend to make green and flowery the banks of life, and to pitch the song of all its shores on the key in which its raptures came.

What a wonderful accumulating and self-registering power is conscience! It stores up both good and evil. The most trivial event can no more escape detection than a single drop of blood can evade the heart. A faithful scribe, he records each moment's work. A polished mirror, it is stained by the faintest breath of evil. We see the foot-prints of time in the granite, and glide back over ages to note the route he took, and the road he traveled. Sin leaves its foot-prints on conscience, and after ages they will be traceable unless erased by the blood of Jesus. The diary of conscience is a minute-book of the life, and from these records the historian of eternity will gather the materials for a faithful history of the generations of time.

What has happened when success justifies its own cheating, when vice is respectable because it is titled, when the steal of millions makes gentlemen out of rogues, and evil-doing pleads the authority of greatness? Evidently the public conscience is warped, and travels over crooked routes, or "else it slinks home by the alleys, and frets because it has lost its right of way." What then is needed? A Samuel to hew the guilty Agags in pieces? Some stripling David to slay the haughty warrior? A John the Baptist, or a John Wesley, to cry in the wilderness and in the crowded city with a voice that wakes the dead? Alas! we forget, perhaps, that it is ours to be simple in the midst of fashion, to be truthful when duplicity meets with flattery, to be sincere when trickery is applauded, and to keep conscience pure when the multitudes are false. Had we, to-day, enough men and women of independence, of strong, quick, robust conscience, full of faith and the Holy Ghost, and steady as the magnetic needle to its pole, a grand reformation would sweep the nation, purge it of its crimes, and make it a very garden of the Lord.

To have a religion of conscience so true in the midst of an evil and adulterous generation, bold enough to plow deep furrows of conviction across continents of vice, to cut out the very heart of sin with the sword of the Spirit, and to sow precious seeds when there are no clouds in the sky and no moisture in the ground, to bear on the cross in the face of opposition till it waves grandly over the ruined battlements of vice, and truth and righteousness go forth to meet the glad welcome of millions—how great the work! Founders of empires never equaled it; explorers of worlds never went so far; warriors never achieved such victories. And though our powers are feeble, our spheres limited, our opportunities seemingly few, let us toil on in the "good old way." We are sowing an incorruptible seed, which will spring up somewhere on the "planet's made soil;" and if not at once, after generations. Not one drop is lost in the ocean. Let us be encouraged. The Gulf-stream sets out upon its journey through the deep, and, after it has gone thousands of miles, may still be tracked by its genial breath; and though it is comparatively small, and has traveled so far, its influence is still perceptible on Greenland's ice-ribbed coast.

Were this not so, it is enough that thrilling duty invites us out upon God's highway of holiness. Opportunities are at hand. Some face of truth looks in upon us, points to her crown of thorns, and begs us wear it awhile; some wail of suffering humanity falls upon the ear to waken our pity; some work, some cross, some self-sacrifice for Christ's sake, is ever and anon knocking at the door. Have we heeded? Is our religion pure and undefiled? Has our faith been made perfect by works? Do we add to inward experience volition and action, according to the requirements of the law of love and the example of Christ? In that day when the Son of man shall sit upon the throne of his glory, and all the holy angels are with him, and before him shall be gathered all nations, shall we hear him say to us, "Come, ye blessed of my Father, inherit the kingdom prepared for you from the foundation of the world; for I was a hungered, and ye gave me meat; I was thirsty, and ye gave me drink; I was a stranger, and ye took me in; naked, and ye clothed me; I was sick, and ye visited me; I was in prison, and ye came unto me?" Amen and amen!

VIII.
THE SUPREME AIM OF LIFE.
BY THE REV. J. D. BLACKWELL,
Virginia Conference.

"Because the gods of the kings of Syria help them, therefore will I sacrifice to them, that they may help me. But they were the ruin of him, and of all Israel." 2 Chron. xxviii. 23.

CONTINUED prosperity and signal adversity are alike unfavorable to true submission to God. "Give me neither poverty nor riches, lest I be full, and deny thee, saying, Who is the Lord, or lest I be poor, and take the name of my God in vain," arraign the wisdom of his providence, and fret against him. Uzziah and Jotham, the immediate predecessors in the kingdom of Judah to Ahaz, had marked prosperity in their reigns. They defeated their enemies, enlarged the borders of their kingdom, built cities in the conquered territory and towers in the desert, adorned and fortified their capital, and strengthened themselves exceedingly. Of Uzziah it is said, "As long as he sought the Lord, God made him to prosper;" and Jotham, we are told, became mighty because he prepared his ways before the Lord his God. Yet, as our context and the first chapters of Isaiah clearly testify, this prosperity, with its power and voluptuousness, engendered in Judah a proud self-confidence, removing from the minds of the nation all sense of dependence on Jehovah.

Ahaz, whom our text brings before us, was assailed by sore misfortunes. The kings of Syria and Israel, the Edomites and Philistines, invaded his land, slew tens of thousands of his soldiers, took possession of some of his cities, and when he sought aid from the Assyrian king, Tilgath-pilneser accepted his gifts and came unto him, "but he helped him not." He was in great straits, and sorely troubled, and our text points to the result: "And in the time of his distress did he trespass yet more against the Lord: this is that King Ahaz. For he sacrificed unto the gods of Damascus, which smote him; and he said, Because the gods of the kings of Syria help them, therefore will I sacrifice to them, that they may help me."

Our text suggests as the theme for our consideration, The wickedness and folly of making worldly success the supreme aim of life. This seemed to be the purpose of Ahaz. He was in great distress. Edom had smitten Judah, and carried away captives; the Philistines also had invaded the cities of the low countries, and of the south of Judah, and dwelt in his land. In his extremity he had hired the king of Assyria to aid him, but this ruler came to him and helped him not; he only smoothed his way for the conquest of Judah by crushing the intervening kingdom of Syria. Trouble, instead of humbling Ahaz, made him desperate and defiant. Tell me not of patience and submission, of trust in the God of Israel; every thing is going to ruin; all will soon be lost. I will try other plans. I must have success, and as these gods prosper those that worship them, I will worship them too, that they may give me prosperity.

In the present age this same device is often resorted to. We are determined on success in business. We rise early, sit up late, eat the bread of frugality, toil with persevering diligence, and yet all our efforts fail. Others succeed, but we observe that they do not sacrifice to the God of integrity and uprightness. They are unscrupulous in their policy. They suppress conscience, and rail at it. "It is a dangerous thing—a man cannot steal but it accuseth him. 'Tis a blushing, shame-faced spirit—it beggars any man that keeps it. It is turned out of all towns and cities for a dangerous thing, and every man that means to live well endeavors to trust to himself and live without it."

> Why should not conscience have vacation
> As well as other courts o' the nation?

Folding up this prying spirit with their Sabbath-robes, they say, Live thou there, and let my business-hours alone. Or they are purely selfish; they gather, but never give. They hoard and gloat upon their treasures, but never open the hand to the needy, or contribute to move the world heavenward. They worship mammon, and seek self-interest alone. Still they prosper. Whatever they touch turns to gold. We fail with our plans and principles; we will adopt their course. Success will atone for every thing. "Because the gods of the kings of

Syria help them, therefore will we sacrifice to them, that they may help us."

Or our business prospers, and we desire social success. We look around, and find that the giddy and frivolous, they who walk in a vain show, are frequently the honored of the world—those who never dream of talent to be improved, or of good to be done; who laugh to scorn the antiquated notions of duty and usefulness, and hold in contempt the idea of labor and sacrifice for others; who seem to value the ornament of the head, the product of the grass and the silk-worm, more than the immortal mind that labors "in the secret chambers of the brain," and spend their time in garlanding the body as an offering on the world's altar; the bright queens of fashion, or the foppish young men, who never resisted a temptation, and never thought of reaching the lofty goal of victory through patient endurance and heroic battle; victims of appetite, and idleness, and *ennui*. We find that these are often the staves in fashion's circle, and we say, Thus they succeed, and we will follow their example. We will worship the goddess of pleasure; we will vitiate the taste, cramp the aspirations of the soul and the expansive energies of the mind within the procrustean dogmas of fashion's god. Because others thus reach that pinnacle of glory, we will adopt their plans, worship their divinities.

Perhaps our lot seems a hard one in the Church. We have much to do and to endure, and yet receive but little present reward—hewers of wood and drawers of water in the camp of Israel. We are sent out as pioneers among the marshes and mountains, the hedges and highways of earth, we sojourn "in the tents of Kedar," and are never permitted "to rest within the curtains of **Solomon**." We are detailed to guard the Thermopylæ of Church and State, to meet and conquer the great multitudes that threaten to overthrow the truth, to evangelize the poor. There we bear, and fight, and fall, but, like Joseph in prison, we are ignored by the Church, or receive only that patronizing notice deemed needful to keep us at our undesirable post. Others refuse to stand there—we should say, do not stand in that Thermopylæ—practically ignore the duty to carry the gospel to the poor, or to the millions of idolaters; equally called, as it seems to us, they appear to flee as Jonah from an unpleasant mission, and take what, to our distorted view, appears a higher sphere of labor, where the world's eye will observe and the world's praise will greet them.

Or, perhaps, with the voluptuous, self-indulgent, and proud, the plain and direct methods and the old doctrines have become distasteful. They demand teachings congenial to their careless mode of life. Pride must be flattered, fancy pleased, the appetite for novelty gratified; all the stern demands of law kept out of view, and Elysian mansions proclaimed as their future homes. And we note that they who seem to neglect the poor, and bow to the demand of those having itching ears, prosper in the world, are applauded of men and crowned by society, and the temptation arises to say, Thus they prosper; these methods, these gods to whom they sacrifice, help them, and we will sacrifice unto them, that they may help us. We find the temptation which ruined Ahaz is very general, and, alas! often triumphant, in the present day. It has broken down many a manly purpose, and wrecked the character of multitudes who still live around us. May the spirit of wisdom and love aid us in an earnest effort to arrest its progress!

In setting forth the wickedness of making worldly success the supreme object in life, we state that Jehovah is acknowledged by us as our God, and the Bible is recognized as our guide. We cannot go back to the heathen worship of ancient Greece and Rome, of Nineveh, Babylon, or Egypt. Judaism, as designed for the peculiar people, Hindooism, Islamism, do not challenge our faith. We can neither worship Brahma, nor receive the Vedas, the Talmud, or Koran, as our rule of life. If we look to the grand attainments and wisdom of this nineteenth century, we find no religion which can for us substitute the religion of the Bible. One of the inventions, or, as it claims, one of the discoveries, of this century is Mormonism. This system evidently does not command our conscience. We feel no obligation to be controlled by the sacred books of the Mormons. Positivism, which is identical in a great degree with the system more recently called the religion of science, claims also to be the result of the investigation and learning of this century.

But this religion makes no claim upon us which we recognize as binding. It is indeed a negation, either denying flatly that there is a God, or asserting, if there be a God, we have no means of knowing either the fact or the nature of his being. As man is the creature of evolution, the result of a force originating this system knows not whence, and moving it knows not whither, we are left, without any sense of obligation, to be what we are forced to be. Nor have all the efforts of modern skepticism availed to loose us from a sense of obligation to follow the rule of life laid down in our sacred book. Indeed, these modern guides, while claiming to be the only advanced thinkers, the only truly wise men released from the shackles of superstition, frankly tell us they know nothing of the great themes which most strongly excite our anxiety. They talk with much complacency of "the future religion of all sensible men," but promptly acknowledge that they do not know what that religion will be. Their investigations do not bring them in palpable contact with Jehovah, and they therefore assure us that there is no God, or none that we need concern ourselves about, as we can know nothing of him. They have, of course, in their system nothing of sin against God, or guilt—nothing of pardon or blessedness from Heaven. They seem not to know that our sacred books taught, thousands of years ago, that Jehovah could not be seen by mortal eye, that the world by wisdom knew not God, that the blessed truths of Christianity were hidden from self-sufficient men—"the wise and prudent"—and revealed only to those who were willing to receive instruction, as from an authoritative teacher. They convince us, with great force of argument, that he who rails at or repudiates the conclusions of science, but will not investigate for himself, can have no claim to consideration; that the man who denies that electricity will shock the system, and yet will not test the truth of **his statement** by placing his hands on the opposite poles of a charged battery, is a vain babbler, unworthy our notice as a teacher in science. And yet, though the Christian system claims to subject its truth to the test of experiment; though its great Author says, "If any man wills to do his will," brings an honest purpose to practice as he learns, "he shall know of the doctrine;" if any man will receive him and trust in him, he shall find rest, peace, joy, and strength. Though Christianity thus declares itself an **experimental science**, these guides laugh at the idea of thus testing our system, and instead of ranking themselves among the unwise for their unscientific course, reversing their own logic, they do not hesitate to place in that list all who adopt the scientific method of receiving as true what they have ascertained by experiment. Though they feel at liberty to place among the unwise all who receive the faith of Newton, and Bunsen, and Hooker, and Milton, and Chalmers, and J. Edwards, and Watson, etc.— men who would be **giants in any age**—and proclaim themselves leaders in thought, yet we, the serious people of this generation, cannot accept them as our teachers in religion. They tell us that our religion, with its Heavenly Father and heavenly home, with its blessed consolations, its rich experiences of strength and joy imparted, is effete and passing away, and yet they acknowledge that they are blind and in the dark. They say, "Never did tempest-tossed mariner long for the haven more earnestly than we for some certain light. We cry aloud in the dark, and the only answer is the wailing echo of our own cry." These men, groping in the dark, wailing in their wretched orphanage, have not only utterly failed to convince us that we should renounce our blessed Christianity for their blank and cheerless system, but they have convinced us that they are totally ignorant of the religion they criticise, furnishing an illustration of the word, "These things are hidden from the wise and prudent."

We can never be convinced that a system, the sum of whose teaching is love supreme to a holy and wise God, and love to our fellow, love such as we have for ourselves, can become effete or out of date. Those Ten Commandments given in the dim twilight of the past, and thousands of years before science had its birth—given, not like the laws of England and America, as the gradual growth of centuries, but as Minerva from Jupiter's brain, wisdom full-formed and perfect—those ten precepts can never be annulled with safety. Written with the finger of God in the rock, the imperishable nature of man, they must live forever. The human mind can conceive of no grander life than such as is the prompting of supreme love to a holy and good God, and a proper love to humanity. Such a rule of life would banish all selfishness, all purposed wrong, exalt mankind to its highest point of excellence, and make of earth a paradise. As well say, Because the soil is now cultivated with more skill, the old king of day has grown effete, and we need a new sun, as to teach that because there is now more mental culture, and because eccentric or self-sufficient men now—as indeed they have done in all ages—fail to see the excellency of the Christian system, we need a new Sun of righteousness. No! no! Man can never be elevated above the claims of the law of love, and will never be so strong that he will not need aid, so that he may measure up to its claims. After all that has yet been said, the truth remains that the serious men of this age and of our country believe that the Bible contains the rule of life appointed by Heaven for man. The evidences of its divine authority are ample and conclusive. Its teachings find much corroboration in our own experience, and we admit them to be true. Now, this word tells us that not worldly success, but a holy, noble character, and right conduct, are the true end of life.

The conviction is in our minds, too, that success and right are entirely distinct—that they may not be found always united in the life of the same individual. Right has reference to the rule and the aim of life—success, to our achievements. He who aims to develop all his powers to glorify God by usefulness to man, under the guidance of the Golden Rule, furnishes an example of right conduct. He who conquers the outer world to himself gains wealth, or fame, and power, among men—secures success. Now, our own nature, that which we feel to be authoritative in our minds, commands us to heed the law of right, whatever may become of success. Our convictions harmonize with the divine law in teaching that the true end of life is that to which we are prompted by love to God and to man; they both unite in the charge—

> Be just, and fear not:
> Let all the ends thou aim'st at be thy country's,
> Thy God's, and truth's.

When, then, we seek success at the expense of right, we not only defy God, but we spurn the authority of our own mind—we trample under foot the law of our own nature. Is there no sin in this? to do violence to our own convictions, and to turn lightly away from the divine command?

How great, how heinous the sin, none can estimate till he is able to comprehend the majesty and grandeur of the divine nature, and to estimate the value of peace, order, and righteousness to a government whose extent is unlimited, whose period is eternity, and whose citizens, with godlike natures, no man can number. God, the Infinite, the Incomprehensible, the Awful One; he who can say, I kill and I make alive, I wound and I heal, I lift up my hand to heaven, and say, I live forever; he who whets his glittering sword, and, taking hold on judgment, renders vengeance to his enemies; he who is merciful and gracious, long-suffering, and abundant in goodness and truth; who built the universe by his word, and upholds its worlds by the might of his will—this grand, unique Being, infinite in nature and absolute in perfection, fearful in majesty and power, has proclaimed himself the champion of right—right under all circumstances, at all hazards, whatever may be its relation to worldly success. To the extent of his resources of wisdom and power has he declared that he will uphold and establish the cause of right. So important did he deem it to the honor and stability of his government, to the interests of his subjects, that no doubt should linger around this question, he spared not his own Son to make it clear. His fellow and equal, his well-beloved Son, undertook the cause of right. But it happened that the path of right led him away from the path of worldly success. To do right in his sphere on earth he must stand alone, and see his wisdom reviled and his counsel spurned; he must be poor, without a shelter for his head, "despised and rejected of men, a man of sorrows, and acquainted with grief;" he must be condemned unjustly, mocked, and scourged, and crucified, amid the hootings of the rabble and the sneers of the rulers; he must endure all that is suggested by the words, "My soul is exceeding sorrowful, even unto death," and by the thrice-repeated cry, "O my Father, if it be possible, let this cup pass from me!" and yet the Father makes no effort to relieve his well-beloved, and the Son makes no effort to dash that cup of gall from his lips. The Father saw the shrinking of his Son; he heard, as the dark cloud gathered over him, his lamentable wail, "My God, my God, why hast thou forsaken me?" and yet, the Father approving, and the Son enduring, they vindicated the right; they taught on a platform visible to the universe, and with an emphasis that made all the domain of darkness to tremble, that any sacrifice, however great, or suffering, however intense, must be endured rather than swerve from the right. We see this effort of the Eternal Father to establish a kingdom of light, strong in truth and righteousness, a kingdom with absolute repulsion, in absolute antagonism, to the kingdom of darkness; we see him interested to the limit of his resources, and to the extent of the sacrifice of his only-begotten Son; we hear his summons to all intelligences to rally to the standard of right; and yet, in the light of this great interest, and of this mighty struggle, and of this authoritative call, we abandon right for a mess of pottage. Our conscience, the recognized regent in our mental nature, sides with God; we feel and know that we cannot answer the questioning of our own nature, nor the demands of Jehovah, if under any pressure we swerve from the right, and bow down to the idols of the Nebuchadnezzars of this world. And can we disregard God and conscience, and be guiltless? Can we adopt the policy of King Ahaz, and because we see others reach worldly success by unrighteous methods, can we worship mammon, or the goddess of pleasure, and say, Because these gods prosper their worshipers we will sacrifice to them, that they may help us—can we act thus and be without sin? Ah, no, my brethren. We need no grand assize, no great white throne, no unerring Judge, to settle this question. Our own hearts—interested judges—in the very days of our success, will ever declare such conduct sinful. As the Jews, to their own condemnation, said, "He will miserably destroy those wicked husbandmen, and let out the vineyard to others," so we shall be compelled to brand as sinful every act which seeks success at the expense of right. Who can draw in colors sufficiently dark the conduct of Balaam, laboring to move Jehovah to curse Israel, to destroy an entire nation—God's chosen ones—that Balaam might secure the wages of iniquity, the reward of Balak? And when the kingdoms of light and darkness, truth and error, are arrayed in deadly hostility, when we recognize that the very existence of order, peace, and blessedness, in the universe, depends on the triumph of the kingdom of truth, and see that God and all the good are staking all on the success of the right, what can be said of us if, for a temporary gain—wealth, pleasure, power—we abandon the right, and ally ourselves with the armies of vice? O brethren, we shall need no word from the King on that day! Our own consciences will stamp the brand of guilt on the soul, and drive us away to the kingdom of darkness.

We remark, that if this conduct of Ahaz is wicked, it is characterized also by signal folly. God has taught, as clearly as the nature of the case will admit, that "he who walketh uprightly, walketh surely"—that the right, and all the friends of the right, will ultimately triumph. In such a world as ours, temporal success to all the servants of God, and because they serve him, would not accord with the highest wisdom. The government of God among men seeks to develop, strengthen, and manifest character. We are unable to see how our first parents could have developed or manifested character if there had been no temptation. Doing the divine will as easily and as naturally as the stream flows down its channel, would develop no character, and secure no commendation. We must have burdens to lift before we can gain strength. Or how could we manifest character—devotion to the right and love for God—if worldly prosperity were invariably the result of obedience to God? Perhaps the strongest desire of the natural man is for worldly success—riches, honors, power. If these should always be given to the children of God, how could it be shown that they who professed loyalty to Jehovah really loved him and his law? When Satan should appear, as he did in the case of Job, and charge that these all serve God because he puts a hedge about them, and prospers them on every side, how could his cavil be met? The most selfish and base would, of course, rally to Christ's standard under this arrangement; the great, carnal crowd, as of old, would be in haste to make him a king, but only a bread-king—not the King of truth and righteousness. The blighting of temporal schemes, the withholding of worldly success, is one of the burdens, one of the forms of trial, to which God wisely subjects his people, that, like their great Captain, they may be "made perfect through sufferings," and demonstrate, under any pressure, in every trial, their loyalty to the right.

Should absolute worldly prosperity be always the lot of the disciples of Christ, there would be no grand character among men constant under pressure and gold in the furnace; no patient endurance, no heroic self-sacrifice, no manifestation of love to truth stronger than love of life, no victorious shout from the scaffold or the stake, "The blood of the martyr is the seed of the Church," no possible way of proving to a gainsaying generation how sweet and all-conquering is the love of God.

Jehovah, in the history of his people, has taught on a national platform the connection of prosperity with righteousness; he has given many illustrations in the case of individuals of prosperity because of fidelity to the truth; he declares, in the most emphatic manner, that it shall be well with the righteous; "that all things work together for good to them that love God;" and he has impressed the conviction on the minds of all his people that the faithful shall be blessed forevermore. And while the man of integrity often fails of worldly success, it is a great slander upon God and his intelligent creatures to hold that selfish principles and corrupt practices are essential to prosperity. The active, enterprising, industrious man, who honors God and loves his neighbor, will most frequently be successful in business. "The very hairs of your head are all numbered," and not a sparrow "shall fall on the ground without your Father." "Fear ye not therefore, ye are of more value than many sparrows." "For your Heavenly Father knoweth that you have need of all these things," and whatsoever success is best for them he will grant to his faithful ones. He has done all that could be done through his word, and providence, and Spirit, to convince us, and he has convinced us, that devotion to right will secure ultimate and eternal prosperity. How unwise, with this conviction upon us, to turn aside from the path that leads to countless riches and fadeless glory, that we may pluck the fruit of Sodom, or obtain "the meat that perisheth!"

The folly of this course will appear more evident when we remember that worldly success at the expense of right conduct is not a blessing, but a curse; not a stepping-stone to aid us in our upward progress, but a millstone to sink us deeper in darkness and difficulty. The divine word says, "They that will be rich fall into temptation and a snare, and into many foolish and hurtful lusts, which drown men in destruction and perdition." "Go to now, ye rich men; weep and howl for your miseries that shall come upon you. Your riches are corrupted, your gold and silver are cankered, and the rust of them shall be a witness against you, and shall eat your flesh as it were fire. Behold, the hire of the laborers, which is of you kept back by fraud, crieth." "He that makest haste to be rich shall not be innocent." These words are not directed against rich men because they are rich. Riches are a talent, and may bring a great reward to their possessor. If wise in their use, he will make friends who will receive him into everlasting habitations. He will secure the approval of the King, and be intrusted with tenfold more possessions. Wealth is a talent of great power. The rich man of the present age occupies a vantage-ground for the securement of improvement to his race, honor to himself, and glory to God, seldom reached by other classes—a vantage-ground of great possibilities, but imposing fearful responsibilities. The warnings of these scriptures are directed to those who, like King Ahaz, make worldly success the ruling aim of life—those who will be rich, who hasten to be rich, who, at all hazards, by fraud, oppression, keeping back the hire, are resolved to accumulate—too restive to tread the sure path of providence, they resort to all tricks and devices—any scheme, any plan, by which they may hasten to be rich.

The wise man, guided by inspiration, says, "There is a sore evil which I have seen under the sun: riches kept for the owners thereof to their hurt. But those riches perish by evil travail, and he begetteth a son, and there is nothing in his hand. As he came forth of his mother's womb, naked shall he return to go as he came, and shall take nothing of his labor which he may carry away in his hand." "And what profit hath he that hath labored for the wind? All his days also he eateth in darkness, and hath much sorrow and wrath with his sickness." What a picture! and how often verified in the life of those who make worldly success their highest aim! Riches gained and kept for the owners thereof to their hurt! Secured by evil practices, they bind their possessors to those evil practices by all the strength of their influence. Their splendid mansions and hoarded treasures stand between them and eternal life. Each one whose success is the result of wrong may well say,

> What form of prayer
> Can serve my turn? Forgive my foul murder!

> That cannot be, since I am still possessed
> Of those effects for which I did the murder—
> My crown, my own ambition, and my queen.
> May one be pardoned and retain the offense?
> In the corrupted currents of this world,
> Offense's gilded hand may shove by justice;
> And oft 't is seen, the wicked prize itself
> Buys out the law; but 't is not so above.
> There is no shuffling, there the action lies
> In its true nature; and we ourselves compelled,
> Even to the teeth and forehead of our faults,
> To give in evidence.

No one can say, with any hope of success, Forgive my foul offense, while he holds with loving clutch the fruits of that offense. To enter the kingdom of heaven, his penitence must be so genuine as to command restoration as far as possible. And how many of the multitude, who have made worldly success their chief end, can receive this saying? The rich young ruler, whose morals were pure, weighing heaven and earth, deliberately turned away from the proffered crown of eternal life, that he might still possess his earthly treasure. But when our purpose at the beginning, and every step onward, is a practical subordination of every thing to the one object of worldly success, how can we, with wrong principles strengthened by life-long exercise, with a conscience seared, with the entire moral nature perverted through the love of gain—how, when called to repentance, can we tear away our hearts, so wedded to our treasures, and restore those treasures for the kingdom of heaven's sake? The man who subordinates all things to worldly success, and is therefore at liberty to gain, and liable to gain, by evil practices, knows not what he does. As the mason, building day by day the lofty tower from whose summit he is to fall and be dashed to pieces, so this man is binding himself, with well-nigh adamantine bonds; and through principles and practices strengthening daily, and with all the weight of his accumulating treasures, he is throwing up almost insurmountable difficulties across the track that leads to life. It is easier for a camel to go through a needle's eye than for such a rich man to enter the kingdom of heaven. And how often these ill-gotten gains bring ruin to our children! With God's curse upon them, too, the same evil practices by which they were accumulated tear them from us— they perish by evil travail. How often does such success vanish as the morning cloud and early dew! It comes, bringing in its train into the household idleness, extravagance, vanity, and pride often, and as it departs, leaving its wretched train, a heritage of woe, it croaks in our ear the sad inquiry, Where is now thy god? "What profit hath he that hath labored for the wind?"

Whether retained or not, their possessor "all his days eateth in darkness, and hath much sorrow and wrath with his sickness." As he nears the end of life, conscience will gather about him the victims of his wrong, who will take up a parable and taunting proverb against him, and say, "Woe to him that increaseth that which is not his own! Woe to him that gaineth an evil gain to his house, that he may set his nest on high! The stone shall cry out of the wall, and the beam out of the timber shall answer it. Woe to him that buildeth a town with blood, and establisheth a city by iniquity!" The great Teacher makes the solemn inquiry, "What is a man profited if he shall gain the whole world and lose his own soul?"

When we survey man as he is — so grand and godlike in his nature that earth, with all its treasures, its Elysian fields, its Tempean vales, its happy isles, its voluptuousness, its magnificence and grandeur, could never satisfy him — when we view him with so vast capacities, and yet destined to live and grow forever, and then think of his deliberately wrecking these immortal energies, and bartering all that is implied in eternal life in the kingdom of heaven for worldly gain—a gain that cannot satisfy, a gain that can last only for a transient flash of time—we are constrained to acknowledge that there is infinite folly in the transaction.

Who in all the range of history has found worldly success at the sacrifice of right profitable? Jezebel and Ahab secured the vineyard of Naboth; Judas got his thirty pieces of silver; but did they bring a blessing in their train? The rich man, who said to his soul, "Take thine ease, eat, drink, and be merry," has no crime laid at his door but that of making worldly gain and its enjoyment the chief end of life; and when God tears him away from his treasures, and, branding fool upon his forehead, sends him out into a dark universe without a farthing or a friend, he but gives another illustration of the great folly of valuing worldly prosperity above right and responsibility.

Again, the success is always transient. Admit, if you please, that it brings a blessing, that we may obtain and enjoy it through life without qualms of conscience, or fears of the future, still we must soon part with this source of enjoyment. We shall retain a remembrance of it, and that remembrance will be a bright background, which will but intensify the gloom of our eternal future. "Son, remember that thou in thy life-time receivedst thy good things, and now thou art tormented." The sad contrast will live forever. But as a blessing, a source of enjoyment, our worldly success, if secured by making it the supreme object in life, parts with us forever at death. To our rank and power, our treasures and honors, at the end of life here, we must bid a final farewell. As a blight to our joy, a curse upon our brow, or a millstone about our neck, these may survive; but as blessings they part with us at the grave. I care not how vast our possessions, or lofty our throne. As we walk in the midst of the great Babylon which we have built by the might of our power, our great success may prompt us to believe that we shall ascend into heaven and exalt our throne above the stars of God, that we shall be like the Most High, that our mountain shall never be moved; but soon the grave will be moved at our coming. Our enemies will break forth into singing, "Hast thou become like one of us? how art thou fallen from heaven, O day-star, son of the morning!" We have surveyed, in the light of history, the great kingdoms which have ruled the world, and we learned that the mighty monarchs, surrounded by their possessions, and guarded by invincible legions, at the behest of the great King each one was compelled to leave all and return to the dust.

Almost in our century a mighty god of war arose, who threatened to subdue the earth. His lowering brow shrouded in darkness the political horizon of the world. At his nod nations trembled. As his humor dictated, he pulled down and set up kingdoms. His disciplined armies, his vast conquests, his stronghold in the affections of his people, his towering genius and invincible will, seemed to promise for him permanent power. Surely, if any could resist the stern rule of fate, and lift his throne above the clouds and the reach of change, it was this mighty god of war. But soon we see him contemplating the setting sun as he throws his lingering beams on the wide waste of waters. His crown dishonored, his scepter broken, his power gone, far from his home and his kingdom, without any army or a soldier, poor and naked, he went down to his grave in a rocky isle of the ocean. We have seen but as yesterday the young man who would be rich. With eager zeal he proclaimed Mammon as his god, and worshiped at his altars. Wealth came, millions were poured into his coffers, yet in the prime of life, forsaken of his own god, haunted by an evil conscience, pursued by men and cursed of Jehovah, in a felon's cell he went down to his grave, " unwept, unhonored, and unsung," and inspiration writes his memorial, " He that getteth riches, and not by right, shall leave them in the midst of his days, and at his end shall be a fool." The world hath seen error and wrong trample down all opposition, and stalk the earth as a mighty giant. Ascending the lofty summit of success, we have seen it crowned, and wave its palm in triumph; but there, on its pinnacle of glory, and amid the exultant songs of its disciples, we have seen it languish and die.

> Error, wounded, writhes in pain,
> And dies among her worshipers.

God's curse rests upon it, and it must be crushed. As Jezebel and Ahab had learned, when the dogs licked their blood and ate their flesh by the wall of Jezreel, and in the portion of Naboth; as Judas felt when the price of innocent blood so burnt in his conscience that he threw it from him and hanged himself; as all the tyrants and monsters of iniquity whom history has branded have learned, under the ruling of Jehovah, so every one, however lofty or low his station, shall be taught, and feel with strong intensity, that any success secured at the sacrifice of right, or through subordinating right to worldly prosperity, is a bitter curse, and *never* a blessing.

Jehovah has declared that he who subordinates right conduct and eternal life to worldly success—chooses his "good things" in this world—shall be bound in the next world by that choice; that he who barters the divine approval and heaven for a mess of pottage shall not be counted worthy to enter his kingdom. He assures us that the feet of such "shall slide in due time," that "they stand in slippery places." While the righteous "shall flourish like the palm-tree," green and vigorous through winter's frost and summer's drought, and "grow like a cedar in Lebanon," whose age is counted by centuries; while they shall stand like Mount Zion, that can never be moved, "the wicked shall spring" only "as the grass," and "the workers of iniquity flourish, that they shall be destroyed forever;" they shall not prosper, a ruin shall overtake them sufficiently awful to send a pang through all the realms of benevolence and love. "I have seen the wicked in great power, and spreading himself like a green bay-tree; yet he passed away, and lo, he was not; yea, I sought him, but he could not be found."

Away, then, with the idea everywhere, that we must have success, wealth, fame, power! These are not necessary; they can never satisfy; if made supreme, they never ennoble, but dwarf and degrade; they perish in the using, and must all be abandoned at the grave. But a good conscience and God's approval are essential. These give a power which all the wealth and armed legions of the world cannot equal, and will sustain in peace and assurance "when suns have waned and worlds sublime their final revolutions told." Away with that demoralizing notion that "nature chooses the fittest"—*fittest* signifying those who gain secular wealth and power; that they alone are valuable, or worthy to live, who can press themselves into the front ranks of worldly success! Away with the unprincipled and cowardly example of this degenerate king, teaching that our methods and our very God may be abandoned in the hope of gaining a success which, like a millstone, will sink us forever! Difficult it is to get beyond the shadow of this world.

Its palpable influence is ever present; the circling waves of its power, as a mighty maelstrom, drive us along their whirling track. Its ease, its wealth, its honors, its magnificence and splendor, its reproach, and scorn, and ridicule, O how they make the brain to burn, and enslave the mind! But we know that another day is coming. The clock of eternity shall strike twelve; the visible universe, waxed old, shall be folded up and laid aside as a garment, and the new heavens and the new earth shall appear. In that hour, as we see our present home, its silver and gold, its honors and power, pass away, and as we take in the vast scope of Jehovah's reign and of eternal life, in what light will appear the choice which now prefers the visible and perishing to the eternal — which sides with the doomed kingdom of evil, repudiating the dynasty of righteousness, whose flag shall wave in triumph forever? How ruinous and wicked then will seem the policy which says, Because these practices secure worldly gain, therefore will I adopt them!

O no! stand bravely by the right, and seek the return of the heroic days, when men of the world could say, "I would rather be right than ruler." I would rather be a door-keeper with the holy than prosper among the wicked! Poor you may be, possibly starve, but the angels who bore Lazarus to the skies have lost neither power of opinion nor loyalty to the will of our Father. Your schemes and plans may all fail, but they fail in the cause and under the eye of Him who knows your wants, and who is pledged to make "all things work together for good" to his friends. You may be the scorn and derision of the prosperous around you, the frown of the world's Cæsars may rest upon you, but you shall have the countenance and the smile of the King of kings. Your names may be unknown to the registry of earth's renowned, but they will live on the abiding records of heaven. No grand mausoleum may stand over your grave, but God will mark the spot, and "when the holy angels come, it surely will be found." And on that day when, Truth's reign secured, she shall raise her pæans of everlasting triumph, you, as the friends of truth, who sold it not, will join in her song of joy, and shout, "They shall prosper that love thee!"

THE REV. W. T. HARRIS, D.D.,
Of the Memphis Conference.

IX.
THE LAST ENEMY.
BY THE REV. W. T. HARRIS,
Memphis Conference.

"The last enemy that shall be destroyed is death." 1 Cor. xv. 26.

WE are in a world of enemies—enemies of soul and body. Some of them are stout, and stubborn, and cruel, and hard to overcome. None may be entirely subdued and conquered without assistance —without divine grace. Our souls have enemies all about, inside of us and outside of us, and they are dangerous. And our bodies have enemies in the earth, in the sky, in the air, in the waters— everywhere.

The great enemy of the soul is *sin*, for all the different forms of evil, and foes of humanity, with all their different phases, and characters, and classes, and degrees, when aggregated and considered, may be pronounced in one word—*sin*.

The body has lustful passions, and libidinous propensities, and carnal desires, and pains, and aches, and many infirmities—all leading to and resulting in death. According to the teachings of the text, the last enemy—"death"—shall be destroyed, shall be counterworked, subverted, and finally overturned. But death cannot be destroyed by there being simply no farther death; death can only be destroyed and annihilated by a general resurrection. Then, if there be no general resurrection, it is most evident that death will still retain his empire. Therefore, the fact that death shall be destroyed assures the fact that there shall be a general resurrection; and this is proof also that after the resurrection there shall be no more death.

1. *The resurrection of the dead is no new doctrine.* It is most clearly and elaborately taught, and fully explained, in the New Testament, and likewise set forth, and with the utmost exactitude, in the Old Testament. This doctrine is as old as the Church of God — believed and taught by patriarchs, and prophets, and apostles—the great doctrine of every dispensation, and of every age of the world.

This heaven-revealed and heaven-attested truth, in the ages long gone, kindled the fire that burned in the heart and flashed in the eye of the prophet of God, and enabled him to rise above the darkling and hurtling clouds of mysticism, and pierce the unborn future, and read on the ghastly mouth of the moldering tomb—light, life, immortality!

Foreshadowed all over the Old Testament. Moses, the earliest writer, and who gave an account of the creation of the world, and man, and all things else, in the infancy of time, when the young world swung down in the warm, fresh breath of heaven, and sparkled in the early dews of eternity, believed it, and looked forward to the day of triumph. How sublime the faith of that grand old Jewish legislator, God's own amanuensis, standing near the burning bush, and calling the Lord "The God of Abraham, and the God of Isaac, and the God of Jacob; for he is not a God of the dead, but of the living!"

And Job, the very embodiment of all physical suffering, and disease, and persecution, in the midst of all exultingly shouted, "I know that my Redeemer liveth, and that he shall stand at the latter day upon the earth; and though after my skin worms destroy this body, yet in my flesh shall I see God."

And Isaiah, the great evangelical prophet, mourning over the devastation and ruin of city, and country, and people, attributing all to the just judgments of a righteous God: "For thou hast made of a city a heap; of a defensed city a ruin; a palace of strangers to be no city; it shall never be built." And of the people he said: "They are dead, they shall not live; they are deceased, they shall not rise; thou hast destroyed them, and made all their memory to perish." Then he rises with the inspiration of hope thrilling his heart and flashing in his eye, and God's own living fire touching his tongue, and in the majesty of unconquerable faith he cries, "Thy dead men shall live, together with my dead body shall they arise. Awake and sing, ye that dwell in dust; for thy dew is as the dew of herbs, and the earth shall cast out the dead." And language equally strong and pertinent may be quoted from Daniel, Hosea, and others.

2. *This doctrine was derided by the Greeks.* When Paul, God's great apostle, appeared in the celebrated Grecian city—Athens—and stood on the renowned

Areopagus, or hill of Mars, in the midst of that pompous court, confronting the learned infidelity and false philosophy of the age, and preached Jesus and the resurrection, a sublimer exhibition of moral heroism, and intellectual grandeur, and unflinching nerve, the world never saw. "It is not possible to conceive a situation of greater peril, or one more calculated to prove the sincerity of a preacher, than that in which the apostle was here placed; and the truth of this, perhaps, will never be better felt than by a spectator, who from this eminence actually beholds the monuments of pagan pomp and superstition by which he, whom the Athenians considered as the *setter-forth of strange gods*, was then surrounded—representing to the imagination the disciples of Socrates and of Plato—the dogmatist of the Porch and the skeptic of the Academy—addressed by a poor and lowly man, who, 'rude in speech,' without the 'enticing words of man's wisdom,' enjoined precepts contrary to their taste, and very hostile to their prejudices."

There he stood, towering above that sea of upturned faces, and fiery, glancing eyes, and infuriated hearts of infidelity—the unmoved, intrepid servant of God, like a beetling rock in mid-ocean, breasting the waves, lashed by the wing of the tempest—the grand, God-sustained, God-honored apostle! And above the low, sullen murmur of dissent, and the sharp, loud clamor of bitter opposition, rang the heaven-inspired words, *Jesus and the resurrection!*

"Then certain philosophers of the Epicureans and of the Stoics encountered him, and some said,

What will this babbler say? he seemeth to be a setter-forth of strange gods. And when they heard of the resurrection of the dead, some mocked, and others said, We will hear thee again of this matter." After their derision and mocking, some believed—and, indeed, all the Jews, as a nation, believed this doctrine—all the Pharisees, all the scribes—only the Sadducees dissenting.

3. *The resurrection of Christ insures the resurrection of humankind.* "Now is Christ risen from the dead, and become the first-fruits of them that slept. For since by man came death, by man came also the resurrection of the dead. For as in Adam all die, even so in Christ shall all be made alive. But every man in his own order: Christ the first-fruits; afterward, they **that are** Christ's at his coming." After the **crucifixion of** our Lord, **his** body was placed in the **new tomb** of Joseph of Arimathea, "in which never **man** was laid." Of course, should a resurrection take place, it must be that of Jesus —it could be of no other person. On the third day **the** tomb was empty. *What became of the body?* We know the plain, unvarnished statement of the evangelists, the straightforward, unembellished way the gospel answers the question, and to the satisfaction of men, and angels, and God. We have gone with the body of Jesus from the cross to the tomb; we have seen the tomb sealed; have left the Roman guard at the mouth of the sepulcher. Now, **let infidelity**, the chief priests, the enemies **of** Christ, produce the body, on or after the third day, in order to silence the clamor of the deluded multitude, and

put this question to rest forever. We have read the predictions of the prophets and of Jesus, and now the eager eyes of an excited world are fixed with intensest gaze upon the result, and all hearts beat with the extremest concernment; *but show the dead body*, and the claims of Christianity are at once and forever hushed: her fair temple totters and falls, and with a crash that sends waking echoes all along down the ages, and through all time! *It was not done.* The soldiers say, "While we *slept* the disciples came and stole it away." Where are the disciples? They have not fled the country, have not attempted to escape; here they are, standing up boldly in the face of the excited multitude, discomfited infidelity, and enraged chief priests, preaching, "He is risen; come see the place where he lay." Why did they not arrest the disciples, and make *them* produce the body? They had all power, all authority—both civil and military—and the bloodthirsty crowd, the influential chief priests, and the strong military arm stretched out for their protection and assistance. Why did they not arrest and crucify every one of them? They put to death the Master—surely they would not scruple to kill the *servants. But this was not done.* Strange, indeed! Why did not the enemies of Jesus, determined to crush Christianity in its infancy, seize upon this wonderful advantage, and blot out every record, every word of the doctrines promulged by the great impostor and his despised disciples? The world was standing on tiptoe, infidelity raging, and the minds of the people inflamed with the most inveterate hate. Why let this best opportunity the world ever saw pass by unimproved? They had the power, the authority, and the sympathy, of the Roman governor and the whole Jewish nation. Under the law, they should have arrested the guards, who were self-convicted and self-condemned—sixty men on watch, all asleep at once—and pronounced upon them the penalty of the law, "Death." *That was not done.* Ah, let stultified infidelity blush with very shame!

What became of the crucified body of Jesus? Infidelity has never answered the question, and never will.

Hear the response of the gospel—the plain, consistent, and harmonious statement of the two angels, all of the apostles, the pious women, and more than five hundred brethren at once—"He is risen." Christianity finds the crucified body of our blessed Lord, *but it is not dead*, but alive forevermore! Christianity saw him at the mouth of the tomb, on the way to Emmaus, on the mountain-top, on the bright cloud, and in the company of marshaling angels ascending to the right-hand of the Majesty on high! Christianity sees him to-day, with the eye of faith, high seated upon the eternal throne of his glory, an exalted and interceding Saviour, a High-priest passed into the heaven of heavens, where he ever liveth to make intercession for us. Pray on, thou risen, exalted, glorified *One!* By faith we see thee.

4. *Order of the resurrection.* The dead saints will be raised first. In that last day of earth, that day

of God's power and glory, into which the destiny of unnumbered millions will be crowded, that day of nameless terror to the wicked, of ineffable joy to the righteous, and of unutterable splendor to all, God will honor his followers. When all the aërial regions, all space between earth and heaven, dazzle with the glory of the descending Lord, and brighten with the flash of angelic wings, God will dignify, invest with honor, and glorify, his trusting saints. "For the Lord himself shall descend from heaven with a shout, with the voice of the archangel, and with the trump of God, and the dead in Christ shall rise first." But what will become of the saints still living, who have never tasted death, never gone into the silence of the grave, still walking the earth, actively engaged with the vocations, and professions, and duties, of this life? In the gospel plan of full redemption they are not overlooked, not forgotten. "Then we which are alive and remain shall be caught up together with them in the clouds, to meet the Lord in the air; and so shall we ever be with the Lord." *Then the wicked* shall be raised; but not until the God-man has gathered up all his *jewels* from the earth, and from the waters, and from every part of the globe, as brilliant stars with which to bedeck his resplendent crown of glory forever. Not until the joyful meeting of the saints with the Lord in the air, shall the deep slumber of a sinner be disturbed, or a grave cracked, or a tomb opened, of the ungodly!

When the wicked do come forth, it will be to shame and everlasting contempt. "They that have done good, unto the resurrection of life; and they that have done evil, unto the resurrection of damnation." They would rather slumber on, hid forever in the thick darkness of the grave, or concealed deep down in the bowels of the earth forever, or go straight to hell, than meet the flashing eye of the omniscient Judge, and see the bursting light of that terrible day. And when they do come at God's command, *pale* and trembling, it will be with a *cry* that will startle the earth, and ring to hell, and thunder to heaven: "Rocks and mountains, fall upon us, and hide us from the presence of *Him* that sitteth upon the throne!"

5. *Nature of the resurrection-body.* We may say but little on this subject, for Paul has treated it with the hand of a master and the heart of a prophet. It will be *incorruptible*, not subject to decay—will live and bloom in fadeless beauty and immortal joy. It will possess *glory and power.* "Sown in weakness, raised in power." How much glory, and how much power, God only knows; and with what celestial brightness and supernatural luster it will be invested, God only knows; and what marvelous strength and wonderful activity, we cannot conceive.

It will be a *spiritual body.* "Sown a natural body, raised a spiritual body." And above all, and grander than all, it will be *like Christ's glorified body.* "For our conversation is in heaven, from whence also we look for the Saviour, who shall change our vile body, that it may be fashioned like unto his glorious body." "It doth not yet appear what we shall be; but we know that when he shall appear, we shall be like him." "I shall be satisfied when I awake with thy likeness."

6. *The resurrection will be the victory over man's last enemy.* "The last enemy that shall be destroyed is death." "Death is swallowed up in victory."

Death, king of terrors! Thou merciless, vaunting, cruel, triumphant enemy of humankind! Broad has been thy empire, stretching from pole to pole, from north to south, from sea to sea, engirding the whole earth! Broad, and firm, and impregnable, and high as heaven, has been thy throne, built of human bones, and cemented with human gore! And the din and noise of thy building was the shriek of widowhood and the cry of orphanage! Innumerable, and active, and cruel, have been the agents, and emissaries, and engines of destruction, at thy command! *Long,* and dreadful, and compassionless, has been thy reign of terror! Thy bloody *scepter,* that waved over dying Abel, has extended to every people, every country, every clime, every tribe, and every home-circle! Where is there a family he has not entered, and broken into fragments? a heart he has not made to bleed? an eye he has not learned to weep? a voice he has not stifled in grief?

And on he strides to-day, building cities, and peopling them with his pale and pulseless victims, and scattering solitary graves all over the land, and filling up the oceans with his slain! No human power can stop his wild, impetuous tread; no human hand can wrench from his grasp the iron scepter; no voice of pleading, nor streaming eye, nor breaking heart, nor bending knee, can move him to pity, or drive him away. O there is but one Power in the universe that can arrest and stop his triumphant march; but one Arm that can take from his hand the bloody scepter; but one Being in earth or heaven that can conquer and drive him away!—*the Lion of the tribe of Judah!* And, thank God, he has undertaken our cause, become the Captain of our salvation, and will fight our battles for us, and overthrow our enemies. "And the last enemy that shall be destroyed is death."

7. *Then death shall be dethroned;* his empire conquered, subjugated; his sepulchral cities depopulated; his solitary graves emptied; oceans disgorged! *When Jesus speaks*, his throne shall totter to the fall, and the king of terrors shall come, with unresisting submission, tamely crouching to his feet!

Our "last" great "enemy" has heard the voice of Jesus before. When death, that tyrannical, gloating, cruel monster, reigned over the grave of Lazarus, and the bending forms, and the pleading cries, and the gushing tears, and breaking hearts, of inconsolable sisters could not move his merciless heart, or make him relinquish his cold and iron grasp, the omnipotent voice of the God-man sounded in his ear, and *then* he quailed, and cowered, and turned him loose!

Jesus met him once in the city of Nain, with his mournful, slow-moving *cortege*, holding his scepter over the only son of a bereaved widow; and when Jesus touched the bier, and said, "Young man, arise!" *death fled*, and the boy sat up, and "began to speak!"

And when the last trump shall sound, and the voice of the archangel shall be heard, and a mighty shout from heaven, the dead, small and great, shall rise. Heaven's gates will open for the righteous; hell's gates will open for the wicked. Then *death* and hell will be cast into the "lake that burns with fire and brimstone" forever!

THE REV. S. A. STEEL,
Of the North Mississippi Conference.

X.

THE SPREAD OF THE GOSPEL.

BY THE REV. S. A. STEEL,
North Mississippi Conference.

"And Jesus came and spake unto them, saying, All power is given unto me in heaven and in earth. Go ye, therefore, and teach all nations, baptizing them in the name of the Father, and of the Son, and of the Holy Ghost: teaching them to observe all things whatsoever I have commanded you; and, lo, I am with you alway, even unto the end of the world. Amen." Matt. xxviii. 18, 19, 20.

THE gospel is for everybody, and it must go everywhere. This was its scope when Jesus gave the great commission to the disciples, and this is its scope now. It proclaimed then, and it proclaims to-day, that the world is the field of its intended expansion, and the fealty of universal man its due. Unlimited enlargement is a necessity of its nature, and the miracle of its progress the sublimest evidence of its truth. God has no favorites.

The main point in the text is the missionary obligation which it imposes on the Church. There are other and important elements in its exegesis, but this is the central thought that lies at its very heart. The imperfect apprehension of these words is the chief obstacle to the religious development of mankind. Whenever they press upon the conscience of the Church, the advance of the gospel is rapid and glorious. Their spirit is like fire in the bones.

The text, therefore, contains the indestructible germ of human progress. The moral antecedents of the world's advancement lie in the crystal depths of this passage. The present activity of the globe has sprung from Christianity, has a deep and essential connection with the gospel, and is a predicted result of the plans and policy of Providence in relation to mankind. As long as that text lives on the page of inspiration there will be a stir on this planet, and hope for our race.

There is a wideness in the idea of the text that befits the mind of God. It is forever conclusive as against every form of moral apathy, religious narrowness, and spiritual repose. It creates an obligation that would stand firmer than adamant against universal unbelief, and imposes a duty as lasting as time itself. The whole thought, purpose, plan, policy, and reason, of the missionary work of the Church originate here. Every aspect of the gospel, every subsequent utterance of its history, every development of its truth in the personal consciousness of the believer, but emphasizes this original disclosure of the aim of the Christian religion. The missionary obligation could have no higher source.

The text gives us this proposition: *It is the supreme duty of the Church to send the gospel to all nations.* We shall try to prove it. We shall analyze this duty into its original elements, and endeavor to show why it is supreme. It has a broad base lying deep in the region of eternal truth, but it has too often been hidden from view by an undue regard for the superficial and incidental reasons of this work. At best, these possess only a temporary and fluctuating value, and we prefer to clear our way through them to the great scriptural truths and facts of Christian consciousness that lie below them, and from whose conclusions there can be no rational dissent. We want a foundation of rock.

I. *This duty originates in the fact that all the world needs the gospel.*

There is a universal capacity for religion in our race. Human nature is a unit, and however modified by external conditions, retains its fundamental attributes. No divergence from the original stock can extinguish the elementary instincts of its being. The moral feeling is constitutional in man, and a moral belief, with its superior motivities, is its necessary correlate. The moment thought unfolds in consciousness, the essential instinct of religion emerges into light as a coëfficient element of human nature; and it grows deeper and stronger, as reason develops, until it asserts supreme lordship over his being, and demands that every thing be sacrificed to satisfy it. No part of our race has been found incapable of mental and moral elevation. Even the lowest types of savages have been lifted up, and civilized, and redeemed. This fact conditions a universal faith, justifies the world-embracing scope of the gospel, and furnishes valid proof of the divinity of a system that, getting back of the multifold manifestations of humanity, plants itself on the primal instincts of our nature as the indestructible base of its operations.

Left to themselves, mankind have always striven to rise out of this darkness. The spontaneous impulse of moral feeling has originated schemes of relief. The grandest efforts of the human intellect have been exerted at this point, in vain attempt to pacify the eternal anxieties of conscience, and fill the vast aching void of immortal aspirations. We can trace the struggle of moral thought and feeling, floundering slowly upward and onward from the base forms of nature-worship to the divinest concepts of philosophical imagination, in mighty but abortive efforts to find out God. Men have found the highest summits of their speculations sheeted in pitiless snows, and have sunk down in voiceless despair on the glacial wastes of error. Paganism is the product of their discoveries. It is utterly inadequate to the moral necessities of mankind; yet it to-day holds under its blighting curse the largest portion of our race, and the fairest regions of our earth. By every rational test, the independent religious movements are stupendous failures; but they show the depth of the moral consciousness of mankind, and are a tremendous argument for the spread of the only true religion.

The depravity of the race is universal. All nations are debauched in crime. The ravages of sin are coëxtensive with the residence of man. The doom of death hangs like a pall upon our planet. The gospel is the only remedy for sin—the cross of Jesus the only hope of our race. It exhibits a perfect correlation with the demands of our universal nature, offers adequate, ample, and available, relief for every human woe, and furnishes the only conception of destiny compatible with the dignity of our being, and commensurate with the range of our desires. The loftiest thought of man has never got above it, or beyond it. Wherever it goes, prostrate humanity rises from its degradation, and begins its appropriate activity. Nations without the gospel have been stagnant from an immemorial period; nations with the gospel have always been restless, aggressive, powerful, borne onward along the path of progress by an internal force which they could not resist; and they are so just in proportion as the gospel gets hold of them, and puts its almighty energy into them. It not only accelerates human progress, but imparts dignity and distinction to all its achievements. Civilization is a product of its power, and is coterminous with its expansion. It is universally and gloriously adapted to the elevation of our race. Repose is guilt in the presence of the awful distress of the world. The displeasure of righteous Heaven must be upon us if we rest on our oars and see unmoved the wreck of our race, while louder than the thunders of the storm the vast, deep cry for help is rolling up from millions going down to death.

II. *This duty originates in the fact that the gospel is designed for all the world.*

Inspiration is burdened with the evidence of its universal scope. Prophecy everywhere, and in the clearest voice, foretold its illimitable range. Its earliest utterances declared that all nations should be blessed in faithful Abraham, and its latest proclaimed that whosoever will may come. The heathen were to be given to Christ for an inheritance, and the uttermost parts of the earth for a possession. He was to be a light to the Gentiles, and the salvation of God to all the ends of the earth. All people, nations, and languages, were to serve him. By the grace of God he tasted death for every man. He gave himself a ransom for all. He is the Lamb of God that taketh away the sin of the world. He is the propitiation for our sins, and not for ours only, but also for the sins of the whole world. He commands the gospel to be carried to all nations. John saw the symbol of the Christian ministry in the Apocalyptic angel, flying in the midst of heaven, having the everlasting gospel to preach to every nation, and kindred, and tongue, and people, that dwell on the earth.

Such is God's purpose in the gospel. It knows no limits but the boundaries of the globe. Shall we nullify the fundamental aim of its revelation? Shall we content ourselves with a selfish monopoly of its blessings, or imagine we are the pets of the Almighty because we have it? Shall we fold our arms in guilty indifference to its spread, and paralyze its progress by withholding our aid, when the whole world is dying for it, and it proclaims by every oracle that it is designed for the whole world, and is the gift of God to all our race? Can we love Jesus and do it?

This aim of universal dominion is peculiar to

Christianity. It lifts it immeasurably above its rivals, attests its divinity, and guarantees its final triumph. It assumed at the first, and maintains from age to age, the position of an exclusive religion, itself essentially right, and all others necessarily wrong, and its destiny absolute and universal supremacy. It refuses to coalesce with other systems. It rejects every offered compromise, and scorns all proposals of armistice. It came to exterminate all other forms of moral belief, and moves steadily onward to realize its aim, guided by the wisdom, and sustained by the power, of God. It overthrew the paganism of Europe, and destroyed that of America, and is invading Africa and Asia, intent on its primal aim. It is the only religion that has followers in every land. It has enrolled representatives of every nation under its banner. Its camp-fires illuminate every region, glitter on the far-off isles that gem the ocean, flame like a zone of living splendors along the vast realm of China, and flash high "up the stainless ramps of huge Himalaya's wall." It is organized, active, aggressive, triumphant from west to east, through all the latitudes of the habitable earth, illustrating its eternal energy in ever-enlarging efforts for the recovery of man. The artificial distinctions of mankind disappear in the light of its impartial love, for it came to make the blessings of redemption flow far as the curse is found.

This design is deep, permanent, fundamental, lying at the very base of the whole economy of moral purpose and endeavor. It is organic in the very nature of Christianity. The missionary obligation therefore springs from an internal necessity of the system, is grounded in the first principles of religion, is inexorable as a moral law, and is of universal and perpetual force. Therefore we cannot be truly loyal to Jesus Christ, and out of sympathy with the sublime and all-embracing purpose of his mission. If we feel no concern for the heathen, and take no interest in the wider and larger range of religious effort, it is the sign of a disastrous defect in our piety, and a melancholy weakness in our faith. Selfishness is sin.

III. *This duty originates in the express command of Jesus Christ.*

"Jesus came, and spake unto them, saying, All power is given unto me in heaven and in earth. Go ye, therefore, make Christians of all nations, baptizing them in the name of the Father, and of the Son, and of the Holy Ghost: teaching them to observe all things whatsoever I have commanded you; and, lo, I am with you alway, even unto the end of the world." The whole genius of the new dispensation flashed forth in that word, Go! No mightier word ever fell upon the ear of the world. Its vibrations have shaken the kingdoms of the globe, and still agitate the ages. The force of an omnipotent imperative is in it. It contains the embryonic possibilities of a world's progress. It is not a suggestion; it is not advisory; it is not instructive; it is not a permission; it is not a commission only; but it is a mandate full and deep as the authority of God.

This lofty commandment was given to the disciples at the special meeting on the mountain in Galilee. It was the most august conference ever held. Jesus Christ himself presided, and settled for all ages to come the functions of the ministry, and the policy of the Church, and gave the plenary commission to subdue the world. Amid the solemn hush of that assembly we hear nothing of the primacy of Peter, of apostolic succession, of pontifical vicarship, of priests, sacraments, or ritual. The thought of the Church was focalized upon one tremendous idea, which not only lay back of all organization, and beneath all outward effort, but was thenceforward to absorb into itself the resources of the world, and direct the progress of the race. In one word Jesus gave the philosophy of the Christian system, and unveiled the rationale of the new and wondrous manifestation of Providence. The grand basal principle of Church-order, the puissant norm of the whole economy of Christianity, is the everlasting itinerancy of the gospel. "All nations" was the wide range of the holy evangel, and the primal appointment secured the perpetual mobility of the ministry to the end of time.

The apostles did not then understand it. It was a revelation which anticipated the profoundest developments of their faith and the grandest reaches of their experience. This sudden burst of the illimitable magnificence of the gospel purpose and prospects blinded and bewildered them. But the baptismal fire of the Holy Ghost on the day of Pentecost swept them into deep and blessed sympathy with the immense conception, and they gradually rose to the unequaled height of its apprehension, and one after another sped away on glorious errand to tell the joyful news.

But we understand it; and we cannot escape the inflexible obligation of a positive commandment, emanating immediately from the Source of all authority and power, and emphasized by the exceptional circumstances of its delivery. We have no discretion in the matter. A divine compulsion is upon us. The inexorable condition of our existence enforces the missionary attitude and effort. Coming over all the mountains, sweeping upon every wind, crossing all the seas and lands, and breaking from the bending heavens, like the thunders of Divinity, we hear the sovereign mandate, Go! The primal obligation has not been lowered, or the primal command revoked. The boundless scope of redeeming love has not been restricted, or the ancient counsels of Almighty Goodness canceled, or the glorious word of the Lord bound. That word is as fresh to-day as when it leaped from the lips of Jesus on the Galilean mount. It is as strong, as glorious, as grand, as when the waiting disciples, in obedience to its divine behest, seized the banner of the cross, starred with the splendors of everlasting light, and startled the nations with their grand advance. We need no other argument for missions. It is injustice to truth to put the claims of this cause upon any lower ground. It is fixed upon us by the fiat of Jehovah. We plant our cause right here, and defy all controversy to lower its claim, or escape the duty it imposes without guilt. Long as the curse endures, the disciples of Jesus Christ must send the gospel to all lands.

IV. *This duty is still more clearly defined and greatly strengthened by the fact that the Church has always recognized it as supreme.*

The outward organization of the Church has always conformed to this inner idea of expansion, and its history has been that of steady progress—it sweeps a wider circle in every age. The providential arrangements for its spread were few and simple, but adequate and effectual. An itinerant ministry was the central idea of Jesus in forming this Church. The apostles became active and invincible emissaries of the cross, who bore the gospel into every accessible region of the earth. Paul, the grandest of the band, was specially set over the foreign work. The wider policy of religious effort, the larger outreachings of gospel progress, required the ripest intellect and greatest heart of the Church. God put the best man the Church had in charge of the foreign field. He sent the most eloquent preacher off as a missionary. He took him away from a large city-station, broke up his settled pastorate at Antioch, and hurried him to the front to lead the van of the infant Church right into the heart of heathendom. Some of our modern objectors to missions would have thought that a great waste of talent. Paul, the man of massive brain, of deep and swift insight into truth, of high and liberal culture, of polished manners and fiery eloquence, of catholic sympathies and safe judgment, could have been useful in any place. Wherever he might have been sent, he would have shaken the very foundations of paganism. But men exist for the work, not the work for men, and God's plan is to send men where they are needed most; so he ordered Paul "far hence." That shows us God's estimate of the foreign missionary work. Is it yours, my brother? If not, who is right?

Ever since then the spirituality of the Church and its zeal for missions have coincided. Left to its natural tendency, Christianity always sweeps straight into this great channel, and flows onward with widening volume and increasing might. It has often been arrested, and its energies diverted to other ends, but with the revival of primal simplicity there reappears the indestructible purpose of expansion. The nearer the Church draws to its center of light and life in Jesus, the profounder becomes the conviction, and more imperative the impulse, to send the gospel to every creature. At the feet of Jesus we are melted into love for all mankind. The moral antecedents of missionary zeal are among the deepest forces of faith in Jesus Christ.

In the light of such facts and principles, what becomes of the objection to missions on the ground that we have enough to do at home? Did the apostles hold such an opinion, or pursue such a policy? Can the objection be reconciled with the Master's words, or the deep and divine purpose of the gospel? We cannot forget that our remote ancestors were pagans; that they were civilized by foreign missions; that our civilization has flowed down from this source. Shall we receive the boon of life, and then not only refuse to convey it to others, but denounce the very policy by which it came to us as a mistake? The objection is unworthy of a rational mind, and betrays a dense ignorance of the gospel. Let it be at once and forever hushed among the people of God, and a generous emulation mark our efforts to extend the Saviour's reign throughout the world.

V. *This obligation is heightened by the unparalleled opportunity offered by the existing state of the world for the spread of the gospel.*

This opportunity is seen in the *political changes* which have opened all nations to its entrance. Christianity has won the freedom of the world. It has access to all lands. There is no legal proscription against it anywhere, except where Rome holds sway. The fires of persecution are dying out, extinguished by the growing spirit of liberty and sense of human rights. The blood of the martyr, it may be, is yet needed to plant the Church in some places; but the public sentiment of Christendom resents religious intolerance as an outrage upon her character and a violation of her rights.

This opportunity is seen in the *improved facilities of travel* which have made all lands easy of access. The most distant regions have been brought near together. Steam-ships and railroads have narrowed oceans and continents, and bade the poles clasp hands in brotherly embrace. The electric telegraph annihilates time and space, and binds the ends of the earth in fellowship. Paul had more trouble getting from Jerusalem to Rome than Bishop Marvin had to circumnavigate the globe. Missionaries come and go between the remotest fields with ease and safety, and with trifling cost. The effect of this commingling of mankind is clearly visible in the production of a higher and broader type of civilization, and the disappearance of exclusiveness, prejudice, and ignorance—all of which eminently favor the spread of the gospel.

This opportunity is seen in the *immense advantages we possess for reaching the people.* The conditions of missionary labor have vastly changed within the past decade, and wonderfully improved. A great deal of preparatory work has been done. Gigantic clearings have been made. The soil has been broken in many countries, and is waiting for the holy seed; in others the harvest has already come, and the ripe grain waits for the reaper's blade. The gospel is now translated into the principal languages of the world; has taken strong root in many heathen lands; has established numerous flourishing centers of expansion; has obtained legal protection, enrolled converts, erected churches, built colleges, organized conferences, founded hospitals, and published newspapers, periodicals, and books. In most heathen lands the whole economy of effort is thoroughly organized, and in active and successful operation. We have not so much to send a forlorn hope to lead the charge, as to support the column already far into the breach.

This opportunity is seen in the *spirit of the age.* Men no longer ridicule the missionary. He is the moral representative of a progress that is widening every realm of thought, and pushing every department of human activity toward the boundaries of the world. The pulse of civilization throbs in unison with his toil. Wherever he goes, Freedom's banner mounts the breeze, and the clarion blast of her bugles rallies our race from the inertia of despair, to lead them up to the high places of life and the wide prospects of immortal glory. He is sustained by the new and nobler feeling of the universal brotherhood of man, which is ascending to control the destiny of our world. Never before have the prevailing sentiments of mankind been so in accord with this work, or did the missionary have behind him such a wealth of sympathy and prayer. The vast, deep river of human improvement is rolling on in grandeur, and its course is bending toward the throne of God.

This opportunity appears in the *great resources of the Church*. 1. *Resources of men and women.*—Our ministry is full of strong young men — educated, gifted, consecrated—who are, or ought to be, ready to go to the front, and toil and die for Jesus. Christian women are ready to go to the rescue of perishing millions in the land of darkness. 2. *Resources of wealth.*—Christianity is the richest religion on the planet. Ours are the gold, and silver, and armies, and navies, and colleges, of the world. We have all the materials of progress. But we squander millions in luxury, we waste millions on lust, we hoard up millions to rust and rot the life out of society. Every dollar belongs to God. He needs it now. It ought to go into the elevation and salvation of our race. 3. *Resources of faith.*—The Church believes more than it ever did in this work. It makes it more prominent, urges its claims more generally and earnestly, and is more liberal to it. It has a deeper trust in God, a nearer view of the field, a more vivid and convincing knowledge of its necessities. 4. *Resources of hope.*—There is not a note of discouragement from any quarter of the field. Success salutes us everywhere. Here and there the forces appear to retreat, but it is only a local maneuver to secure a larger advantage and a quicker victory. Along the whole line the ringing command, Forward! breaks above the clang of clashing steel and roaring thunder of the strife, and the tramp of the conquering legions shakes the gates of hell. Tidings from the front, my brother, and everywhere we win the day!

This age is the crisis of the world. The gospel never had such a chance as now. Every circumstance conspires to facilitate its progress and hasten the period of its universal sway. God speaks by his opportunities. They are the oracles of his providence. He prepared the world to receive the gospel. The union of so many different countries under the imperial sway of Rome; the large security of law; the safe and rapid means of transit; the cosmopolitan activity of commerce; the general hush of the world's strife; the giving way of the older forms of thought, and the deep and universal desire for higher and better things, and the vast forward impulse of humanity—which was a resultant of all these moral and political causes—all this was in providential coincidence with the advent of the Son of God. But ours is a yet greater, a far grander opportunity. Every thing that has gone before has been preliminary to the universal advance we are called upon now to make. O Church of the living God! throw thyself forward upon this wide and glorious opportunity! Go up and possess the land which the Lord thy God hath given into thy hand!

VI. *Finally, this obligation is intensified to a degree absolutely painful by the fact that we are responsible for the spread of the gospel.*

Paul says, "How shall they believe in him of whom they have not heard? and how shall they hear without a preacher? and how shall they preach except they be sent?" The gospel will go only where we send it. There is no other agency for its promulgation. God will not work a miracle to convey it to the heathen. He has done every thing that infinite goodness ought to do. He has redeemed us by his own precious blood; he freely gives us the offer of salvation; he enables us to send it to others; he opens wide the opportunity; he commands us to speed it on its all-embracing mission. The solemn responsibility is upon us. We cannot evade it. We are utterly without excuse for failure to comply with the highest injunction of our risen Saviour—the last benevolent appointment of his love. The world ought to have been converted long before now. No decree of God has kept it back. He does not mock the sorrows of a world by blocking the way of its deliverance. He has moved the heavens to save us. Nothing hinders the universal spread of the gospel now but the unbelief and apathy of the Church. God is ready; China, India, Africa, are ready; but we are not, and the whole work halts, and the progress of the gospel is retarded, and millions grope on in darkness, and sink into hell!

My brethren, while we recline in our soft places, while we feast on the gospel in our cushioned pews, while the sacramental chalice is at our lips, and, amid the altar's holy hush, we say, "Our Father, who art in heaven," the distant wail of dying millions breaks upon our ear. A lost world's appeal for help sweeps up over the roar of all the storms, and rebukes the unchristlike indifference of the Church. It is no fiction of thought. It is not a fancy picture. We make no appeal to the imagination. We state sober facts, and address the honest reason of every professed believer in Jesus Christ. We defy the world to show why we are not guilty of our brother's blood! If the gospel is true, if our religion is not a solemn sham, if life itself is not an illusion, and universal depravity a conceit of the enthusiast, then, in the name of all that is in earth and heaven, we are fearfully recreant to our trust, and disloyal to our Lord, in that we monopolize the benefits of the gospel, and will not give it to all the world!

We submit our argument. We are willing to abide by the verdict of the intelligent conscience. The whole world needs the gospel; the gospel is designed for the whole world; Jesus Christ commands us to send it to the whole world. The Church has always regarded this as her chief work; she never had such a chance as now; on every principle of equity she is responsible for the result; *therefore it is the supreme duty of the Church to send the gospel to all nations.*

If, then, this is our duty, let us faithfully discharge it. We may not be able to do much, but we can do something, and God will recognize and hallow all we do. By earnest faith, by joyous hope, by fervent zeal, by the power of Christian sympathy, by the offering of our wealth and the riches of liberality abounding out of our deep poverty, by the benison of self-sacrifice, and the benevolence of the Christly spirit, let us have a part in the uplifting of our race.

There is no prospect like that of a world at the feet of Jesus. Everywhere the scene of moral renovation unrolls upon our vision, and the watchers herald the approaching dawn from all the towers of the field. Nearer and yet nearer sweeps the glorious victory of the Son of God, when every knee shall bow, and every tongue shall confess his everlasting name. Lo,

> 'Tis coming up the steep of time,
>   And this old world is growing brighter;
> We may not see it dawn sublime,
>   Yet high hopes make the heart throb lighter.
> We may be sleeping in the ground
>   When it awakes the people's wonder;
> But we have felt it gathering round,
>   And heard its voice of living thunder.
>   Christ's reign—ah, yes, 'tis coming!

Ay, it must come! The tyrant's throne
   Is crumbling, with men's hot tears rusted;
The sword, the great have leaned upon,
   Is cankered, with men's heart-blood crusted.
Room! for the men of love make way!
   Ye selfish great ones, pause no longer;
Ye cannot stay the opening day—
   The world rolls on, the light grows stronger—
     The Master's advent's coming!

XI.

THE HINDERANCES OF THE GOSPEL.

BY THE REV. A. W. MANGUM, D.D.,
North Carolina Conference.

"But suffer all things, lest we should hinder the gospel of Christ." 1 Cor. ix. 12.

In this language St. Paul presents an example of self-denial worthy of universal admiration. While vindicating his rights as an apostle, he farther teaches that such was his devotion that he willingly yielded his own just claims to earthly reward for his labor, and unmurmuringly suffered all things, lest he should hinder the gospel of Christ. But in this he was simply consistent. He was a member and minister of the Christian Church, and the one divinely-appointed work of that Church is to evangelize the world. The principle involved in his example commends itself to our most careful consideration. The duties and privileges of the gospel of Christ have been transmitted to us. The work of evangelization, so nobly begun, so heroically prosecuted, now rests upon those that constitute the Church of to-day. After all that has been done in the long centuries, a great part of the human race are still without the word of God, or the institutions of Christianity, while vast numbers in this and other

Christian lands are wandering in the ways of sin, and dying in the horrible gloom of rayless unbelief. The Church, in its various divisions, though still making high professions, and still presenting an imposing array, is sadly unsatisfactory in moral influence, and alarmingly slow in conquest. With more educated mind gathered around the cross than in any preceding age, with unprecedented auxiliaries in the printing-press, in the means of rapid intercourse, and in the wide-spread diffusion of knowledge, there is ominous necessity for fierce struggles on the part of Christianity, that it may maintain its ground, and win even slight and occasional advantages over the opposing world. The love of many of the professed followers of Christ is cold, the faith of many is weak, the fears of many are tormenting, the conduct of many is wicked. No wonder that the language of the enemies of the gospel becomes bold and threatening. True, the Church continues to grow, but, alas, how slowly! Surely it is incumbent upon those that sincerely believe and teach the gospel to ascertain, if possible, the causes of this sad truth.

I. *What are the hinderances of the gospel in our day?*

It is not within the compass of the text, and it is not necessary, to consider at length the palpable and acknowledged opposition of the ungodly world. Sin is older than the Church, was the occasion of the whole economy of redemption, but cannot be at once removed by the will and effort of the servants of God. In all our calculations respecting Christian progress we must incorporate as a factor the truth that sinners are free agents, and that if they will not yield they cannot be saved. It is enough for us to know that we have the perfected plan of salvation—the power that can and will overcome the world. We are chiefly concerned in the hinderances for which the Church is primarily responsible. What are they?

1. *Formality—having the form, without the power, of godliness.* This evil appears most flagrant in the extravagant ritualism that is so great a reproach and curse to some other divisions of the Church. It is the miserable delusion from which earnest souls escaped before Methodism could be founded, and it has never been able successfully to tempt us to return to its baleful influence. With us the danger lies rather in too complacent trust in those forms of worship that are in themselves proper, commendable, and even indispensable. Many, while criticising and pitying the ritualist, vainly linger in those mere ceremonials, through which they ought in consistency to pass, until they apprehend the glowing spiritual realities that constitute the only genuine object. There is too much dependence on nominal membership and the mechanical, or conventional, observance of the externals of piety. The public worship is well attended, the demeanor in the church is unexceptionable, the words of moving hymns are sung, some reverent posture in prayer is observed, respectful attention to lessons and sermon is seemingly paid, the contributions to the holy cause may be promptly offered, and the ministers, institutions, and doctrines, of the Church are es-

teemed and defended, but, alas! how faint the signs of spiritual life! how slight the appearances of hungering and thirsting for the things of God! how rare the actions that tell of a holy love for the brethren! how feeble the efforts to sustain the tempted, reclaim the backslidden, and bring sinners to Christ! Think of the waste of precious means and talents in the worship of a single congregation that seeks no fervor, shows no inner life, and makes no direct assaults on Satan! The assumed conflict between such a Church and the powers of darkness does not rise to the dignity of a mock-battle. It is the orderly dress-parade amid flying shot and shell, while duty shouts for the spirit and struggle of the field. It soon becomes but the brandishing by deluded prisoners of beautiful but worthless weapons in the walls of what they deem their camp, but of what is their prison, lorded by their wily and triumphant foe. What rational hope can there be for victory?

2. *Sectarianism.* True loyalty to one's denomination is highly praiseworthy. No one can voluntarily become and continue a member of any organization and knowingly neglect the obligations assumed without downright inconsistency. This is preëminently true of the Christian and his Church. But there is a tendency to pay excessive regard to what may be relatively called the non-essentials in the denominational economy. The prosperity of the individual Church often appears as the supreme object. There is not sufficient care to make the denominational interest contribute directly to the

achievement of the one ultimate purpose of the divine religion. He is not a true friend to his own Church who does not desire and strive above all else to secure the salvation of souls. Whatever his profession or belief, he is an actual foe to the cause he nominally espouses. Too much sectarian feeling invariably implies too little love for the real kingdom of Christ. Are there not those who are more jealous of the success of other Churches than of the dread *conquest* of souls by Satan? Have we not reason to fear that there is a kind of sectarianism that is less disturbed by the prevalence of spiritual declension and death than by the knowledge that showers of revival grace are descending upon other divisions of Zion? By such the peculiar ritual and creed are recklessly magnified and exalted above the true, essential spirit and aims of Christianity itself. They love their individual Church more than souls, more than the gospel, more than Christ. Surely this is the deadly ichor of ungodly selfishness, a daring violation of the supreme duties of the child of God, a direct and shocking contradiction of all the impulses of an enlightened conscience. It involves a deplorable misapprehension of the character and design of evangelical agencies. Mere instruments are prized and honored, while the author and wielder of the instruments is disregarded or forgotten. The melting hymn and fervent prayer win ready compliments to the sweet singer and eloquent suppliant. There is eager demand for fine sermons, and the worth of ministers is measured solely by the degree of their reputed eloquence. When elegant periods, beautiful imagery, and fascinating originality, have wooed and won the fanciful admiration of those who have "itching ears," every tongue praises the excellent preacher as a model, eulogizes his lofty discourses, and by every available art fosters in him the dangerous ambition to be noted and lauded for his superior learning and brilliancy. In accordance with this misguided opinion and influence, the main reliance is placed upon the minister's power to make a display of his extraordinary endowments. The earnest and devout believers, that walk humbly before God, draw near to the mercy-seat, and bring down the blessings of divine love, are simply tolerated, instead of being gratefully esteemed. The long-tested instrumentalities, that have so often aroused slumbering consciences and imparted new life to the languishing hopes of the children of God, are deliberately abandoned for empty, popular attractions. The paramount idea being to please and to be pleased, but little attention is given to that which aims directly and only to humble and save.

3. *False ideas of religious culture.* Complacently cherishing the persuasion of their superiority, and diverted from the character of true religion, deluded members of the Church give more and more regard to that which the world loves and envies. The restless fancy roams delighted in the vision of splendid churches, artistic music, and large, wealthy, and cultivated, congregations. Elegance, refinement, fashion, become the cardinal virtues, para-

mount to all spiritual requirements. The loftiest spire, the loudest bell, the grandest organ, the costliest chandelier, the richest carpet, the most luxurious pews, the most spacious nave, the most operatic choir, the most sensational pulpit — these become the leading objects of interest, while simple-heartedness, humility, self-denial, and Christlike sympathy and devotion, are relegated to those who are not too high in the world, or in their own estimation, to be in earnest about the verities of religion. The æsthetical is thrust out of its proper relations to the cause it is intended to subserve, and is installed in the chief place in the temple of human excellency. Here links on the whole mechanism of changing fashion — all that misguided enthusiasm associates with the sentimental theories of higher culture. Under such a reign of the exquisite taste of deluded pride, there is no time or room for the cry of the mourner, for the wrestling prayer in the altar, for the stirring revival-hymn, for the joyous exclamations of the young convert, or the rapturous shouts of those that are baptized anew with a Saviour's love. Alas! such are the life and conduct of some Churches that, without being either unreasonable or unkind, one may ask the question, Is it not generally true that the intensity of spiritual devotion is inversely as the measure of worldly wealth and social position? It is not surprising that in such Churches the ministers sometimes yield to the prevailing influence, and turn away from the infallible word of God, to dazzle the minds of admirers with brilliant displays of pleasing but powerless and unsanctified learning. Let it be remembered that these congregations, as united bodies, and many of their members, as individuals, owing to their social prominence, are sure to impress their peculiarities, to some degree, upon the multitude of their susceptible, imitative observers. Should we wonder at the slow progress of the cause of God?

4. *Want of self-denial.* The surrendering of all for Christ is the beginning of all genuine religion, and the constant subordination of all that one controls to the will of God is indispensable to a religious life. In this we have the secret of the hard struggles of the penitent, and the reason why there is necessity for faithful watching and prayer throughout the life of the Christian. But, alas! how hard it is to give up the world! Often, when conscience and self-love drive the imperiled soul into the visible Church, the continued love of that which is forbidden leads to the lowering of the standard of religion to the plane of worldly indulgence. There is a restless effort to make unauthorized compromises with sin. There is an unwarrantable blending of those principles and practices that are unmistakably incompatible. Self-denial is pledged in profession, but self-indulgence is betrayed in the conduct. Christian duty is blindly wedded to ungodly custom. The card-table and the communion-table, the prayer-meeting and the ball-room, the theater and the sanctuary, devotion to the crucified Saviour and to the "pride of life"—these all appear to be placed unblushingly in the same category. But no man

can serve two masters. The experiment always results in peculiar but positive service to the world, and direct and terrible injury to the real interests of the Church. But this inconsistency is not limited to that alone which is generally designated by the name of pleasure. There is much self-indulgence under the garb of reputable business. In this stirring age, multitudes are devoting to their secular employment much of the time and care that justly belong to their religious duties. There is fearful potency in the charm that the daily occupation fastens upon every power of the soul. The eager rush of trade-life, the stimulus of fierce competition, the abundant pretexts of professional engagements, the exacting demands of social customs, the claims of numerous enterprises and societies—with specious names and purposes—the unresisted sway of partisan feelings, and the presumptuous dictates of one's political party—these, each and all, make tremendous drafts upon the time, talent, and treasure, that are due to the paramount interests of immortal souls.

5. *Loss of the sense of responsibility on the part of the private members of the Church.* There is very much greater capability for moral achievement in the vast multitudes of private members than in the comparatively few that are ministers, or that hold official positions. The general spread of useful learning, the extensive dissemination of religious intelligence, and the peculiar genius of modern society, render it possible for all classes in the Church to exert a telling influence, and perform highly

effective service, in behalf of the vital interests and leading objects of Christianity. Hence, the principle of wise economy unites with the law of the talents in requiring every professed disciple of Jesus to do what he can, not only in working out his own salvation, but also in extending all possible aid unto others. But what do we see as the usual policy of Churches respecting this main department of their strength? While they zealously contend for the right of private judgment, and to a degree accept the doctrine of personal accountability to God, there is still a tendency in congregations and in individuals to impose nearly all of the many and arduous duties involved in religious work upon those who hold some official position. The Church is an army in which many seem to think the leaders are to do not only the planning and directing, but also the fighting. Multitudes of those who consider themselves the servants of God have little, if any, appreciation of the labor to be done. Though they bear the name of the children of God, they do not realize the fearful obligation resting upon them to look after the interests of their Father's kingdom. As they have no experience in Christian effort, they live and die without a practical knowledge of the methods and means of Christian usefulness. As they do not exercise their special gifts, they never attain unto godly skill, or learn for themselves, or reveal to others, their latent powers. As they do not faithfully cultivate Christlike sympathy, intercession, toil, and sacrifice, they develop no glowing zeal, feel no assurance of Heaven's approving smiles, and enjoy no inspiring prospects of glorious reward. They are burdens when they should be blessings. They are stumbling-blocks when they should be helpers. Their talents are buried. Their work is undone. "Clouds they are without water;" "trees whose fruit withereth, without fruit." Verily, the inactivity of the laity is a great hinderance to the gospel.

6. *Errors respecting public opinion.* The common judgment of society, when based upon a reasonable degree of interest, integrity, and information, should be respectfully considered. But when public opinion, as often obtains, means merely the wayward, popular voice, or the general sentiment of the mingled multitude, without regard to their qualifications to form an intelligent judgment on the subject in question, it must not be admitted as a potent factor in deciding the words and actions of one who is pledged to the right. Yet it is a deplorable truth, that many members of the Church deliberately determine the course they will pursue in servile deference to what they believe others will think and say. They do despite to that authority which their vows at God's altar bind them supremely to respect. The imperative dictates of conscience are traitorously ignored for the voice of the unregenerate world, and of cold, unfaithful professors. This false regard for public opinion has often prevented the confession of penitence, sealed the lips to prayer and praise, checked the tears of holy sympathy, suppressed the voice of Christian counsel, turned the feet into forbidden ways, seduced the heart to sinful

pleasures, left the truth without defense, and even caused the soul to deny its Lord.

7. *Forgetfulness of the immediate providence of God.* The word of God assures us that "all things work together for good to them that love God, to them that are the called according to his purpose."

There are some who embrace this doctrine in a spirit of unwarrantable self-esteem, appearing to believe that the Father of all is gracious and loving to them in a peculiar sense and extraordinary degree. This is selfishness, and selfishness is sin. Others rashly assume the merciful interposition of divine favor in their behalf, although they are conscious of frequent willful violations of the commandments of God. They boldly claim the promises, while they constantly neglect the conditions. The man that does not lead a Christian life has no right, in self-complacency, to say of any event that "all's for the best."

But the most common error in respect to divine providence consists in the failure to recognize the active presence of God in all the interests and facts in common life. It is difficult to appreciate the extent to which this error prevails. It permeates the whole body of our language. Every page of the English lexicon shows "a mingling of accident with order, of chance with design." Common speech not only expresses but influences and fashions common thought. Thus our ideas pass from mind to mind on a bridge composed in part of language-skepticism. The very word "providence" supplants the idea of God, and often gets between the mind and the divine presence. Men that are learned in many respects often substitute the mere name *law, law of nature*—which is but the name of the methods of an ever-present, acting God—for the real divine agent by whose immediate will all of nature is unceasingly upheld, directed, and controlled. Multitudes of those who profess to be Christians too often form their opinions, guide their actions, and interpret events, by their own or other human judgment, without the slightest recognition of Him who governs all things from the least unto the greatest. It is distressingly common for avowed believers in Christ to show, by word and deed, that they place more reliance on the temporal, the natural, and the human, than upon the word and providence of their Heavenly Father. Thus they come to think of God as far off. By this dim, cold, distant idea of him, they are inspired with superstitious dread rather than peaceful confidence and grateful love. Forgetful that God is supreme, and that his promises cover all the possible, they murmur at reverses that are trivial, stagger under crosses that are light, and recoil before opposition that the weakest Christian need not fear. Surely this is not vital Christianity. It ought to be called pitiful infidelity. It contradicts the word of the Lord. It most grievously affects the influence and progress of religion.

8. *Neglect of proper discipline.* When a person joins the visible Church, he thereby enters voluntarily into a formal covenant. His vows at admission bind him to a faithful obedience to the specified requirements, and to a consistent exemplification of

the doctrines, by a godly walk and conversation to the end of life. As long as his vows are maintained, his ecclesiastical rights cannot justly be taken from him; but as soon as his vows are violated, his claim to membership is essentially forfeited, and he remains in the Church only through neglect or toleration. But the benign spirit of Christianity moderates the discipline that untempered justice would inflict. That spirit dictates that the offender shall be dealt with in reference to the threefold object of his own restoration, the admonition of others, and the vindication and protection of the Church. When an offense is committed, the first object should be to induce the offender to recover what he has lost, and to repair, as far as possible, the injury he has done. When the forbearance and effort that are consistent with both charity and integrity have failed to accomplish this, his positive excommunication is the only reasonable alternative. It is then necessary to the safety and success of the Church. Purity is an indispensable condition of moral influence. Gross infractions of the laws that God has instituted for the regulation of the spiritual life will surely lead to the shame and overthrow of the Church that tolerates them. There is no consistent judgment or mercy in the blind forbearance that shields an offender to the injury of religion. The Church of Christ was never intended to be the resting-place of those who are traitors to the sacred cause. The word of God and the history of his Church prove that if those members that bring reproach on their profession are permitted to hold their places, and continue their demoralizing course, it is impossible for the Church to which they belong to maintain its influence with Heaven, or to exert its full measure of saving-power upon the world. While this is unmistakably plain to all, we must with sorrow say that there are some Churches in our land that do not have a discipline as high as the merely moral requirements of the Decalogue. How many are subject to covetousness! and "covetousness is idolatry." How common in Churches are those "works of the flesh, ... hatred, variance, emulations, wrath, strife, seditions, heresies, envyings, ... revelings, and such like!" "They which do such things shall not inherit the kingdom of God." How often do members escape even admonition, not to say prosecution, when they are known to be guilty of profaning the Sabbath, or drinking or selling spirituous liquors, or practicing dishonesty in business, or indulging in ungodly conversation, or patronizing wicked amusements, or violating their plain obligations in trade-life, or withholding what God requires for the poor, or wasting their time in idleness or folly, or neglecting the plainest and most important Christian duties—such as attending the public worship, taking the sacrament of the Supper, holding family-prayer, observing proper secret devotion, and studying the Holy Scriptures!

9. *Want of consecration.* True religion means all the heart, and all the powers, and all the life, for Christ. No man becomes a Christian until he gives all to God; no man continues a Christian, with power to prevail at the throne of grace, any longer

than he maintains this attitude of complete surrender. How does the average Church-life compare with this? Nominal Christians possess abundant strength, influence, property, and education, to secure the rapid progress of Zion, and the speedy evangelization of every nation on earth; but, alas! the spirit of *entire* consecration is wanting. This subject rises into stupendous significance when we consider that whatever is withheld from God is thereby unquestionably added to the resources and agencies of the world-power that is essentially arrayed against the cause of Christ. How can it be said that one belongs to the Church while his time, and money, and skill, and influence, and effort, are constantly given to the world? Who wonders that the world is not conquered?

II. *The duty of the earnest Christian in view of these hinderances.*

First, it should be remembered that there have been hinderances throughout the history of Christianity. While their phenomenal forms have changed from age to age, their real nature has continued the same. What sins can be mentioned that did not brand the character of individual disciples and blot the name of Churches in the apostolic age? Greater crimes were more common among the professed disciples of Jesus then than now. What sickening depravity has been revealed by the Church itself, in every Christian land, from the first century to our own day! It is a bold declaration, but confidently made, that, in view of all involved, there is relatively less opposition to genuine religion in this day than in any other of its career. The power and prestige of the Church have been incalculably augmented. Christianity is now so interwoven with the language, character, aims, customs, laws, and interests of the mightiest nations on earth, that its complete overthrow and eradication may justly be declared an absolute impossibility. Its achievements in the salvation of men, in the exaltation of nations, and in the promotion of all human welfare, stand forth in the brightest light of history as an unparalleled glory, and an unanswerable vindication of its claim to superhuman origin, spirit, and power. To-day it has more disciples, greater advantages, and mightier instrumentalities at its command, than it could have claimed in any other age. There may have been times when a larger proportion of the world's powers were professedly devoted to its interests, but those powers were directed too much by worldly ambition or deplorable fanaticism. Its eventful past and fortified present are the convincing prophecies of its victorious future. Its sufficiency under indescribable sufferings in the periods of its comparative weakness assures us that there can be nothing too formidable for its strength in these grand years of its disciplined power and stupendous development. There are shadows, dark shadows, now and then, but the sun shines on, and, when the clouds are driven by the winds, the undimmed radiance gleams over mountain and plain. The unprecedented advancement in art and science in this century of wonders has furnished corresponding facilities for the advocacy and dissemination of divine truth. While the doctrines of the great Teacher are constantly tested and verified by thousands of the wisest and best of our race, there is a most auspicious ecclesiastical enterprise, in the main peculiar to this century, that gives cheering promise of invincible organization and glorious progress for the Church of God in the next generation. I refer to the work of the Sabbath-school. Before science can bewilder, or fashion delude, or wealth corrupt, or vanity inflate, the impressible minds of the children are preöccupied with the ineradicable convictions of the truth, the efficacy, and the preciousness, of the gospel. Thus all the insidious plans of the enemies of the soul are wisely forestalled. Better means are provided for the godly training of the young to-day than have been furnished by the followers of Christ in any land in any other age. In this grand movement the men of God are like the wise Highlanders in their plans to extinguish the tornadoes of fire that were blasting their forest-hills. With purpose bold and hearts of hope those hardy peasants rushed away before the defiant flames, and cut the broad lane through the crowded wood, so that the baffled fire sought in vain for fuel when it reached the scene of their battling toil. Thus, when the multiplying millions of the Sabbath-school children are reached by the threatening forces of shameless vice and arrogant infidelity, the well-trained host will be prepared, with both heart and skill, for determined and triumphant resistance. It may reasonably be doubted whether the history of Christianity furnishes, since the day of Pentecost, another chapter so full of all that should inspire confidence and exultation as that which is presented in the work of the Church for the children in our day.

Secondly, in view of the hinderances, the paramount duty—that which stands as an absolute prerequisite to all other duties—consists in individual fidelity to God's righteous requirements. There must be a consecrated purpose to have life and power in personal devotion—zeal and activity in one's own work for religion. Simplicity, fervor, and whole-heartedness, must characterize the prayers and deeds of every disciple. Above all claims of creeds, all teachings of example, all tendencies of fashion, all allurements of the world, all demands of business, all pressure of the multitude, there must be prompt, unwavering obedience to the commandments of the Lord in respect to purity in one's heart and life, and to enthusiasm and sacrifice in labor for the salvation of souls. This involves faithful seeking for the testimony that God is well pleased with the condition of the heart, the character of the motives, and the methods of the work that is performed ostensibly for the sake of Christianity. Yes; the true test is in the consciousness—in the heart. The religion that withstands temptation and persecution must be sustained by indubitable assurance—resting on intellectual conviction and correspondent feelings. First, there is faith in the truth of God's word; then, holy impulses to duty; then, self-surrendering trust in the Father of Mercy, through the merits of Christ. This trust, which is the free-will's offering of self and all to the Saviour, is what is called saving faith. It is followed immediately by some measure of peculiar peace and joy. Hope is kindled. Love wells up in the soul. There is a sense of the warming of the heart toward God. When we feel that we love God, we feel sure that God loves us. The knowledge of his love fortifies us against all evils and foes, and prepares us for sacrifice, toil, and suffering, in his cause. It makes the heart feel "I can do all things through Christ that strengtheneth me." Profound consciousness of the divine favor is the true panoply of the soldier of the cross. Without that consciousness he is weak in desire, purpose, and effort; but with it, he is an invincible hero. Those who wish to be useful as Christians must, by maintaining humble trust and singleness of purpose, have in themselves continually the all-sustaining testimony that they please God.

As a necessary condition of peace, welfare, and usefulness, it is the privilege and duty of the Christian to apprehend the doctrine of God's providence in all things. The realization of his loving presence makes faith stronger, and hope brighter, and love intenser. When thoroughly realized, it restrains the soul from sin, perpetually impresses the necessity of purity, keeps the heart aglow with the fervor of grateful love, and stimulates to a watchful and zealous performance of the divine will in every duty. It sweetens the simplest pleasures, it ennobles the humblest tasks, it illumines the darkest hours, and solves the gravest problems of human life. It is the vital breath of prayer, the basal faith on which all other Christian faith must rest, the grand, essential requisite for loyal work and triumphant success in the service of God. Under its inspiration, every object that is beheld utters a voice of more than earthly significance; every pleasure, small or great, is rendered precious by the ennobling benediction of Heaven; every trouble is softened and subdued by the melting smiles of Redeeming Love; and the whole spiritual nature, kept in lively exercise, finds in every experience something that stimulates its energy, expands its capacity, and furnishes new weapons and skill for godly achievement. Thus God becomes "a very present help," a constant companion, feeling ever nearer and nearer, growing ever dearer and dearer. The soul, enjoying a perpetual consciousness of infallible security and unearthly peace, by day and night, in all possible changes, in toil or rest, in hope or fear, in pain or pleasure, in smiles or tears, may exultantly exclaim, *My Saviour knows, directs, and sanctifies it all!* In such a state the heart beats always in holy trust to the heavenly refrain of *"All is well!"*

But the safety and usefulness of the Christian absolutely require fidelity in maintaining good works. He must have that mind in him that was in Christ Jesus. He must take up his cross and follow Jesus. The only work of Jesus is to seek and to save the lost. If we expect his companionship, sympathy, and coöperation, we must be engaged in the same purposes and efforts in which he is engaged. If we enjoy the presence and help of the Holy Ghost, we must be aiding in his work of seeking to consummate the glorious enterprise of the world's salvation. To work sincerely for God is to work with God. To work with God is to become more and more partakers of his nature, to grow more and more like him. It exalts every act in life to an ennobling relation to the heavenly. It links every day in life by the golden chain of obedience to the grandeur of the everlasting. It gives to human life on earth much of the genius of immortality. It makes the voices of memory mingle in sweet harmony with the songs of hope and the benedictions of Sovereign Mercy. It enables the soul to look back and know that it has done something for God, and laid up some treasure in heaven. Be not cast down, though you may be feeble, faint, and poor. The Lord will help you to work. He can and does work by few or many, by great or small. Do what you can—God will require no more. Pray for the right. Pray in faith and love. Be true in all things, that you may be able to prevail when you pray. Talk for Jesus. Be a consistent Christian, that your words, though broken and plain, may ring with the superhuman eloquence of piety and truth. Live out pure and undefiled religion before the world, that your example may be an effectual instrument of salvation in the hands of Almighty Love. I entreat you, I implore you, I warn you, before you go to the bar of final judgment, strive to do more, to do better, for the cause of Christ, than you have yet done. Let what remains of your life of probation be more wisely spent. Be not dismayed by the coldness of the Church, the assaults of skepticism, or the wickedness of the age. All this is but the peculiar form of trial for the Church of God in our day. There have always been great trials for the followers of Christ. Sometimes there is bloody persecution; sometimes, dangerous worldly prosperity; sometimes, wide-spread apostasy; sometimes, fanatical heresy; sometimes, bold and powerful attacks upon the Bible; but God's grace has always been, is to-day, and will forever be, *sufficient for all.* There is no just cause for alarm. The Church has been a safe refuge in the past—it will be a safe refuge to the end of time. It will never be destroyed. It is the only institution on earth whose foundations are eternal. It is the fold of Christ; and the omnipotent Shepherd never slumbers. It is the "habitation of God," and therefore the very *home-love* of the *Infinite* will defend it. It is the "body of Christ," and has therefore already passed through the final resurrection unto immortality. It is the "strength and glory of God," and that strength is unbounded, and that glory everlasting. O, then, cling to it, pray for it, toil for it, live for it, die for it! Its ruler is the Lord of lords and King of kings. Trust in Him, and faithfully serve Him, and you shall enjoy His richest blessings on earth, and His endless salvation in heaven. Let the most anxious cry of your longing spirit ever be:

> O Father, haste the promised hour
>   When at His feet shall lie
> All rule, authority, and power,
>   Beneath the ample sky;
> When He shall reign from pole to pole,
> The Lord of every human soul;

When all shall heed the words He said,
    Amid their daily cares,
And by the loving life He led
    Shall strive to pattern theirs;
And He who conquered death shall win
The mightier conquest over sin!

THE REV. MORGAN CALLAWAY, D.D.,
Of the North Georgia Conference.

XII.

CHRISTIAN COMMUNISM.

BY THE REV. M. CALLAWAY, A.M., D.D.,
North Georgia Conference.

"Therefore let no man glory in men: for all things are yours; whether Paul, or Apollos, or Cephas, or the world, or life, or death, or things present, or things to come; all are yours; and ye are Christ's; and Christ is God's." 1 Cor. iii. 21-23.

A CLUSTER of paradoxes. We are not to "glory in men;" nevertheless, "Paul, and Apollos, and Cephas," are ours, and ours rejoicingly. "The world, and life, and things present," are ours; yet elsewhere we are taught to "love not the world, neither the things of the world;" to "take no thought for our life, what we shall eat, or what we shall drink, nor yet for our body what we shall put on." "Death and things to come" are ours, yet we are to "take no thought for the morrow, for the morrow shall take thought for the things of itself." And death is spoken of as a shadow, a terror, an enemy, the last to be overcome. Stranger than all, this group of properties is ours because "we are Christ's, and Christ is God's."

What means the apostle? Evidently he purposes to rebuke the party spirit then prevailing, to harmonize the rivalries, to heal the divisions forming and threatening the unity of the Church, to correct the tendency to saint-worship, and to indicate the untrustworthiness of men as spiritual guides. He would fix forever in our memory a reminder that Christ is the head of his own Church, that he alone is its lawgiver, and that he only is worthy of worship. The admonitions are generally as well as specifically just, for the Church at Corinth is not by itself in unseemly variances and in unchristianly followings. The history of the Church at large is largely the history of the Church at Corinth. "Who shall be greatest?" had been asked with reference to the coming, and doubtless felt as to the present kingdom, by those who stood nearest Jesus while on earth, and now thoughtless Christians are vaunting devotion to men as zeal for Christ. All down the Christian centuries this shameless folly is repeated, for rarely has the Church been without men ambitious of leadership, or of those who were ready in unholy subservience; nor is it to-day, though growing in grace, so spiritual as to follow men only as they follow Christ.

Our own heart-history, it would seem, should suggest the probability of human error, unless, forsooth, we rely confidently on our insight, feel no confusion from doubts, and no shame from sins. If, however, we be conscious of vitiated powers, and of a perverse use of them at their best estate, we shall at once accept the warning of the apostle as timely and deserved.

Important as this admonition is, it is but preliminary to a broader, deeper truth of the text. Paul is urging the Church to review her possessions, and contemplate her pledged inheritance, and in so doing the cluster of paradoxes becomes a coronet of pearls. As the resultant teaching, he presents what we shall designate *a doctrine of Christian Communism*.

We transfer the term from a civic to a Christian office, premising that communism in name is modern, but in spirit ancient—as old, indeed, as populous cities and poverty. In its last analysis communism is self-indulgence at the expense of others. By its advocates it would be defined as the championship of the rights and interests of the many as against the wrongs and tyrannies of the few: by the people it is understood as the proposed universal pooling of estates for equal redistribution.

Christian communism essays to appropriate the possessions of all Christians to each, and of each to all, with loss to none, but gain to all. In the matter of doctrine and representative men it declares, "Whether Paul, or Apollos, or Cephas, all are ours." In the Christian family, and probably not elsewhere so unmistakably, does community of interest work good to the individual, and the individual interest work to the good of the community—where the happiness of one person is in sharing the property of all, and all in contributing to the happiness of each. Communism receives the Scriptures as a whole, but a whole made up of parts; as "profitable for doctrine, for reproof, for correction, for instruction in righteousness," but not all delivered in one book, by one man, or class of men; that one doctrine is not to be magnified to the overshadowing of another; that one true representative man is not to be heeded to the discount of another; that all measures of inspiration, all grades of culture, all orders of talent, so far as intrinsically and operatively good, are to be counted worthy of study and imitation.

Passing without pause the unbrotherly dispute of Paul and Barnabas, the blameworthy lapses of Peter, the necessity to Apollos of having "the way of God more perfectly expounded," it may be truly said that no one of them so knew "the truth as it is in Jesus," or had so experienced of his grace, that he should alone present the doctrine of the cross in its fullness, or furnish in his own life illustration for all of the largeness of its blessing. Were one person sufficient to construct the canon of truth, but one would have been inspired; were one life adequate for the illustration of Christian biography, but one would have been portrayed. Were these eminent three able to compass in their life and teaching the sphere of Scripture verities, the Father would doubtless have omitted the anointing of others for sacred writing and speaking. Not to mention the writers of the Old, the New Testament is distinctly distributive of topics of history and doctrine, of experience and discipline, as forming the full-orbed gospel of the Son of God. So marked, indeed, is this feature of Holy Writ, that the least learned see it when pointed out. The synoptic Gospels, for instance, are notably occupied in narrating the life of the Son of man, while the fourth Gospel engages us with the Christ, the Son of God. Not, indeed, that the divine nature of our Lord is unnoticed in the synoptic, or that his human nature is slighted in the fourth; gleams of the divine-human appear in both, but the Son of man is the subject of the former, the Son of God of the latter. "Of the generation of Jesus," opens the one; "In the beginning was the Word, and the Word was with God, and the Word was God," is the lofty exordium of the other. Nay, moreover, in the expansion of the teaching of the Gospels, in the Acts, and in its discussion too in the Epistles, order and progress are observable, not unbroken, it is true, by rehearsals of facts and principles previously stated. The stream of Christian story meanders, but it moves, and deepens as it moves in its enriching flow. As the evangelists in the Gospels, so the apostles in the Epistles, and in the Revelation, formulate their own teaching, and after their own manner. The teaching is as *unique* as the character and capacity of the several authors, and no one character is the counterpart of another, no single mind emphasizes the same phase of truth as another, no single school measures the circle of Christian science.

Paul was much engaged in deducing Christian doctrine from Scripture narrative, and, we may say, in modifying it by the richness of his own experience, more, probably, than all other New Testament writers, and, by consent of theologians, more successfully. His conspicuous conversion, his ready submission, his unselfish surrender, his personal "perils," his extraordinary labors, together with his forceful statement and eloquent defense of Christian doctrine, constitute him the hero of Protestant Christendom. His prominence, however, and his learning, and even his apostolic call, did not free him from the disabilities of the race; he was yet but a man, and, as such, subject to the limitations imposed by the Creator on the knowledge of man. He saw not, it may be, "through a glass darkly," but he "knew but in part, and prophesied but in part."

Before science had declared the form of our earth, or the Northmen, followed by Columbus, had popularly verified it by the discovery of the Western Continent, one might have complacently but ignorantly supposed the Eastern Continent the whole of our habitable planet. Realizing its existence as we do, it is hard for us to understand how men could so long be ignorant of its place and power in the equipoise of the universe. Did we not know of the fourth Gospel, and the Epistles of John, and of Peter, and of James, we might content ourselves with the other Gospels and the Epistles of Paul; but we have listened to the "beloved disciple" in his narrative moods, and in his high discourse of the *Logos*, and, following him in his Epistles, we have heard like simple, deep, soulful utterances. He wins our heart mayhap as, leaning on his bosom, he communes with the Master; or draws us by the stronger but kindred reason that, in his way, he gives us the comforting last words of our ascending Saviour; or in his Epistles, as his heart, not so much toned by time as mellowed by holy fellowship with Christ, he illustrates more intimately his special doctrine, and pleads the more winningly with us, "Little children, love one another, for love is of God;" or he impresses us with his cordial and brotherly greeting of the "elect lady;" or, as elsewhere, he buoyantly but unboastfully reminds us who we are, and intimates what we shall be, confirming our faith by the ardor of his own; or, without modifying our estimate of his theme, still warmly appreciative, and undisturbed in our reverent love, he establishes himself in our heart by vindicating his suppressed manliness and sense of right, when justly aroused and dealing with willful wrong, as a "son of thunder" he righteously flashes indignation on the offender. As the foliage of our American forests, beauteous in the emerald of spring, becomes resplendently so in the gold and scarlet of autumn, so, advancing in years, but clearing in prophecy, John caught, as it were, from the lips of the Master, messages to the seven Churches of Asia, commending the good, rebuking the bad—messages so manifesting the scrutiny, and yet the compassionate watchfulness, of Him who "walked in the midst of the golden candlesticks," that we conclude that the communion of John and Jesus is closer now than when they reclined in brotherly intimacy at the feast of the Passover in the upper chamber; and that, as he neared the city of his vision, he took on more of the character of its citizens and more of the likeness of its King.

No; as much as we need Paul and his gospel of faith, we cannot do without John and his gospel of love.

Besides grasp of doctrine, there are happy surroundings, providences of position, personal knowledges, which fit the minister of every order for labors, clothe him with potencies, and adapt him for exigencies, which otherwise could not be so fortunately met. And so of the apostles.

In the nature of things, Paul could have no acquaintance with Jesus as man with man, or as living disciple with living Master. In all that pertains to the heroic, his life is rich in incidents, but to some it may be fearful in tragic impressiveness. To Paul it was not granted to look upon the face of the Son of man, only as veiled in blinding light; nor to hear his voice, only as rousing a Pharisaic conscience to Christian wakefulness, or in answer to agonizing prayer. As he went up to Damascus, Paul saw the light and heard the voice that wrung from him recognition and obedience; and again, as he was crying with self-repeating earnestness to be delivered from the "thorn in the flesh," the same voice said, "My grace is sufficient for thee." These two occasions were enough to bring home to him Christ's power to convict, sustain, and save. Besides, "Blessed," says Christ to Thomas, "are they that have not seen (me), and yet have believed."

John, however, writes "of that which we have heard, which we have seen with our eyes, which we have looked upon, and our hands have handled," and, at the same time, "of that which was from the beginning, and was the Word of life." John sees and knows Jesus as Mary and they of Bethany knew him; is with him as he "goes about doing good," as he teaches, or as he works miracles; is one of the honored *coterie* with Jesus in the death-chamber of the maiden, in the garden of the "bloody sweat," and in the overpowering splendor of Tabor; is at Calvary, too, sustaining Mary, and giving all he could express—the sympathy of his presence to the Crucified; there, furthermore, to take upon him, at the request of the dying Son, the care of the **holy mother**; is with the eleven when the risen Saviour makes himself known unto them; and later he enters anticipatively the New Jerusalem, walks its streets, numbers its gates, counts its towers, stands near the throne, bows with the elders before the Lamb, and with the one hundred and forty and four thousand swells the song of the redeemed. So favored a mortal—an intimate of Jesus, a man holy, a disciple teachable, an apostle faithful, a saint honored—his life can **but be** exemplary and stimulating to **the** brotherhood, as his doctrine is vital to the creed of the Church.

Stress is placed on the life and labors of Paul and John because, though, of all writers of the New Testament, they are most able to stand unsupported, and most nearly embrace the cardinal tenets of our religion, differing widely, as they do, in temperament and scope of inspiration, and yet are indispensable to each other and the system of truth; for **the** greater reason every other writer needs the support of all the canonical writers. We merely formulate what is partially disclosed in the discussion when we say that the Christian ministry, in its variety of gifts and grace, learning, zeal, and eloquence, is a benediction. But how blessed soever each teacher and doer of the truth may be to the Church and the world, no one of them preaches the whole gospel, or discharges all its holy ministries. If Paul is to be sustained by John, and John by Paul; if Peter, and James, and the rest, is necessary to supplement the truth as taught by Paul and John, may we not wonder at the bigotry of sects that blinds them to their own deficiencies, and enlightens them as to the supposed deficiencies of others? nay, may we not "do well to be angry" with the ecclesiastic who assumes the exclusive shepherding of God's flock, the lording it over his heritage, whether he sits in the Vatican of Roman power, or rules the chapel of some mean village?

Christian Communism must be discriminated from Optimism, who is so kindly in spirit that she discerns no faults and foibles, and is too complacent to be wise. Her glasses are rose-colored, disclosing to her naught but images of beauty. Were she not so amiable, we should be disposed to laugh at her mistakes. Communism is amiable too, but not blindly so. Her eyes sparkle as she looks abroad on the goodly heritage of the Church, and her face beams at the evidences of its prosperity; but objects to her return their true color, and a shadow therefore sometimes flits over her countenance. She is seeking the good, and, of course, comes at times on the evil; but she delays, not as the mud-wasp, to take up a soil, but only as a bee, to carry off a sweet. Her censures, then, are negative, but none the less pointed, for praise of virtue is condemnation of vice.

Religious narrowness is an offensive weakness, for it comes of ignorance of self and of society, and is damaging to the spiritual growth of the individual and of the Church. Paul is here commending broadness of view, catholicity of sentiment, and of consequence denounces narrowness and sectarianism. The philosophy he inculcates is in accord with that of the thirteenth chapter, "it thinketh no evil." It significantly, on the one hand, rebukes the Protestant who denounces Romanism unqualifiedly, by pointing out her good works, and discriminating properly between perversions developed and wrestings maliciously devised; and on the other hand, the Romanist for his sweeping denunciation of Protestantism, by showing that the policy of Protestantism toward learning and freedom is based on the Rock of Ages. Again, it rebukes Protestantism because in her own family the daughters differ in the theory and use of the sacraments and ceremonies of the Church; and Romanism again, because she excommunicates all who refuse to subscribe to the primacy of Peter; and the Church at large, because she neglects to take sisterly notice of other religions, especially of Judaism, the schoolmaster that brought her to Christ; because, secure in her own faith, she is severe on the doubting and disbelieving, admitting the worth of no half-truths nor half-virtues, shutting off theism and pantheism abruptly—though the one adoringly seeks to remove God from possible contact with sin, the other solacingly to bring him home to every burdened heart—haughtily exclaiming to all, Christ or nothing!

This doctrine of communism leads us to honor Christ, by acknowledging his presence in the germ, flower, and fruit, of Christian growth; in the shrinking but loving woman who bathed his feet with her tears; in the busy Martha and contemplative Mary; in conservative Thomas and aggressive Peter; in every state of grace, and strength of faith, finding something to admire and imitate, causing us to reach forth the hand of welcome, and utter words of greeting to all who "name the name of Christ." Christianity knows no differences of race or color, no forms of government, civil or ecclesiastic, as peculiarly deserving its favor, or qualifying for a monopoly of its blessings. "There is neither Jew nor Greek, there is neither bond nor free, there is neither male nor female; for ye are all one in Christ Jesus." It is implied in the doctrine of the text that nations may be better than their religions, and that Churches may be orthodox in practice, though heterodox in belief, just as French morality is superior to French religion, and the piety of the Kirk of Scotland is below the standard of the catechism. Communism obeys the injunction, "Prove all things, hold fast that which is **good**;" claims the theologies of Christendom as ours; and that we can no more exhaust the truth by our requisitions than the air by our breathing; that it is common property, and if divided and sequestered we have the warrant of the King for its search and restoration to the commonwealth. Our interest in the truth is commensurate with our desire, and as attainable as our efforts are earnest. It is not to be carried off as gold in bags to the loss of depositor or depositee. Its method of communication is reciprocal. Like the duplex interchange of messages on the wire, its giving and receiving are virtually one. As the earth draws upon the sun only as she can utilize his light and heat, so truth is dependent on the receptivity of the seeker for what is given out, and the quality of its display. Christian truth is a possible universal property, for it is the most needed form of knowledge, and is self-generating.

The Church is unconsciously and slowly, but steadily and surely, rising to the height of this argument of communism. Here and there, now and then, a word is spoken, or a work done, in its furtherance. Now we see hints of closer fraternity by sects of the same creed, but of sometime variant usage; now a call for an evangelical, now an ecumenical, council. In the fellowship of the Spirit we sing the classic "Rock of Ages," and "Jesus, lover of my soul," little caring whether Toplady and Wesley side with Calvin or Arminius, and pray as expressive of thankfulness, or of wants unsupplied, in a common language, just as the one hundred and twenty, invoking the descent of the Holy Ghost, demonstrated the probability of a common tongue through the heavenly motion of a common sentiment. The Spirit makes us free and one.

Communism leads us out of Christendom, for Christianity, which it seeks to spread and develop, is not exclusive. It visits the Ganges as well as the Jordan, for there is something sacred in the one locality as in the other, for Buddha is a prophet as well as John, and though he saw not "that Light," yet he longed for its illumination; that in the Vedas and Koran, as in the Bible, there are truths, buried it may be in a matrix of error, but truths giving promise of potency which the Christian philosopher slights at the risk of dimming the brightness of his own jewels; for honor to the Master is interest in men, and forgetfulness of men is a slighting of God. "By unduly depreciating all other religions," says Max Müller, "we have placed our own in a position which its Founder never intended for it; we have torn it away from the sacred context of the history of the world; we have ignored or willfully narrowed 'the sundry times and divers manners' in which in times past God spake unto the fathers by the prophets, and instead of recognizing Christianity as coming in the fullness of time, and as the fulfillment of the hopes and desires of the whole world, we have brought ourselves to look upon its advent as the only broken link in that unbroken chain which is rightly called the divine government of the world. Nay, more than this, there are people who, from mere ignorance of the ancient religions of mankind, have adopted a doctrine more unchristian than any that could be found in the pages of the religious books of antiquity, viz.: That all nations of the earth, before the rise of Christianity, were mere outcasts, forsaken and forgotten of their Father in heaven, without a knowledge of God, without a hope of salvation."

"The world, life, and things present, are ours." The blessings of our religion are for to-day as well as to-morrow. We do not forget the seriousness of life, our dependence on our Lord, as beneficiaries of his bounty, as subjects of his grace; but he nowhere requires us to repress the cheerful, hopeful, joyous elements of our nature, for religion **is for men. Earth is as much** our home now as heaven shall be hereafter. Something richer **hereafter,** something rich now. No chancery delays to keep us out of possession and use: prospective increase, consummation, but no break, no interregnum of **disorder, no** orphanage or widowhood, no isolation or ostracism, but peaceful occupancy and home-felt joy. With the remembrance of the intervening curse, Christianity repeats the declaration of the Creator, that the earth is good—its streams, mountains, forests, birds, beasts, men, are good, and that whatever is bad is of the enemy; **that there** is no flower, **or fruit, or soil, or mineral, or living creature,** but may **be made to minister to man's** happiness and God's **glory; and to him** "who hath ears to hear" there comes **a** response from Nature joyously confessing God, as he has gladly recognized her:

> Tell the silent sky,
> **And** tell the stars, and tell yon **rising sun,**
> Earth with her thousand voices praises God.
> God! let the torrents like **a** shout of nations
> Answer! and let the ice-plains **echo God!**
> God! sing, ye meadow-streams, with gladsome voice,
> Ye pine-groves, with your soft and soul-like sound.
> And they too **have a voice,** yon piles of snow,
> **And in their perilous fall shall** thunder God!

But this, perhaps, is the least important of the lessons of the passage. With a purpose of rational indulgence, the Christian life does not separate us from the world; for in trade, it is not buying and selling, but "bulling" and "bearing," that is censurable; in business, it is not diligence, but dishonesty, that is denounced; in home politics, it is not the advocacy of the rights of the people, nor even the platform of a party, but the foisting of an unworthy person on the suffrages of the citizens, that is to be condemned; in foreign politics, it is not diplomacy, but deceit, that is reprehensible; in war, it is not so much the hot blood of the field, as the bad blood of the council-chamber and the cabinet, that is open to the criticism of the Christian. Among the pleasures, it is not the grace of the dance, but the "german" of it, that is sensuous; it is not the smile of innocence, but the smirk of wantonness, that is frowned at; not joyous laughter, but such as suggests the "crackling of thorns under a pot," that is ranked as a folly. In racing, it is not the speed and bottom of the horse, but the jockeying and gambling, that is vicious; in the fruit of the vine, it is not its refreshing and strengthening properties, but its epicurean and excessive indulgence, that constitutes sin; in society, it is not the gleam of humor, the flash of wit, the sparkle of repartee, the glance of affection, the look of admiration, but the coarse mirth, the unfeeling sneer, the satiric sting, the wily coquetry, the empty adulation, at which Christianity shakes her indignant head. No inhibition against joy or activity, except such as grows out of our weakness or waywardness. Charged with the grace of Christ, the heart is responsive to all tokens of his presence, and appropriative of all communicable good. "God giveth us richly all things to enjoy." Christianity does not cloister her devotees; superstition does that. She rather invites them to walk through the marts of business, the forum, the senate-chamber; wherever men "most do congregate" she would introduce her representatives, for her concern is for men; and though she moves a queen among them, she manifests all the sympathy of a sister, keeping her garments unspotted, and indicating by her own walk the better way of religion. She "renders unto Cæsar the things that be Cæsar's," and thinks it no crime to discuss his policy; it is only exaggerated religiousness that does. She knows full well that without government strong and stable, the things of God are endangered, and that without the binding power of religion, government becomes disorganized. She takes part in the industrial enterprises of the day, directly or indirectly managing many of them. She invests in rails and engines, in wires and batteries, encourages the tunneling of the Alps, the bridging of the Mississippi, advocates the opening of Suez and Panama, that the nations may be neighborly, and the peoples flow together like long-barred oceans, and that the continents of heathendom may come to Christ. She takes stock in the learning of the day and its achievements—not simply editing the Bible, works of theology, and religious journals, but supplying authors and editors for scientific and literary treatises. She muddies no stream of truth, clogs no wheel of progress, puts no veto on investigation, interdicts no work of litera-

10*

ture, lays no embargo on the press. If, as is the fact, an *expurgatorium* has been kept, it is but charity to say that it originated in a misguided zeal "for the faith once delivered to the saints," or is chargeable to men who audaciously arrogate the vicarship of Christ.

She does not array herself against science; ignorance does that. Her energies and resources are specially devoted to the science of religion, but as contributory to this she draws from all. Strictly speaking, she is no specialist, though she smiles on specialists, for her elective instinct conducts her to the best. The illustration, if not the embodiment, of many sciences, she patronizes them all. Hammer in hand, she walks over the earth with Lyell and Miller, taking the "testimony of the rocks," harmonizing geology and Genesis; or, with Bopp and Grimm, cons the grammars of the races, that philology may corroborate the ethnology of Paul, that "God hath made of one blood all nations of men for to dwell on all the face of the earth." She accepts the demonstrated, though her cheek mantle at the memory of the now historic blunders of her zealous but sometimes inconsiderate adherents. She may not be able at all times to demonstrate, or even discern, the relations of the several sciences to herself, but she is a philosopher, and trusts to the ultimate solution of the revelations, as she does to the vindication of God, for God is truth.

The progress of religious thought and sentiment, and their climax of influence in our present civilization, she considers; but, that she may estimate rightly their share in the elevating process, she considers also, in the interest of her chief work, the value of the fine arts. She exercises not merely her taste, but her godly judgment, in choosing from ancient and mediæval art such excellences as may be promotive of refinement and worship, holding surveillance over the sensuous, lest in her love for the æsthetic she be imposed upon by that which is insidiously harmful. She enters—for nothing forbids, except the sour severity of Puritanism—the galleries of paintings, the studios of sculpture, the conservatories of music, and appropriates whatever of inspiration or suggestion they have to offer. She does not hesitate to subsidize the genius of a Mozart for the expression of praise, admires the majesty of the "Moses," meditates on the ennoblement of womanhood in the "Madonna," or the glorified humanity in the "Transfiguration;" but since God is a Spirit, and is to be worshiped in spirit, and jealous of the displacement of her Christ, she refuses them a niche in the house of his worship.

But "the world, life, and things present," are ours specially, because the present is the only time when the Christian life is really lived, and the cross glorified in the victories of its followers over sin. We are invited to inspect the armory of Israel, and make requisition for what is needful for the warfare. "Other men labored, and we are entered into their labors." We stand in our lot, we enter on our labors, we shirk not our duty. We take part in the enterprises of our Zion, we build up her walls, we restore her waste-places, we go up against her enemies, we contribute to her resources, we pledge her our energies, and dedicate ourselves to her service. Under the charter of liberties, as laid down by the apostle in Philippians, "Whatsoever things are true, whatsoever things are honest, whatsoever things are just, whatsoever things are pure, whatsoever things are lovely, whatsoever things are of good report—if there be any virtue, and if there be any praise, we think on these things," and on these things act.

We come now to solve a paradox not always understood by the regenerate, and never by the unregenerate.

"Death and things to come are ours." If it require some consideration to induce us to perceive that "the world, life, and things present," are ours, much more in this case shall the heart hesitate until the eye of faith scan the character of this property, and the conditions of its conferring and acceptance.

A property? Is it not that over which we have control for our advantage as against contingent disadvantages? Death bring us service? Is he not the universal robber rather? A friend? Who understands him as such? Has he not defied the descriptive powers of pagan and Christian poets, and yet remains, not the riddle of the sphinx, but the enigma itself of the universe? Dreadful in the favoring distance, and in the irrepressible forebodings of the soul, how shall we endure him in the horror of his actual presence? Are we not his at the meeting? comes he not, and sees, and conquers?

There are no answers to these race questions outside the gospel, for death is its mystery and majesty too. And so deaf and dull are we that not always do we hear the oracles distinctly, nor understand them rightly. To some, the dread of death vanishes as ghosts before the dawning day, for to them the gospel gives forth no uncertain sound; with others, fear lingers as the twilight of the Arctic regions, for the heart is yet divided in its trust. "According to our faith," so is our fear. Christ's victory over death shows us God. No wonder the resurrection, the proof of the victory, was the theme of the apostles and early preachers; it is the heart of the gospel. If Christ be not risen, then is our preaching vain, and your faith is also vain, and of all men we are most miserable. But Christ is risen, and Christians are of all men most blessed.

> Strong Son of God, immortal love,
> Whom we, that have not seen thy face,
> By faith, and faith alone, embrace,
> Believing where we cannot prove;
> Thine are these orbs of light and shade:
> Thou madest life in man and brute;
> Thou madest death; and lo, thy foot
> Is on the skull which thou hast made.
> Thou wilt not leave us in the dust.

What Christ hath done for himself he hath done for us. He died, that we may live; he lives, that we may die in assurance. "For we know that if our earthly house of this tabernacle were dissolved, we have a building of God, a house not made with hands, eternal in the heavens." He who cannot look into the new tomb of Joseph and believe, has no quieting for his instinctive fears but fatalism, and fatalism is death.

But we have looked, have we not? and believed; not, perhaps, with the eagerness of Peter: we may have required the articulate tests of Thomas; but yet we believe, and are going on to believe the more. We have feared death, but we are fearing him less. Our faith in the miracle of Christ's death satisfies us with the mystery of our own. His power over death is our power over life. Needful was it for Christ to die, else he would remain unglorified; needful for us, that we may be glorified with him. As Christ in the flesh manifested something of his divine nature, so we who have "known him in the regeneration" manifest something of the Christly character, and that supremacy of composure which comes with the new life. Really, we have already entered upon our heritage. The retroactive power of our property is seen in our wise and happy appreciation of the "world, life, and things present." It has made us strong, and gentle, and true, and loving; for the great issue is settled, and in our favor. The relief it brings fills the world with beauty and gladness for us. A righted judgment, a wider knowledge, a freedom from restraint, a conscious at-homeness, a restored soul, an insight and security as to the uses and objects of life, rob death of his power to threaten at a distance. Nay, this is scarcely different from the dialect of the unconverted. Death is to us a Master of the Rolls, who issues our patent of nobility, conducts us to our manor, and will in due time introduce us to the

King and his court. A marvel of mercy in this ennobling graciousness is, that the disaffected and disloyal share now in the munificence of the provision. The security of civil government, the sanctities of home, and all that these imply, are bought with a price for those who disregard, if they do not disdain, the sacrifice. But to us who believe Christ is precious, and his work paramount — bound together by the sacrament of death, but death robbed of his sting, there grows up among us a oneness of sentiment, a holiness of joy, a peace in believing, deep, settled, prevailing.

There is much significance in the record of Luke that, after the resurrection, but while the miracle was fresh in the minds of the disciples, and the closing proof of the Messiahship of Christ was descending in the cloven tongues of Pentecost, "All that believed were together, and had all things common; and sold their possessions and goods, and parted them to all, as every man had need." The highest spiritual state comes of assurance of power over death, and makes the resultant blessings common. This is "the law and the testimony." The death of Christ is the seal and sanction of Christian Communism.

Prospectively of death what shall we say? Casts it a shadow athwart the hereafter? and does the valley of the shadow deepen and descend into Stygian wave and darkness? Not for us, not for us! By a fiat as omnific as that which said, "Let there be light, and there was light," the gloom of the grave has been kissed into gladness, and its darkness made all luminous by the light of the Sun of righteousness. Yet scant are the reports of the inheritance of the saints. Moses and Elias came back for a moment to dazzle us with their garments of light; but an Eshcol token of the goodliness of the Canaan is ours. Even John, as we have seen, when in the Spirit on the Lord's-day, chiefly reveals to us the objective glories of heaven, whatever reserve, like Paul, he may have made of "unspeakable words, which it is not lawful for a man to utter." He speaks as inspired, and we can but study the attractive but unsatisfying picture, until, from the opulence of our "faith, hope, and charity," it shall glow in the soft beauty and spiritual home-likeness of our Father's house, secured to us through the sacrifice of his First-born, our Elder Brother. We rest on the coincident and cumulative testimony of David and John: "I shall be satisfied when I awake with thy likeness;" and "We shall be like him; for we shall see him as he is."

Our Father, however, fetters us not in our efforts to rise to the conception of the blessedness and engagements of the heavenly state. As the angels, we desire to look into the "sufferings of Christ and the glory that shall follow." We have been rapt in the Spirit; have gone up in the luminous clouds of contemplation; have breathed the high air of heaven; have felt, as we stood before the throne, the hush of reverence, the awe of majesty, the holiness of the sacrifice, the Godhead of the Lamb. Whatever may be the engagements of the unfallen and redeemed — ministering to the untranslated, and solving the delayed problems of life, or in carrying the gospel to other worlds, and the projection of new and godlike enterprises—we shall share them, and share them in the vigor of conscious capability; for our ignorances no longer cramp and disqualify us, the mists of error dissolve, and truth stands out in the bold relief of the everlasting mountains. "We know even as also we are known." The supernal light vivifies and deifies our intelligence. Verily, "now are we as gods, knowing good and evil." The fell work of the deceiver is more than met by our walk in the light of the Lamb. He shall lead us through the courts of celestial learning, and all the desires of our souls to know and to do shall be satisfied. "We follow whithersoever he leadeth."

Our sins shall shame us no more; we are washed from them in the blood of the Lamb, and are made kings and priests unto God and his Father; and through the ages he shall be the ever-present memorial of our interest, and guarantee of our right to the blessedness of the sanctified and the saved. "One faith, one Lord, one baptism," on earth; one joy, one throne, one salvation, in heaven.

XIII.

THE INEQUALITIES OF LIFE, AS ILLUSTRATING THE WISDOM AND GOODNESS OF GOD.

BY THE REV. WHITEFOORD SMITH, D.D.,
South Carolina Conference.

"For the poor shall never cease out of the land." Deut. xv. 11.

"For ye have the poor always with you." Matt. xxvi. 11.

MANY of the evils which afflict society are the result of our efforts to make better what God made good. Not satisfied with the order which Infinite Wisdom has established, men have vainly imagined that it was susceptible of improvement, and in their endeavors to convert a system of beneficence into what they conceive would be a system of optimism, "after the manner of the giants, they have warred against the laws of the universe, and the wisdom that created it."

The successive disappointment of these attempts has not deterred from their repetition, and the exploded follies of one generation have been adopted by another, to result only in the same disappointment and mortification. If these experiments were harmless, and made only on insensate matter, they might be the subject of ridicule, and excite but a smile of contempt at their absurdity; but when they disturb the relations of society, and introduce confusion and discord, awakening hopes only to be disappointed, and promising good which can never be attained, they are too serious for laughter, and deserve a stern denunciation.

Conspicuous among these vagaries of the human mind is the attempt to set aside the immutable law of Nature which has established the inequality between man and man. Under the specious guise of philanthropy, it is sought to establish, not what Heaven ordained a law of universal brotherhood, but—as if there were something degrading in being a younger son—a law of *universal primogeniture*.

It might be supposed that the glaring absurdity of such a proposition would carry with it its own confutation, and render needless any reply; yet it is not less true than surprising that many, whose intelligence would seem to place them beyond the reach of deception, have been beguiled by this Utopian dream. The voice of Nature, even in the inanimate world, declares against universal equality. From the lowliest shrub to the stateliest tree, the law of inequality prevails; while, by the beneficent provision of a gracious God, each in its place subserves the end of its creation, adorning the earth with a beautiful variety, and administering to the gratification and happiness of man. The midnight heavens proclaim—alike to the infidel astronomer and to the believing Christian — that "one star differeth from another star in glory." And so far as it has pleased the Almighty to reveal to us the secrets of the invisible world, it has been declared, "So also is the resurrection of the dead."

When the Israelites, having been delivered out of the land of Egypt, and led through the wilderness for forty years, were about to enter upon the possession of the promised Canaan, Moses, while directing and exhorting them to the duties which would insure their permanency and prosperity, uttered the remarkable and prophetic declaration, "*The poor shall never cease out of the land!*" There might seem something strange in such a declaration at such a time. Were they not about to inherit a land of promise, lovely for situation, salubrious in its climate, and fertile in its productions? And was not that land, for plenty, described as flowing with milk and honey? Was it not about to be divided to their tribes and families according to the principles of a just and impartial distribution? And was not the patrimony of every man to be secured by a homestead law which rendered it inalienable, so that if necessity drove him to sell, he might redeem it at any time, and if unredeemed, it reverted to him or his family at the year of jubilee? How, then, should there be any rich or any poor among this people? Whence should arise those inequalities which should clothe one in purple and fine linen, and spread for him a sumptuous table every day, while another should be in rags, a beggar at his gate? Was this peculiar people, under a theocracy, to be subject to the same contingencies to which all other people were liable? Yes; the unalterable law of Heaven, decreed as well in kindness as in wisdom, was neither to be abrogated nor suspended even for them; the inequalities that existed in Egypt under the Pharaohs should exist in Judea under David and Solomon; and the rich and the poor, the strong and the weak, the wise and the ignorant, the master and the servant, should be found as well upon the banks of the Jordan as by the waters of the Nile.

And when, after long centuries, the Prophet came of whom Moses spake, like to himself, but greater far than he, he confirmed the truth of the ancient lawgiver's words when he said, "The poor ye have always with you." The experience of every age and every clime attests the truth of the divine utterance; for since the primeval bankruptcy in Eden, when the wealth of innocence and the divine similitude were lost, where have not the poor, beggared children of our race been found, wandering in the deserts, or crouching under the shadows of the rich man's palace, asking for sympathy too oft denied, for charity too oft withheld? Even where civilization and refinement most prevail, and where the sublime teachings of Christianity have done most to mitigate the evils of our fallen condition, the alms-house, and the orphan asylum, and the widow's home, standing beside the lofty dwellings where the children of affluence reside, bear their perpetual and emphatic testimony to the truth, "The poor ye have *always* with you."

Shall we be told that these are but the artificial distinctions of society? that they are no part of the divine economy, but an infraction of the great order of Heaven? Why, then, let us ask, have these inequalities in wealth, and wit, and worth, been always found among all people? It is not alone where a rank civilization has fostered an unnatural growth that these inequalities are found. On the contrary, they exist everywhere. The Indian acknowledges for his chief the brave whose strength in battle has won the victory for his tribe, and yields a superstitious reverence to the aged seer whose sagacity and experience have distinguished him among his people. The inequality between man and man is found in the submission rendered to the leader of the robber-band, and of the pirate-crew, as well as in the honors conferred upon the gifted few in the higher ranks of civilized society. It is seen not only in the forum and the senate-house, where genius wins unfading laurels, but also in the dungeon, where true greatness bears with dignity its cruel sufferings, or on the scaffold, where conscious innocence triumphs over the doom to which tyranny consigns it.

To test the soundness of this wild conceit of universal equality, let us imagine for a moment the experiment to be made. Let us suppose it possible that, on a given day, the entire wealth of a nation should be divided, upon principles of the strictest justice, impartiality, and equality, among all its people. How long could this condition of things remain? How many disturbing causes would operate immediately to destroy the nicely-adjusted balance? The skill and ingenuity of one would soon augment his share, while the ignorance and thriftlessness of another would make him the victim of his more crafty neighbor. The ordinary casualties of life would deprive one of the ability to labor, or a protracted and wasting sickness would utterly exhaust his means, while his robust and healthy brother would be rapidly increasing in wealth. The family of one would be numerous and expensive, while that of another would remain unenlarged. The father of one family would be taken away by death in the midst of his years, and a widow, perhaps feeble and sickly, be left to struggle for the support of numerous children, too young to provide for themselves. What principle could be introduced into this system to prevent or correct these occurrences, which would be constantly destroying the desired equality? Would you rectify the aberration by a new division every year? Then you remove every incentive to industry; for no man would labor only to distribute the fruits of his toil among the unfortunate, the idle, and the vicious.

Nor are the inequalities of life confined to the circumstances of our physical condition. They are equally apparent in all that relates to our intellectual being. Nearly a century ago, a French philosopher advanced the theory that in each individual his talents and his virtues are not the effect of his organization, but of the education he receives. In our own day, precisely the reverse of this has been taught by those phrenologists who have found all human talents and virtues located in the several divisions of the brain, and, by an examination of the head, profess to tell at once the character and future history of the man. Thus error is always found oscillating between opposite extremes, while truth, like the polar star, maintains its permanent and unalterable position. Surely the mind must be blinded by prejudice until it is incapable of any just perception that does not recognize the infinite diversity of intellectual gifts with which the Creator has endowed our race!

How variously diversified are the intellectual gifts of men! In one, the fires of imagination burn with uncommon luster, and burst forth in the highest displays of poetry and eloquence. In another, the strong powers of argumentation or reasoning are displayed, carrying conviction to the minds of the multitude. In one, the genius for music displays itself, and listening thousands are entranced by the sublime oratorios of "Creation" and "The Messiah;" while another, investigating the profoundest truths in science and philosophy, gives to the world a "Novum Organum," or reveals the great secrets which for ages had been buried in the bosom of Nature. And will it be pretended that all these have been endowed with no higher gifts than the multitudes among whom they lived? Why, then, does not every age and every clime boast its Demosthenes and its Homer, its Shakespeare and its Milton, its Plato and its Aristotle, its Paley and its Whately, its Handel and its Haydn, its Copernicus and its Galileo, its Bacon, its Newton, and its Locke?

Talk of mental equality as a law of the human race! The school-boy, who witnesses daily the triumphs of genius in the contests of the school, will give the lie to the ridiculous proposition. How admirably has an eloquent writer denounced this absurd hypothesis: "Law! if the whole world conspired to enforce the falsehood, they could not make it *law*. Level all conditions to-day, and you only smooth away all obstacles to tyranny to-morrow. A nation that aspires to equality is unfit for *freedom*. Throughout all creation, from the archangel to the worm, from Olympus to the pebble, from the radiant and completed planet to the *nebula* that hardens through ages of mist, and shines into the habitable world, the first law of Nature is inequality. . . . . No; while the world lasts, the sun will gild the mountain-top before it shines upon the plain. Diffuse all the knowledge the earth contains over all mankind to-day, and some men will be wiser than the rest to-morrow."

Education can, doubtless, do much to lessen the difference between mind and mind. To a certain extent it can arouse the imagination, strengthen the reason, improve the judgment, elevate and purify the taste; it may fit a man to move with ease and grace in the society of the wise and learned, but it never has made, and never can make, a philosopher of a fool—a Solomon of a Rehoboam.

They who have studied well the nature of man in the light of experience have been constrained to acknowledge the inequality among men in morals as well as in mind. While the theologian maintains that all are fallen, and finds no exception in the race, from the effects of the primeval sin, he will not deny the differences that exist between the amiable and the morose, the gentle and the turbulent, the meek and the passionate. It may safely be admitted that the influences of education and religion can and do exert a larger power here than elsewhere. It has been wisely and mercifully arranged that they should, for however little the true happiness of man may depend upon his fortune or his intelligence, it does depend upon the soundness and purity of his morals. Yet even here a judicious observer cannot fail to notice the differences that exist even among those who are acknowledged to be good men. The homely saying, that a peck of grace will go farther with some men than a bushel with others, is only a confession of the natural inequality which marks the race. That parent must have been unobservant indeed who has not recognized this great law as manifesting itself among his children at an early age, when the gentlest rebuke will suffice to correct an evil in one which the severest chastisement will scarcely correct in another. Every teacher, too, must often have noticed among his pupils the different effects produced upon them by his appeals to their sense of honor, or propriety, or to the gentler sympathies of their nature.

It is not our purpose on this occasion to enter at any length into the question of the political equality of men. Such an investigation, properly and thoroughly conducted, would require more time and space than the limits of this discourse will allow. Perhaps it is sufficient, in connection with this argument, to say, that the history of the past, as well as all just and sound views of government, would exhibit the doctrine to be as wild and visionary as any other phase of human equality. From the patriarch who exercised authority over his family—from Nimrod, who sought to extend that authority into the rule of a king, and became a hunter of men—down through the ages to the present hour, men have been subjected to the government of their fellow-men. Whether that power has been exercised *jure divino* or *jure humano*—whether the popular voice has called to the throne, or the right to dominion has been founded on might, in all ages, and among all men, savage or civilized, political inequality has existed always and everywhere. No matter upon what principles government may be founded, whether monarchical, aristocratical, or republican, the very elevation to power marks the inequality, and places man over man.

> They tell thee in their dreaming school
>   Of power from old dominion hurled,
> When rich and poor, with juster rule,
>   Shall share the altered world.
> Alas! since time itself began,
>   That fable hath but fooled the hour:
> Each age that ripens power in man,
>   But subjects man to power.

But why multiply illustrations of a truth which stands out conspicuously written on every page of the history of our race? a truth which must commend itself to every mind not warped by prejudice, or blinded by error? A far more grateful task awaits us, to contemplate the infinite wisdom and benevolence evinced in this seemingly partial arrangement, and to hush into silence those murmurs of envy and discontent which this eternal law of Nature is so apt to excite.

It is only because the spectacle never has been, and never can be, presented to our sight, or because we have not calmly considered what the effect would be if it were possible, that we do not realize how great a curse the wished-for equality of men would be. Let us endeavor to bring the matter home to our minds by a contemplation of such a state of things as actually existing. Suppose, then, that the Creator, listening to the repinings of his weak and erring children, should reverse the law he has established, and gratify their foolish desires by making all men equal—equal in wisdom, equal in goodness, equal in physical strength, and equal in fortune. Suppose an angel from heaven commissioned to bring to our world the intelligence that the law of human inequality was abrogated—that henceforth there should be no poor in the land to utter their plaintive cries and supplicate a brother's help—no rich to look down in the pride of their opulence upon their poorer brethren—no weak to depend upon the aid of the strong—no strong to look with pity or contempt upon the feeble. Let the proclamation be made, as the fiat of the Almighty, "All men are equal." Let us imagine the announcement received with acclamations of joy by the whole family of man, as the inauguration of a new era in the history of the race, perchance, as the dawn of the long-expected Millennium. Methinks no band of angel-minstrels would hover over the world to repeat the song they sung over the plains of Judea long centuries ago, "Glory to God in the highest, and on earth peace, good-will toward men." O no; for that song proclaimed a birth of poverty, and celebrated the swaddling-clothes, the stable, and the manger. But methinks, rather, the loud laughter of infernal fiends would be heard, as they contemplated the utter ruin of that world, for the mastery of which they had so long contended.

What would be the first effect of this new law of universal equality? What, but the independence of every man upon his brother-man, and the introduction of the most complete and unmitigated selfishness? The bond which now holds society together, in all its various and beautiful relations, is Sympathy. Its chords are struck by the cry of distress, from whatever source it comes, and the appeal for help from the desolate and the suffering awakens the noblest sensibilities of the heart. O blessed human sympathy! how it speaks to the mother's heart in the feeble wail of her dying babe! How it weeps with those who weep,

> When, sorrowing, o'er some stone they bend,
> Which covers all that was a friend!

How it hears the faint cry of the famine-stricken, borne across the great sea, and vibrates with a deep emotion as it loads its ships with bread for the perishing!

O human sympathy! how it binds up the bruises of the wounded, and speaks the words of comfort, and recognizes even in a fallen foe a brother-man! How glorious are the exhibitions which it everywhere presents, binding families together in holy love, maintaining the peace of States and nations, ministering in hovels and hospitals where wretchedness may be relieved and vice reformed! What is it but the regulator of human society—the salt of the earth which preserves society from moral putrefaction?

But the establishment of universal equality would drive it from the world—there would be none to need it, there would be none to give it. Universal equality would be universal selfishness. And what darker doom could be visited upon the world than to give it over to the dominancy of this ungodlike passion? Imagine every individual of our race cut loose from all those sympathies which now bind us together, each bent only on what he thinks will advance his own greatness or fortune, and determined to pursue his own interests independent of all around him. Every generous impulse of nature would be destroyed, and the spirit of selfishness would be the prolific mother of a brood of evil passions, which would make every man an Ishmaelite, whose hand would be against his fellow. Where, then, would be all those beautiful relations which now adorn and sanctify human life? In the present constitution of things, there is none so rich, or so exalted, that he is independent of the services and sympathies of others. The rich are dependent on the poor, as well as the poor upon the rich. What the genius of the wise may invent, the skill and strength of the common laborer may be necessary to execute. How many alleviations of our miseries come from the sympathy and aid of the weak? It was the little captive handmaid of his wife, whose pity, on beholding the leprosy of Naaman, suggested the prophet in Samaria as the healer of the Syrian captain. And the affectionate remonstrances of his servants overcame his proud rage when he scorned the direction of the prophet, deeming the rivers of Abana and Pharpar better than all the waters of Israel.

The man who does violence to this great law of our nature—the law of universal sympathy and dependence—who, aiming only at his own aggrandizement, seeks to live to himself alone, passes through life devoid of the sweets of friendship, and descends to the grave, "unwept, unhonored, and unsung." But he whose life is given to deeds of benevolence, whose path is radiant with acts of noble generosity, is greeted everywhere as the friend and benefactor, lives in the affections of those whom he has blessed, and leaves behind him a name embalmed in the hearts of men. A community where the names of friend and benefactor are unknown, where the tear of compassion never flows, and the smile of gratitude is never seen, would resemble the arid desert, where no verdure blooms, no gushing fountain springs, and no bird of morning greets the traveler with its joyous song.

What would be the condition of society, let us ask, if there were no intellectual inequality? "Universal equality of intelligence, of mind, of genius, of virtue! No teacher left to the world? no men wiser, better than others? Were it not an impossible condition, what a hopeless prospect for humanity! . . . . The few in every age improve the many; the many now may be as wise as the few were, but improvement is at a stand-still if you tell me that the many now are as wise as the few *are*. . . . . And *this* is not a harsh, but a loving, law—the *real* law of improvement—the wiser the few in one generation, the wiser will be the multitude in the next."

Will not these observations apply with equal force to those moral inequalities that meet us everywhere? In the Scriptures themselves these inequalities are recognized as the order of the divine administration. The master, who was leaving his house for a season, intrusted his goods to his servants, not upon the principle of an equal distribution, but he gave to one five talents, to another two, and to another one—to every man according to his several ability. And the responsibility of each was proportioned to his endowments, for he who had improved two talents was commended in the very same words with which he was applauded who had improved five.

The world is to be instructed and elevated, not by precept alone, but by example also. Nothing is more encouraging to one who is struggling for a higher condition in virtue than to see that condition made attainable by the examples of others around him. Without such incentive he might willingly acknowledge the excellence and desirableness of the state, but yet regard it as impracticable. To teach by example is the noblest mode of instruction; and He who alone of all our race exhibited the perfection of every virtue, summed up the essence of all his lessons in one injunction, "*Follow Me.*" But admit the theory of universal equality, and there can be no example of superior virtue to excite our emulation, or to encourage our exertion. Then the value of history as philosophy teaching by example is lost; for why commend the patience and labor, the self-denial and perseverance, the generosity and magnanimity, the benevolence and unselfish devotion of those whose names are illustrious in the calendar of patriots, philosophers, philanthropists, or saints, if there be nothing above or beyond us to which we can attain?

But the law of human inequality orders otherwise. The bright examples of the past are not in vain. Over the generations that follow they weave their spell and wave their enchanted wand. The plains of Marathon, and the bay of Salamis, and the pass of Thermopylæ, identified as they are with the names of the men who have made them illustrious, and the noble deeds of which they have been the theater, awaken the inspiration of patriotism, and excite a holy emulation in the hearts of posterity. In the retirement of his closet, where the student toils over the hardest questions of science and philosophy, the shadowy forms of the mighty, who have trod this path before him, beckon him on, and cheer him in the pursuit. In the busy struggle of daily common life, the recollection of the virtuous triumphs of predecessors in the same field of labor counteracts the weariness of the conflict, and encourages the hope of similar success. Everywhere rise up the forms of the wise, and the great, and the good, animating the soul to persevering effort, by pointing to the dangers they have braved, the obstacles they have overcome, and the laurels they have won.

Is it hard to discover the benevolence of the Deity in this arrangement of our human condition, "that to every station there should be its care—to every man his burden?" In the eloquent words of the author already quoted, "If the poor did not sometimes so far feel poverty to be a burden as to desire to better their condition, and (to use the language of the world) 'seek to rise in life,' their most valuable energies would never be aroused, and we should not witness that spectacle which is so common in the land we live in, namely, the successful struggle of manly labor against adverse fortune—a struggle in which the triumph of one gives hope to thousands. . . . If all men were equal, if there were no suffering and no ease, no poverty and no wealth, would you not sweep with one blow the half, at least, of human virtues from the world? If there were no penury and no pain, what would become of fortitude? what of patience? what of resignation? If there were no greatness and no wealth, what would become of benevolence, of charity, of the blessed human pity, of temperance in the midst of luxury, of justice in the exercise of power? Carry the question farther: grant all conditions the same —no reverse, no rise and no fall, nothing to hope for, and nothing to fear—what a moral death you would at once inflict upon all the energies of the soul! and what a link between the heart of man and the providence of God would be snapped asunder! If we could annihilate evil, we should annihilate hope, and hope is the avenue to faith."

Accept these inequalities as the behest of Heaven, and how wide the field for the exercise of every virtue! and how rich the records of the race in these sublime achievements!

How palpable, then, are the great moral lessons which this condition of things is calculated to teach! Let the lowlier children of our race in poverty and sorrow, struggling with the evils of their hard estate, remember that this estate is not one of their own choice, but the allotment of Infinite Wisdom; that the Universal Father, who has assigned them this position for reasons and for ends they cannot now discern, but which they shall fully comprehend hereafter, is equally pleased with their patient acceptance of his will as he is with the obedience and service of the principalities and powers in the heavenly places. Discarding the envy which they may be tempted to indulge toward those in higher or more favored positions, let them learn the lessons of contentment and submission. Forget not, ye children of want and misery, that the fragrance of the lowly violet is not less precious than that of the more gorgeous flower; and that when the chilling blasts of winter have disrobed the roses of their glory, the humble violet still blooms in beauty, and regales us with its sweet perfume.

Let the rich and the great remember the uncertainty of all earthly good, and, while they rejoice in the possessions of the present, forget not the possibilities of the future. The times in which we are living have forcibly illustrated before our eyes how frail is the tenure by which we hold our earthly goods. The rich of to-day may be the poor of to-morrow. The sovereign who feels his throne secure, and may be contemplating still larger acquisitions of territory, that he may leave a boundless empire to his heir, may read in the history of no very remote times how near is the scaffold to the palace, or how soon the scepter of power may be exchanged for the exile's staff.

Away, then, with boastful pride. Let the rich be clothed with humility. Lay to heart the admonition of the prophet, "Let not the wise man glory in his wisdom, neither let the mighty man glory in his might; let not the rich man glory in his riches." There is one terminus to all the inequalities of life, and to that the rich and the poor, the wise and the ignorant, the great and the mean, are all rapidly approaching. There is but one true leveler, who effects his purpose, not by elevating the humble and abasing the proud, but by laying low alike all the hopes of the greatest and meanest of mankind. The distinctions of life are swept away by his power, and over the common ruin he rears the memorial of his conquests. Proudly he rebukes the restless ambition which frets at the inequalities of life, and asks:

> Can monarchs compass aught that hails their sway,
> Or call with truth one span of earth their own,
> Save that wherein at last they crumble bone by bone?

Let us not forget that the poor are the representatives of Christ on earth; that he has scattered them through all the lands to give opportunity to those who love him to minister to their wants, and that he will declare in that day, "Inasmuch as ye have done it to one of the least of these, ye have done it unto me." Surely, if there be any thing by which our nature is most exalted, and in which we may be godlike, it is in the noble privilege of doing good to others, of being the benefactors of the poor, of emptying ourselves that we may enrich others, as He who, "though he was rich, yet for our sakes became poor, that we through his poverty might be rich."

There is yet another particular which vindicates the wisdom and beneficence of this divine order in the affairs of men. If the happiness of man were dependent upon fortune, or power, or intelligence, then indeed there might seem to be some cause of complaint at the inequalities of which we have been speaking. But the law of compensation seems to be commensurate with the law of inequality. If poverty deprives a man of many of the advantages which wealth confers, it also exempts him from its cares, its anxieties, and its responsibilities. If a humble position in life debars him from the honors and prerogatives of power, it saves him from being the object of envy and malignant hate. If it condemns him to labor and to toil, it blesses him with health, and brings to him the welcome visits of refreshing sleep. If it denies him the advantages of high mental cultivation, it frees him from a thousand perplexing doubts, and from much study, which is a weariness of the flesh. For, alas! the records of our race are but too replete with illustrations of capacious minds wrecked upon the dark rocks of infidelity and skepticism, or perishing in the fires which their own genius had enkindled.

The traveler who scales the summit of the highest Alps may look down for a moment with enthusiastic delight upon the world beneath him, and in the temporary delirium forget the pains and perils of the ascent, and all the dangers that await the downward way; but the humble peasant of the vale below may have enjoyed an equal feast, where Nature smiled in perpetual verdure.

He who takes a broad and philosophic view of men in all the various departments of life, from the highest to the lowest, cannot fail to be struck with the fact that, however different may be the pursuits and fortunes of men, happiness is distributed among them with a wonderful equality; for, while the poor may often feel the emotions of envy arising within them when they witness the pomp and pageant attendant upon wealth, it is equally true that from the pride of place and the pinnacle of power the opulent and the mighty look down with envy too upon the tranquil enjoyments of the poor. Could we see into the hearts of men, and read all the repinings that are written there, it is probable that this uneasy feeling of discontent would be found as often among the one class as the other. It is not wealth, or fame, or power, or the noble gift of high intelligence, that brings to the mind that sweet content and cheerfulness of heart that constitute what the world calls happiness. Alike from the palace and the hovel proceed those vain regrets and murmurings against our earthly lot, which bear a constant testimony to the dissatisfaction and restlessness of man. It is virtue alone — virtue, in the highest, widest, and noblest acceptation of the term, embracing all the good which religion teaches and enjoins—which can still these wild cries of discontent, and bring to the heart the blessed solace and the soothing balm.

> For not with natural or mental wealth
> Is God delighted, or his peace secured;
> For not in natural or mental wealth
> Is human happiness or grandeur found.

If we confine our views to the present state of man, and contemplate him only in reference to this life—if we divest our earthly condition of all its relations to the eternal future—if, in a word, we shut our eyes to the immortality which religion reveals, then indeed is human life, with all its varieties and inequalities, an unsolved and inexplicable enigma. We are but feathers wafted by the wind, bubbles tossed on the great sea of life. The only appropriate superscription over the great panorama of the world would be the bitter expression of disappointment and regret, "Vanity of vanities, all is vanity and vexation of spirit."

But when life is viewed in the light of its connections with another and an endless state of being, where virtue shall receive its appropriate reward, and vice shall meet its just condemnation—where these rewards shall be measured, not by the splendor which may have shed a false halo around the act, but by the motives which have prompted it, and the proportion it bore to the ability of the agent—where earth's mightiest and most renowned shall stand revealed in all their selfishness, the objects of disgust and loathing, while the humble and unknown, who have labored only for the good of others, and been the ministers of mercy to the suffering of their race, shall be honored as the truly great—all these inequalities we now behold are but little mole-hills on the surface of society, not to be noticed when they are past, or only remembered as manhood in the fullness of its intellectual strength remembers the trifles of childhood which perplexed its feeble powers, or disturbed for a moment its infant glee.

If, then, at any time the scene of human disappointment shall tempt us to adopt the beautiful but sad lines of Gray—

> Full many a gem of purest ray serene
> The dark, unfathomed caves of ocean bear,
> Full many a flower is born to blush unseen,
> And waste its sweetness on the desert air—

a nobler inspiration shall prompt us to add,

> But raised by power divine, each gem shall shine;
> Each flower exhale in heaven its rich perfume;
> Each owned by thee, Eternal Sire, as thine,
> Shall with effulgence glow, with beauty bloom.

We may indulge in the pleasing anticipation of a time when the oppressions of tyranny shall cease throughout the world—when the tocsin of war shall be heard no more, and no more shall be seen the garments of warriors rolled in blood—when the repinings of discontent shall be hushed in perpetual silence—when the gifts of genius shall never be prostituted to the service of licentiousness and sin, nor the lights of science lead into the mazes of doubt and error—when the glorious principles of truth and virtue, coming forth triumphant from the conflict of ages, shall assert their high-born right to universal supremacy. But even then, in the bright millennial reign, the blended notes of the high and the low, of the rich and the poor, of the wise and the simple, of the master and the servant, shall still be heard, mingling in sweet concord, full of peace, and exultant hope, and everlasting joy.

XIV.

THE INTELLIGENCE OF FAITH.

BY THE REV. T. J. DODD, D.D.,
Vanderbilt University.

"At thy word I will let down the net." Luke v. 5.

This act of casting the net has sometimes been referred to as an instance of *blind faith* upon the part of Peter. A blind faith, however, is a thing which has no existence. "The eye of faith" and "the visions of faith" are figures which had never been used but for the fact that faith *sees,* and is *intelligent.* There is a faith which *takes God at his word,* believing and obeying immediately, without hesitation or objection; but this is really the most intelligent faith that is ever exercised. It is immediate, because it instantly perceives the grounds upon which it should proceed, and acts accordingly. Just in proportion as we fail to perceive these grounds will be our hesitation either to accept the promises, or to obey the commandments, of God.

There is no such thing as faith *without a reason.* The reasons for belief may be very different for different individuals, and even for the same individual at different periods of his life; but whenever one believes, his mind must act in consequence of that

THE REV. THOS. J. DODD, D.D.,
Of the Kentucky Conference.

which appears to himself, at least, to be a sufficient reason. The little child believes in God because of his confidence in the superior wisdom of those who have so instructed him, just as the Romanist, for a similar reason, accepts with full confidence many of the teachings of his priesthood. Most of the earlier belief of us all arises from our submission to authority recognized as the source and standard of our faith. There is a time when we are perfectly satisfied with this, and our belief is just as positive and assured as if resting upon the best-ascertained facts of history or science, or as if settled by ourselves only after the most painstaking and impartial investigation. As we advance, however, in the use of our intellectual faculties, and realize the necessity of having, each for himself, a foundation for our faith, we throw aside the influence of instruction or authority, and seek other grounds of belief; but, after all, we attain no conclusions more satisfactory, or more reasonable, than at the time was the simple, confiding faith of our childhood. Now, in the maturity of our years, we read, we think, we travel, we explore, we pile fact upon fact, and we have our own reasons for accepting God and the Bible; yet these are no more reasons, relatively, than was the artless recital to which our little hearts responded as we sat upon our mother's knee, and heard her tell of God and Jesus.

At whatever period of life, whatever the degree of our intellectual or moral culture, and in whatsoever realm of thought or knowledge, if we believe at all, we believe for a reason; and this is saying no more than that faith, like all things else, must have a cause. Nor is there a faith *opposed* or *contrary* to *reason*, or a faith that is *above* reason. If we do not believe without a reason, much less can we when reason is against us; much less, again, can we disregard reason, forming beliefs in a realm that is above it —reason entirely out of view, not consulted, ignored.

In saying this, we do not mean that we never believe that in which, or of which, we do not perceive the *reasonableness;* in other words, that which we cannot comprehend. We are compelled to believe in thousands of instances where we may never expect to understand. Out yonder is a landscape—wide-spreading, beautiful; it is taken in by the eye, and impressed upon the retina; we believe that we behold it there, pictured like a painting on the wall, and we also believe that all others who look upon it behold the very same thing; yet the vision itself no man can comprehend. We cannot understand the omnipotence, or the omnipresence, or the self-existence, of our God; yet we find not the least difficulty in believing that he is possessed of these attributes. Just so in regard to all of our most familiar and most dearly-cherished beliefs—those in the simplest equally with those in the most recondite truths of nature, experience, providence, God.

Right here we may determine, to some extent, the *province* of reason in its relations to the revealed word of God. The question, here, should not be as to the reasonableness, to us, of the *contents* of the book, but as to the *evidences* which can be found of its being, indeed, a divine revelation. Upon this point we are to satisfy our reason, whatever be the kind or degree of the argument required. To say that we must take the book *upon faith* is merely telling us that we must believe the book to be from God; but the question comes up, *Why so believe?*

The volume accepted as of God, we should admit its statements in whatever light they may appear to us. We cannot believe that God would utter that which is either untrue or unreasonable, and it is highly irrational in us to expect to understand all things in the divine word, while there is such an infinitude of things about us in daily life which far transcend our comprehension, but which, nevertheless, we must accept with the most assured conviction.

As regards faith in the promises, and obedience to the commands, contained in the book, the province of reason is to fix the *meaning* of these—not to ascertain the grounds upon which they have been based of God. We have no right to call God to account, and ask him why he has commanded thus; nor may we require of him *how* he can verify his promises to us. Ours is to obey the commands, and to trust the promises, as we understand *them*—not as we understand the divine counsels concerning them. There doubtless are many instances in which we think we can see the grounds of the divine requirements, and the means by which God accomplishes his purposes in our behalf; but these are not proper subjects of inquiry on our part—at least, of such inquiry as determines to relax pursuit only when a satisfactory result is attained. What has God ordered? what promised? what does he *mean* in his revelations to the world? These are the subjects upon which we are to employ our reason; and it is thus only, assisted, of course, by the Divine Spirit, that we can either believe or obey the word of God. We can neither trust nor obey that which, in this sense at least, we cannot understand.

There is no such thing as an *unreasoning* faith. On the other hand, every act of faith is the result of a process of argument in all regards the very same as takes place in investigations of a most strictly scientific character. In that faith which is immediate, we do not perceive the successive actions of the mind; but this is because of our rapid darting from premises to the conclusion. There are courses of reasoning through which we work our way toilsomely and slowly: we are distinctly conscious of every mental operation involved, because we have to weigh evidence, to examine the bearings of propositions and fit them together, as it were, before our minds can arrive at the general result. This is usually the case when we are not previously familiar with the subject-matter of the occasion, or entertain beliefs opposed to the conclusion to which the argument would conduct us. At one time it required labored demonstration to convince the world of the revolution of the planets; but let a new planet now be discovered, and we immediately believe that it revolves both upon its axis and around the sun; yet this latter belief comes from a process of ratiocination as real, though different in kind, as that in the former belief, accepted only after years of painful doubt and fearful apprehension. Were one wholly destitute of all idea of God to receive, for the first time, instruction upon the divine existence, attributes, and providence, we may readily conceive that much time might elapse, and much argumentation be required, to induce him to trust His promises or order his life by the precepts of His law; while the man who has long known God, and really believed in his character as revealed, trusts and obeys with a readiness almost equal to that of opening the eye to sight or the ear to hearing. When truths have been long established in the mind, we may instantly perceive their logical relations when brought together as premises; and then we form our conclusions without either conscious effort or consciousness of time—just as the light shoots across the heavens without our observing its pathway, or taking note of the duration of the transit. In general, this rapid, unconscious argumentation makes up the greater part of our lives, and is really the most logical, accurate, and reliable, in which our minds are employed. Let any thing occur which checks the mind in its rush from the premises to the conclusion, and we very clearly perceive the process through which it has advanced. When there is no cause for apprehension or suspicion, we accept the national currency without in the least considering that such acceptance is the result of an argument drawn from our confidence in the financial character of the Government and the genuineness of the bill; but let suspicion once arise as to either of these things: then, being arrested and thrown back toward a consideration of the honesty or ability of the Government, or the possibility of counterfeit in the currency, we immediately see that a regular train of reasoning must take place before the promissory note is accepted in lieu of gold or silver. The reasoning is of the very same nature, when, without check or hinderance, the mind, with a single bound, leaps to its conclusions; and this is true whether the subject-matter be of a secular or religious nature. Every act of faith is a distinct logical process.

The phrase, *unreasoning faith*, is, however, perfectly allowable, if by it we mean the faith which does not object to, or dispute with, the word of God *understood* as such. In this sense Abraham believed and obeyed with an unreasoning faith; so Peter in the history which contains our text; and so all who have exhibited the faith that pleases God. This is the faith which takes God at his word, and obeys *because it is his word*.

The faith of Peter appears to have been *blind* and *unreasoning*, in the ordinary use of the terms, (1) because he nowhere seems to have doubted or entered into argument with Jesus in regard to the command which he had given, and (2) because it seems to have been a faith *against* reason. The reason of things, the nature of the case, appeared to be against all farther effort at fishing, at that time and place, and, accordingly, the fishermen had given up their enterprise, and were preparing to rest from their labors. But if we look a little more closely at the transaction, we shall see that reason was upon the side of Peter, and that his faith was the direct result of an argument as real as that by which any conclusion in life is attained, or any act performed. No one would suppose that, after having toiled all night and taken nothing, Peter would have hearkened to the word of any other one than Jesus. His reply, most probably, would have been: "Sir, it is useless to fish here any longer; we are going home!" But to Jesus, while he asserts their want of success so far, he takes a second thought: "*Nevertheless*, at thy word, I will let down the net." *At thy word.* We see here exactly how Peter reasoned upon the subject. He saw clearly what, in ordinary circumstances, had been the folly of regarding the words just spoken; on the other hand, he knew Jesus — knew his character, his power, wisdom, loving-kindness — knew that in every command of his was implied power, and the promise of successful obedience, to every one who *would* obey. He knew that while Nature might refuse the demands which he himself might make, she could not refuse to hearken to the voice of the Master. Time and again Peter had seen Nature yield immediate obedience to the word of Jesus. In his own little village he had beheld him, with a word, expel an unclean spirit, so that the spectators cried out, amazed, "What a word is this, for with authority and power he commandeth the unclean spirits, and they come out;"—in his own humble home he had been with Jesus, when, by the utterance of a word, his wife's mother was healed of the fever; and that same day, as the sun was setting, he had seen all that were sick with diverse diseases brought forth before him, and Jesus had restored them all. Peter thus understood that Jesus was the Lord of Nature, and at his word was ready to do that which, but for such knowledge, had appeared in the highest degree absurd. There is no blindness here on the part of Peter, no faith without reason, no faith against reason, or without *reasoning;* the faith and the obedience are, in every sense, intelligent, clear-sighted, rational: *not* to have believed and obeyed had been blind, irrational, insulting to reason.

There was another thing that assisted Peter's faith in the case before us. He *desired* to believe—belief lay along the line of his interests. Generally, we are not aware to how great a degree our beliefs are assisted by our interests, our affections and desires. Arguments which, on ordinary occasions, are of no weight or value whatsoever, present themselves with a most persuasive eloquence when we find it greatly to our advantage to become convinced. We may now understand one great element, perhaps the distinguishing element, of what is called *saving faith* in Jesus; it is the interest which we have in the matter of salvation—our desire, our determination to be saved. The chief reason why so many persons have no faith at all, not even the mere historical faith, so called, is that they have no desire to believe, and oftentimes their determination is *not* to believe, in Jesus. Others really have such faith, believing as truly as any of us the great doctrines of Christ and his salvation, yet are conscious to themselves of having no such faith as saves the soul.

This is because, though believing all the truths of the gospel, they are almost wholly without concern or interest as regards the responsibilities therein involved. The great difference between those who have the mere intellectual assent, and those who believe to the salvation of the soul, is that the former merely *believe*, while the latter are more properly said to *trust*. We must be careful not to confound these two acts of the mind.

One may believe that a certain enterprise, diligently pursued, will conduct to ease, wealth, fame; but he cannot be said to *trust* the enterprise so long as he wholly disregards it, and devotes his energies to a different one. The trust comes in only when we desire, seek, determine, *act* in the case. The devils referred to by St. James really believed, as did likewise those indifferent members of the Church to whom the apostle wrote, but neither the one nor the other trusted, because they *cared* not, and were not intent upon securing to themselves the benefits of their faith. It is *trust* in Jesus which brings salvation, because the sinner, awakened, desiring to flee from wrath, seeing no help in himself, no help in his fellow-man, none in ordinances or works of his own, throws himself upon the mercy of God in Christ as his only but all-sufficient refuge. He that merely believes will never come to Jesus a penitent, sin-smitten soul: he that desires release from sin, and resolves that eternal death shall not become his doom if there is any possible way of escape, will never rest in mere belief; he will determine upon eternal life; will repent; will renounce his sins; will cry out, "God be merciful to me a sinner;" he will seek the promises graciously given; he will find peace by trusting in the Son of God.

Is this faith that saves any the less intelligent than that which merely believes? or is its intelligence of a different character from that of the mere intellectual assent? Some would throw the matter of faith entirely out of the realm of our intellectual powers by calling it the *belief of the heart*, meaning thereby, if they really attach any definite meaning to the phrase, belief of, or by, the emotional nature. But the emotions do not believe, neither can the *heart*, as the word is used by us of the modern day. Belief is the action of the heart, as the term is employed by St. Paul when he declares that with the heart man believeth unto righteousness; but Paul, like the rest of the Hebrews, used the word *heart* in the sense in which we employ the *intellect, mind, reason, understanding.* This meaning of the term we might illustrate by numerous references to the Sacred Scriptures, but a very few must suffice: "An heart to *perceive*"—Deut. xxix. 4; "The heart *knoweth*"—Prov. xiv. 10; "The heart of the rash shall *understand* knowledge"—Isa. xxxii. 4; "A man's heart *deviseth* his way"—Prov. xvi. 9; "Thou shalt also *consider* in thine heart"—Deut. viii. 5; "The former shall not be *remembered*, nor come into mind" (heart)—Isa. lxv. 17; "The *imagination* of man's heart"—Gen. viii. 21; "Every *imagination of the thoughts* of his heart"—Gen. vi. 5.

Even allowing that we might believe by the emotions or affections, these are not the action of the heart, as we understand the word, for this can no more have emotion than the arm, foot, or leg. There are certain emotions which make themselves felt at the heart, but so there are those which are felt in other parts of the body—in the knees, for instance, as when Belshazzar, seeing the hand writing upon the wall, felt the joints of his loins loosed, and his knees smiting together, but no one would suppose that the monarch's knees were affrighted at the thought of the impending doom. Emotion is the movement of the mind, and in no sense of the heart, unless in the use of the term we, like the ancient Hebrews, designate all the powers and achievements of the spiritual man, with no exclusive or even partial reference to the emotional nature.

In this we are not saying that there is no emotion attendant upon the exercise of faith—that trust which saves the soul. There must be emotion both antecedent and auxiliary to it, and it is utterly inconceivable that no emotion in the way of joy or hope should arise consequent to the realization of its power upon the soul. We have just endeavored to show that where no interest or desire is felt—and these are emotions—there will be no coming to Christ; and when one does trust, in the evangelical sense of the word, it is because of his conviction of sin, and his desire of pardon and eternal life. There can be no religion without emotion—not by any means, necessarily, emotion displaying itself by any particular marks or demonstrations, but emotion in the sense of feeling—such feeling as desire, purpose, hope, love, adoration, joy. But it must be borne in mind, nevertheless, that all these are exercises of the mind, not of the heart —of the very same mind that reasons, thinks, calculates, forms plans, concludes. When God requires of us the heart, he means the entire spiritual nature, the complete manhood, intellect, reason, judgment, understanding, conscience, imagination, thought, purpose, faith, love.

Let us here remark upon several terms popularly used to express the religious life and character— *spiritual religion, religion of the heart, old-fashioned religion, scriptural holiness,* and others of like import. These phrases may develop, each, certain distinctive aspects or features of the religious life, yet there is really but one kind of religion—that which has just been referred to—by whatsoever name it may be known or called. If one has religion, in the very nature of things it must be a spiritual religion; it cannot consist in any mere *bodily* sign, movement, or expression; it cannot be of the voice, in either song or shout, nor of the eye in tears; it must likewise be a religion of the heart, comprehending both the intellectual and the emotional faculties of our nature; it must be an old-fashioned religion, at least as old as Jesus, Paul, and Peter, as old as David, Moses, Enoch, Seth, Adam; and it must be scriptural, for we know of no other religion than that which has been taught us in the Scriptures of divine truth. All religion is summed up in "Thou shalt love the Lord thy God with all thine heart, and with all thy soul, and with all thy might," and "Thou shalt love thy neighbor as thyself"—the entire manhood, in all its powers, consecrated to God.

The question is sometimes asked whether we have the exercise of faith under our own control, the idea being that we are *compelled* to believe or disbelieve, according to the nature of the evidence brought before us. We have no hesitation whatsoever in saying that every man may either accept or reject the gospel of Jesus, just as he prefers or determines. It cannot be that God has required us to believe in Christ at the peril of our souls, while at the same time he has failed to give us either sufficient evidence of his being the Saviour of the world, or ability properly to appreciate the evidence bestowed. If God has commanded men to believe, he has certainly given evidence upon which we may found belief, and likewise the power so to employ the evidence that we may arrive at the knowledge of the truth. This is not saying that one can, by an immediate determination or resolve, persuade himself of the truth of the gospel, and then, by another exercise of will, attain the faith which is accounted righteousness: what we mean is, that one, desiring and determining to believe, may put himself upon a course of inquiry which will terminate in the desired result. Here we revert to our statement that our beliefs are largely dependent upon, and modified by, our special interests and affections. One has certainly had but little experience of his reasoning powers not to have perceived how easily he may feel the weight of evidence, or not feel it at all, according to his predisposition as regards the proposition in hand. It is this predisposition adhered to and followed out, oftentimes unconsciously, through the investigation, which largely accounts for the great variety of conclusions to which men arrive in their inquiries. The evidence is the same as presented to all, but far is it from being the same as perceived by all. A determination, or even a little preference for disbelief, if allowed to influence the mind while weighing evidence, will almost surely conduct to a rejection of that which, but for such preference, or with preference the other way, had been admitted among the most positive convictions of the mind. How natural it is for men who have placed certain conclusions before themselves, toward which they are going to argue, to find a thousand convincing considerations of which their opponents had never dreamed; while these latter, on the other hand, draw forth just as many, and, in their own estimation, far more convincing, in support of their denial of the point in question; and, at the close of the strife, each party withdraws more firmly set in their previous beliefs, and wondering at the dullness or dishonesty of their adversaries. We forbear to say more in proof of the power of interest, or preconceived result in the formation of our beliefs. We think our statement will be accepted by all—that we have never known a man come to a saving faith in Jesus while his thoughts, reasonings, inclinations, predilections, were running the other way; nor have we known one to fail of the attainment of such faith who has perseveringly and sincerely sought the same.

There are, we know, numbers who inquire into the evidences of Christian truth who never come to an acceptance of it, while their inquiry is frequently made in the spirit of candor and impartiality; but these men have not been seeking *Jesus* so much as the *evidences of his life and mission*. There is a broad distinction to be noted here. To attempt to know the truth in Jesus by investigating the difficulties of the Mosaic record, by the study of protoplasm, of the nebular hypothesis, or the monuments of Egypt, is beginning too far off—away out in the darkness and the cold. Christ himself is the light of men, and in his light are we to see light. The command is, Look unto me, Come unto me, Call upon the name of the Lord. One may not believe, but let him call. God is near; his ear is open; he is a present help: Him that cometh unto me, I will in nowise cast out. What one needs, who desires to believe, is repentance of sin, and calling upon God for pardon. This is the way to Jesus—the shortest way, the scriptural way, the only sure way—a way in which no man need err.

But the power to come to God no man can have until he comes, *starts*, or *resolves*, to come. He need not bewail his weakness; he need not call for help until he says, I will arise, I will go to Jesus— and then! there is no weakness then! *Arise, take up thy bed*, and the man arose. He did not parley; he resolved to obey, and with the resolution came the power. *Stretch forth thy hand*, and he stretched it forth. *Ephphatha!—be opened*, and his ears were opened, and the string of his tongue was loosed, and he spoke plain. When God commands, he bestows the grace, if one *will* obey; when Jesus calls, he imparts the power, if one *will* only come; when one cries, Save, Lord, I perish, the Hand that made the worlds is extended to bear him up.

Faith is not a mere *arbitrary* appointment of God as the condition of our salvation. The *reasonableness* of it is seen in the fact that, in matters of this *present* life, it is the great bond of union between man and man—the great agency, or power, by which almost all of our interests are subserved. It is by faith in our fellow-man, by faith in the working of natural law, and in the general connections of cause and effect, that all the departments of business are conducted, and all the varied enjoyments of social and domestic life experienced. In ordaining, then, that the just should live by faith, and that by faith we should be first inducted into the hopes and privileges of the gospel of Christ, God required of the world the exercise of no new faculty, nor any new method in the exercise of a faculty long since known; he only required that a power, familiarly used in matters of the secular life, should be employed in the interests of the life to come—that he himself, through Christ, should be made the great object of trust, and that the all-prevailing sacrifice of Jesus—not any so-called righteousness of men—should be looked to as the ground of our salvation.

Faith, therefore, is the *means* by which we enter and continue the service of God, as well as the *condition* upon which Christ's death is made available to us. It must, consequently, be regarded, not as an *end* toward which we are to aspire, but as an agency by which, once admitted into the household of God, we are to abide dutiful servants and loving sons, ever accomplishing the will of the **Father in the use of all our powers** to the **glory of His name. It is not the consummation,** but the beginning **and the instrument,** of the Christian life. Hence, we are **exhorted to** leave the principles of the doctrine of **Christ, not laying** again the foundation of repentance from dead works, and *of faith* toward God, and **to go** on to perfection! Whatever *perfection* here may mean, it means advancement, growth, development, ascent; height on height, Alp **upon Alp, the Christian character** rises high above any elevation we have thus far attained. **Let us not yet count ourselves to have** *apprehended;* forgetting **those things which are behind, and reaching forth unto those things which are before, may we press toward the mark for the prize far** on, ahead and **above!** We **have every** assurance that, by grace, through faith, **we** may make an ever-onward progress. The entire eleventh chapter to the Hebrews is a bright array of the triumphs, by faith, of those who have gone before us, and **the twelfth opens by** exhorting us to lives of like earnest, energetic, lofty achievement, **in the service of God:** "Compassed about with **so great a** cloud of witnesses," testifying the power which they, under God, had wielded in his cause, **let us** be confident, hopeful, bold, **determined.**

The cloud of witnesses! how sublime! how inspiring **the conception!** The **long roll of** the sainted dead pressing round us, giving testimony to what they had severally done through faith! Abel—that through faith he had offered the sacrifice by which he obtained witness that he was righteous; Enoch —that by faith he had been translated, that he should not see death; Noah—that by faith he had prepared the ark, saved the race from annihilation, and become heir of the righteousness which is by faith; Abraham, Sarah, Jacob, Moses, Gedeon, Barak, Samson, Jephthae, David, Samuel, the prophets—that through faith they had subdued kingdoms, wrought righteousness, obtained promises, stopped the mouths of lions, quenched the violence of fire, escaped the edge of the sword, out of weakness were made strong, waxed valiant in fight, turned to flight the armies of the aliens!

Compassed about with so great a cloud of witnesses, and their testimony sounding in our ears, shame upon us if we halt or falter in our course! Let us lay aside every weight, lift up the hands which hang down and the feeble knees, make straight paths for our feet, and look to Jesus. He is the author and the finisher of our faith, and to us is secured, through him, all needed grace and strength, for we are *complete* in him—the Head of all principality and power. Rooted, and built up, and stablished in the faith — the word of Christ dwelling in us richly in all wisdom—we seek those things which are above, where Christ sitteth at the right-hand of God. When Christ, who is our life, shall appear, then shall we also appear with him in glory.

XV.

FAITH IN CHRIST.

BY BISHOP PAINE.

"Let not your heart be troubled: ye believe in God, believe also in me." John xiv. 1.

The whole history of our Lord is full of sublime incidents. Wonders crowded his life, presaging and accompanying his birth, and crowning his death with demonstrations of his divinity. The circumstances under which he used the language of the text impart to it a specially impressive significance. It was on the night of his betrayal, and between the institution of the Eucharist and his mysterious agony in Gethsemane. It was the beginning of his valedictory to his disciples, who were soon to be bereaved by his death, uttered in tones of tenderest affection, yet enjoining a duty which, to them, and to all men to the end of time, is conditional of salvation.

Foretold by prophecies which pointed to this period, and to the place and circumstances of his advent, and described with wonderful minuteness his person, his offices, and the leading incidents in the history of a life that never had a parallel, the majority of the Jews had been ready to come by force and make him their King. They recognized in him the *realization* of their *ideal*, the great Antitype of the signs and symbols hitherto veiled by gorgeous ceremonies and obscure rites, the complement of a thousand apparently incongruous parts lying (as the *disjecta membra* of prophetic conceptions) all along the line of their inspired books and daily ceremonies. In *him*, and him only, all these seemingly incompatible parts united to form an harmonious, grand, and all-perfect character. But alas! while "the common people heard him gladly," and, prompted both by patriotism and piety, were anxious to hail him a lineal descendant of David, and heir to the Messianic throne, yet, misled by their ecclesiastical rulers, and deterred by the iron despotism of Rome, the popular enthusiasm subsided, and Christ's enemies were now determined and united.

The tribes had assembled to celebrate their greatest national feast. The recent raising of Lazarus from his grave within two miles of Jerusalem, followed by his arrival with his disciples at the house of the newly-raised man, had stirred the hearts and concentrated the attention of all. The crisis had come. Impelled by curiosity, and stimulated by hopes founded on prophecies, through the gates of the city, and from the thousand tents which dotted the valleys and hill-tops about Jerusalem, a living stream was moving toward Bethany to see the man who had been dead four days, and the more than man who held the keys that unlocked the hitherto impregnable gates of death and hell.

Who is he? where is he? will he come to the feast? were on every lip, from the Sanhedrim to the dwellers in the mountains of Lebanon and the desert of Gaza. The company from Bethany, headed by Jesus, and accompanied by Lazarus, Bartimeus, and others who had joined the little band of his disciples, met the surging throng, and, after a pause on the summit of Mount Olivet, slowly swept down to the eastern gate, amid the shouts of thousands, in which the clear, sweet voices of innocent children mingled, bearing into the holy temple the "King of Israel," the "Son and the Lord of David." Assuming the office, he at once exercised the authority of King of Zion, by exposing the corruption of the hierarchy, expelling by force the mercenaries who infested the temple, and proclaiming the subjects and laws of the mediatorial kingdom. He had accepted the position, and no longer postpones the trial; but, the time having fully come, he moves to the front to meet the momentous issues involving the interests of heaven, earth, and hell.

Twice afterward did our blessed Lord seem to shudder and draw back for awhile from the fierce and terrible ordeal—once, late in the night, after our text had been spoken, the night of betrayal and blasphemy, when, alone in grief and agony inconceivable, he had thrice uttered those words which no man should ever hear without shame and awe— "Father, let this cup pass, if it be possible;" but that involuntary outburst of grief and prayer having been answered of his Father by the strengthening presence of an angel, the sufferer at once became calm, and, rising up, went forth to meet the conspirators, saying, "*Thy will be done.*" Again, at the memorable ninth hour of the day, when, after a night of unparalleled horrors, tried, rejected, insulted, condemned, crucified—having hung three hours on the cross in such bitter agonies as only his pure and sensitive soul could feel under the burden of the sins of the world—he was forced to confess himself forsaken by his Father: "My God, my God, why hast thou forsaken me?" To this appeal no strengthening angel nor assuring answer came; but the sky grew darker; the vail of the temple was rent; an earthquake shook the frame-work of the globe; rocks burst asunder, and graves yawned. Amidst all these scenes, and notwithstanding these portents, the brave and still confiding Son exclaimed, "Father, into thy hands I commend my spirit!" and, bowing his bleeding, thorn-crowned head, gave up the ghost.

> O Lamb of God, was ever pain,
> Was ever love, like thine!

No; Christ could not withdraw from the conflict —or, if ever it might seem to have been possible, certainly not after he had "come up openly to the Passover." He had committed himself and his helpless followers, and put himself and them in the power of his foes. Henceforth every thing rapidly converges to the great end. Foreseeing all the scenes in the progress of this drama, and submitting to endure them not the less willingly because he foreknew them all, the meek and blessed Prince of Peace seeks to counterplot their diabolical aims by inspiring and arming his followers by his last address. It was all that he could now do, and what he only could do. *"Let not your heart be troubled: ye believe in God, believe also in me."* How appropriate to the condition and circumstances was the theme! There were troubled hearts in that room "on that dark and doleful night." The sudden retreat of Judas after he received the sop, and heard the significant admonition, uttered in tones inaudible to the other disciples, "What thou doest do quickly," followed by the rebuke to self-reliant Peter, and the prediction of his denial of the Master before the third crowing of the cock, must have troubled and startled them all. No wonder the disciples "looked upon one another" in alarm. A wolf in the fold! To add to this, and worse than this, he had just told them that it would be only "a little while I am with you;" and, worst of all, "Whither I go ye cannot come." Could they hear this unmoved? Was not the Master also troubled? Often had he been grieved before, but now the dagger is from the hand of a trusted friend. What a spectacle! a deeply-troubled heart pouring out its pent-up sympathies in soothing others! And who so competent to minister to the sorrowing and suffering as he who has himself "felt the same"? An indispensable qualification for the high-priesthood of our troubled and tempted race is to have realized "in all points" the trials and troubles of humanity. The supernatural loveliness and adorable perfection of Christ's character are most impressively seen in the closing days of his life. Well might he then say, "Now is the Son of man glorified, and God is glorified in him." The last rays of closing day are the more precious because they are the last. The last words from the pale and quivering lips of a loved and honored friend are treasured imperishably in the memory of survivors.

"Let not your heart be troubled." But what is meant by this prohibition? Is it such a stoicism as renders us indifferent to passing events? a stolid condition of mind, which deadens our emotional nature, and paralyzes action? Is it a Dead Sea state of the heart, without wind, waves, or current, when the sluggish soul floats and drifts without aim or effort? or is it merely want of thoughtfulness as to the present and future welfare of ourselves or others? Nothing could be farther from the meaning of the text. He knew they would have tribulation in the world; their faith and patience would be tried. It must be so—so while life should last. It had been so with him, and he was just then descending into an abyss of darkness and trouble which extorted even from him the confession, "My soul is exceeding sorrowful unto death!" This mystery of mysteries can only find its solution in the vicarious character of the Sufferer, the necessity of his personal experience to fully qualify him for the office of the priesthood, and to demonstrate, by passing triumphantly through this last great trial, his just claim as Son of God and Saviour of man. The text does not say, Let not your heart be sensible of grief and sad on account of your present condition or prospective trials, but be not so distressed and cast down as to abandon your vocation and disqualify you for duties. You must temper your natural sorrow by a supernatural joy—may be cast down without being destroyed. Judas may betray me, Peter deny me, Caiaphas and Pilate unite to revile and crucify me, and men and devils hold a jubilee over my death and your martyrdom; but keep heart and hope. It is only for a little time. "I will come again." My degradation is a preliminary to my exaltation—our temporary separation to my speedy return and our eternal reunion. In order that this end may be attained, it is necessary on your part that you shall not only believe in God, as you do, but you must " believe also in me." From which we infer that a *belief in God is not sufficient to relieve the heart from trouble, but that a true and abiding faith in Christ will do* it.

No Christian can deny the existence of God. It is the foundation-doctrine of all religion as well as of all true philosophy. The atheist is a heresiarch in theology, a sophist in science, the foe of all order, moral, social, and political. He ignores the relations between beings—the fatherhood of God and the brotherhood of men, and their consequent mutual obligations, and, by thus destroying the basis of duty, resolves all virtue into policy, and consigns a life evolved by chance to a grave unillumined by hope. His creed, if he may be said to have one, is such a monstrous contradiction of the laws of evidence, of the dictates of reason and common sense, and the instinctive cravings of the human heart, that we need no argument to show its fallacy. Its philosophical absurdity is equaled only by its horrid impiety. And yet he *has a heart* which will throb with troubles that will not down at his bidding. He can no more prevent it than he can resist the law of gravitation. He is isolated from his normal relation to his great Father, and his soul cries out for divine sympathy, but it is a cry in a desert. No answer comes back but the echo of his own despairing wail. There is none to reply. Whether there are really any theoretical atheists, and whether the belief in God is natural or educational, it is not necessary to argue. It would be as difficult as useless for our purpose to test the question. While "the heavens declare the glory of God, and the firmament showeth his handiwork," and "things that are made make known his eternal power and Godhead" to all who in any way may have attained the conception of a supernatural being, yet, whether such a concept would *originate* in the mind, is thought very doubtful. Nor is it probable the experiment has been or will be made. Tradition, and revelation in some form, have traveled with the race, insomuch that no considerable number of people have been found together who have not received the great primal truth of history. But what if Nature could teach the superhuman origin of the world, can it make known God's will, his character, and his designs, with sufficient clearness and authority as to constitute that idea a rule of action and a solace in trouble? It is a mere negation, and consequently is utterly inoperative.

Nor can deism, any more than atheism, meet the wants and relieve the troubles of the human heart. No view which simple deism presents of God, providence, and futurity, can satisfy it. The disciples to whom the text was addressed were Jews—they believed on God—it was the highest type of theism, vastly higher than that held by Mohammedan or pagan philosophers. They believed in the one true, only Lord God—the God of the old covenant—but still their minds and hearts were deeply troubled. Like the eunuch reading Isaiah, they needed an interpreter. Is Nature a competent one? Are there thousands of gods, as then taught in the mythology of the most cultured and noblest nations in the pagan world? Or is he *"One"*? Is he to be loved and trusted, or feared and shunned? If propitious, how can his favor be retained? if forfeited, how regained? Is he good essentially and unchangeably? or capricious, by turns kind and cruel? Does Nature satisfactorily answer these questions? We assert that reason, unaided, does not—it never has. Can it reconcile the present condition of our world with infinite wisdom, power, and goodness, without assuming the historic truth of the Bible? Who is so blind as not to perceive that, amidst the displays of wisdom and goodness in the physical universe, disorder and evil on our planet are equally apparent?

See the *ocean!* What a mirror of the glorious stellar world! Imagination hears in the gentle heaving of its billows, ceaselessly chafing its resounding shores, the pean of its great Creator; but when the heavens grow black with clouds, and the tempest, with its blazing and blinding lightning, its crashing thunder, and the deafening roar of its wild waves, comes down upon its late peaceful bosom, lashing it into a furious and destructive whirlpool, ingulfing innocent thousands who look up and cry in vain for rescue, what lesson does this scene of death and ruin teach? Is this the voice of the great Creator in tones of wrath or mercy? Do the doubts and fears of the troubled hearts subside into filial trust? If we turn to the *sky*—the heavens which declare his glory when calm and transparent by day, or when gemmed with countless stars of radiant beauty at night, shedding down their twinkling sheen upon mountains and vales, rivers and rivulets, tombs and turrets—it may easily be imagined that we catch the low, sweet notes of a celestial minstrelsy,

> Forever singing as they shine,
> The hand that made us is Divine.

But when every heavenly light is eclipsed, and the dread monotone of the coming tornado is heard approaching, interrupted only, as it rolls on its pathway of clouds, by coruscations of lightning and bursts of thunder, until, presently, it sweeps in resistless fury, like the very genius of destruction, through venerable forests, cultivated plains, and marts of commerce, does it not seem that the prince and power of the air has assumed his throne?

Nor does the *earth* itself, the abode of our race, which, according to the Bible, was adorned and beautified as a paradise of fertility, beauty, and purity—fit home for our ancestors, "who were made only a little lower than the angels"—the antechamber of heaven itself, where God held audience with them—more clearly solve the great questions of the character of its Maker, when unassisted reason becomes Nature's interpreter. Its changing livery, as the seasons succeed each other; its undulating hills and valleys; its mountains, rising into the region of perpetual snow, and glittering in mid-heaven like icebergs in a great aërial ocean; its unbroken ranges of frowning ramparts, which stretch across whole continents; its majestic rivers; its cataracts; its silvery lakes; its murmuring rills; its verdant plains; its grass, herbs, flowers, and fruits, proclaim his goodness and his power. But these mountains have been thrown up by deeply-seated internal fires, and three hundred active volcanoes now throb and glow in the interior, and anon pour forth rivers of blazing lava to devastate the land. Not more than one-tenth of the earth's surface is fit for the comfortable residence of man. Rocks and desert wastes, frozen seas and burning sands, precipitous cliffs and frightful chasms, make up a large portion of its crust. The nutritious products of the earth of spontaneous growth are few, even in the most favored latitudes. The sweat of the brow is the price paid for daily bread, and many fail to obtain it even at that price. The irregularities of the seasons, storms, depredations of insects, floods, and other unavoidable casualties, frequently frustrate the honest, hard toilers, leaving many to suffer, and some to starve. Every year gaunt Famine, with hollow eyes, emaciated, outstretched hands, and sepulchral voice, lifts the wail, "Come over and help us ere we die!" Even to-day, before the cry of the Irish famine has died away, or the ships that bore them the generous gifts of fraternal sympathy have returned, there comes the same appeal from the cradle of our race: Millions in Asia perishing for bread! Surely earth has long ago lost her paradise, and it has not yet been regained.

But consider *man* himself. If his present condition is the direct result of divine agency, as deism must maintain, how does his physical, intellectual, and moral state illustrate the character of his Maker? Discarding the biblical history of his creation and fall, infidels have not only been sadly puzzled to account for his origin, but scarcely less so by his recorded history. "Fearfully and wonderfully made" as to his physical organization, invested with astonishing powers of mind, and a still more mysterious moral sense, taking cognizance of right and wrong, and approaching a loftier order of beings in his capabilities and aspirations—alas, how often are these noble endowments subjected to the despotism of passion and beastly instincts, illustrating the fable of the Centaur—half-human and half-beast! History shows war to have been his occupation, sensuality his chief enjoyment, and self his divinity. The exceptions to this rule have been so few, especially out of Christian countries, as to prove the rule.

But it is held that the uniformity of Nature's laws furnishes sufficient ground as to the character of God as to induce to piety, trust, and filial love. We deny it. While there is a general uniformity in the operations of the material universe, we deny that to man, individually, it is so obvious as to remove doubt, and relieve the heart from trouble upon the momentous issue of his present relation to his Creator, or his final welfare. God's providential dealings with man, viewed from a deistical stand-point, do not harmonize always with the doctrine that he is the object of divine favor. Whence come sorrow and suffering? and, if suffering is *natural*, why may it not be perpetual? Why is disease in various forms universally prevalent? Whence those terrible epidemics which spring up suddenly and sweep away millions to an untimely grave? Infantile innocence and hoary age, the pure and the vicious, the benefactors and malefactors of society, statesmen, poets, orators, patriots, female beauty, maternal gentleness, and manly nobleness, suffer and die alike. "There is no house without a skeleton," no hearth-stone without a shadow. Often the fairest flowers are the first to fade—the most worthy and useful the first to die. Is not some revelation wanted to explain these apparent contradictions, in order to assure our faith and assuage our grief? Does a kind father treat his children thus, and leave them ignorant both of the *cause* and *design* of their condition? Nor let it be thought sufficient to reply, as to the cause of this disorder and suffering, that "Deity is not bound to explain, nor to interfere with, the course of events;" for, if we might forego a knowledge of the cause, may we not, with good reason, reverently urge to know if there is a *remedy*, and, if so, what it is?

Heretofore our remarks have had reference mainly to the conflict between *Nature*, as seen in the condition of our planet, and more especially in the physical infirmities and afflictions of men, and our conceptions of the Deity; but when we consider man in his higher and nobler relation of a moral, spiritual, and accountable being, the question assumes a graver aspect. How deep and wide the chasm yawns between what he might be, and ought to be, and what he is! Who can bridge that abyss? Human reason, conscience, and laws, have all tried it for ages, and failed. This difference between the ideal and the real of human character and conduct proves his guilt and consequent degradation, and presents him in an attitude toward his Maker which no other creature on earth sustains. Vegetables and animals, in their natural state, attain their legitimate end, and, after their kind, reach perfection. But man is the *anomaly.* He, alone, fails to fulfill the purpose for which his intellectual and moral attributes adapt him. In him only conscience resides, and is in ceaseless antagonism with passion, and is often its victim. He believes in God, but, ignoring him, neither fears nor loves him—with capabilities which assimilate him to angels, he too often resembles the infernal spirit, and counterplots his Creator. An eagle, made to roam the sky, he dabbles in the mire of the barn-yard for the filthy muck-worm. A lion, and "monarch of all he surveys," he is the degraded vassal of ignoble animal instincts, notwithstanding all the restraints which can be found in civilization, example, and the denunciations of "eternal judgment."

Let it not be objected that this picture is darker

than the reality. Would that it were! but, alas! we know it is not. Nor let it be said that, while atheism and deism, as formerly inculcated, may be inadequate to the demands of the mind and heart, the late discoveries in science and theology have developed in pantheism, naturalism, and rationalism, a solution of the problems of humanity. But while these several systems differ apparently from those already discussed, and also from each other, they are only the same old theories of infidelity modified to suit the emergency—the rallied remnant of the defeated cohorts falling back to a new position—their names changed, but not their identity, nor their *animus*. Their common origin—and their " name is Legion "—is atheism under different *aliases*. Old-fashioned atheism denied God; pantheism denies his personality; rationalism, while in words it acknowledges his existence, banishes him to a distant solitude, and practically dethrones him. The naturalists talk flippantly about him, and yet substitute the laws of nature for him, as if laws enact and execute themselves. In fact, the latest theory of the advanced scientists—the evolutionists—have practically discarded an actual God, and reverted to bald atheism. Spiritualism, as taught by some who wear the name and livery of the Christian ministry, is only baptized rationalism. It admits only a nominal difference between natural and revealed religion, their favorite maxim being that "every man possesses in his own mind the *absolute truth*, and that the objects of worship are accidental circumstances peculiar to the age, sect, nation, or individual;" and finally, that "the next great reformation is to deliver us, by philosophical spiritualism, from the two great idols—the Bible and Christ," "as Protestantism delivered us from the tyranny of the Church and the pope." May we not respond, in the name of God and humanity, From such reformers "good Lord deliver us!"

Having looked in vain into these empty cisterns of philosophic speculations, and found in them no water of life for famishing and sorrowing souls, the great question recurs, *Is there any remedy?* May deliverance be found and felt—deliverance from doubts of mind and troubles of heart, from the domination of evil passions, the crushing sense of guilt, and the foreshadowing dread of avenging justice? To the agonizing soul which asks this question there comes from all the schools of philosophic speculation no reliable reply.

Having attempted to show that the contemplation of God without reference to Christ cannot relieve the heart of trouble, we proceed to explain—

How the Christian revelation accomplishes this end.

1. *It exhibits the true character of God*, and the real condition and wants of man. As the basis of every system of religion is the character of its God, so, to err here, is to err fundamentally. It is an error which cannot be eliminated from the system, but is inseparably interwoven with the whole theory of its doctrines, precepts, and practice. A bad foundation ruins the whole superstructure. While gratefully accepting the truths taught us in Nature—that first

volume of revelation—and in those great historic and theocratic developments of his character made in the inspired writings of the Old Testament, and, therefore, like the disciples, we " believe in *God*"— we hold that these revelations, however true and sufficient for their time and purpose, were incomplete. They marked out the foundation and reared the frame-work; but to beautify, perfect, and fully utilize the great temple, the Lord himself must come into it, and fill it with his glory. We must see his glory as revealed in the Son, " the only-begotten of the Father, full of grace and truth."

The deistical view of God represents him as the *cause*, and the biblical view as also the *Father* and *Governor*, of the universe; and, while the former stops there, and practically neutralizes the efficiency of this great doctrine, the Bible announces that, " in the unity of nature in the Godhead, there are three Persons—the Father, the Son, and the Holy Spirit —of one substance, power, and Godhead." To the first is ascribed creation and preservation; to the second, redemption and mediation ; and to the third, regeneration and comforting. Now, inasmuch as infinite perfection excludes all imperfection, or whatever is essentially different, so any number of infinitely perfect beings must be alike. They cannot differ in nature, and thus must be in reality one Being. *In this sense,* " *these Three are One.*" Between these Three there is a *distinction* of *personality*, without a *difference of nature*. This distinct personality is not to be understood in a strictly philosophical sense, or of official *relations*, but to each distinct volitions and works are ascribed, and worship offered, as to the Supreme Divinity. As to the manner of their union in the Godhead, that is, of course, incomprehensible to a finite mind.

The necessity for a farther revelation of God than Nature can give grows out of the fact that sin has been introduced, and it is to explain the discrepancy between the character of the Creator and the condition of his creatures, and at the same time present through Christ an all-sufficient remedy for sin, and all the troubles and ills flowing from it. The entrance of sin into the world is the key that unlocks the mystery of the present state of the moral and physical world. Every form of speculative philosophy ignores this fearful factor in the solution of the problem. The Bible only furnishes it. It shows that moral evil was introduced by an act of a human free agent, to forcibly prevent which act would have destroyed his freedom and his responsibility, and would have been a virtual admission that the divinely-instituted plan of the creation, endowment, and government of man, was wrong. With sin, this *new* element, "came death and all our woe." It teaches that this sin, being the act of the first man as a probationer, and the federative representative of his race, not only brought guilt upon himself, but death also upon his posterity; and that it is not merely a negative thing, a defect of positive goodness, but a positive evil in the heart, affecting all the mental powers, and manifesting itself in the conduct of all men. May we not say reverently that, in this great emergency, only one of two things remained—either let the divine economy proceed to the full execution of the penalty of the violated law, and thus sustain its dignity and the authority of its Maker, or *intervene* in such a manner and degree as to attain this end of the divine government, and at the same time provide for the rescue of the culprit, and the salvation of his hapless descendants. If the *latter* could be done without detracting from the authority of the law, obscuring the majesty of the Lawgiver and the heinousness of sin, it would seem to be a reasonable conclusion that it would be done. If the penalty incurred should be executed on the transgressor to its full extent, then, as we apprehend it, the race would have terminated by the death of the personally guilty. How this result would have affected the subsequent history of our planet, or what course the divine economy would have adopted in substitution of the original one, belongs to the realm of speculation, into which we do not choose here to intrude. Suffice to say, for the present, that the resources of the infinite God were equal to this momentous emergency, and the alternative of *redemption* was projected by the All-prescient Mind.

2. It offers a competent Saviour and a full salvation upon reasonable conditions. Intervention, or redemption, by *power* alone would be ineffectual, because it would only act externally; and the remedy must also be intellectual, moral, and spiritual, to meet all the demands of the case. An advocate was needed—a redeemer, a ransom, and reconciliation. It must be by one not himself disqualified by sin—not a disloyal advocate of traitors. In nature

and character he must rise to the dignity of his high commission, and yet not be insulated from the lowliness and infirmities of those whose cause he represents. He must know both parties—fully comprehend the law and facts—must be in sympathy with both, and the equal of either. While, as an actual sinner, he could not be heard at the bar of supreme justice, he must be the sinless, piacular substitute of a world of sinners. Above the law, its claims and curses, he must come *under* it, and atone for its violation. He must be more than man, and less than God, and yet be truly God and man. Where can such a one be found? In whom may such seemingly paradoxical and incongruous characteristics inhere? Where is he? From the throne of the doomed prince, hell, and the wide domain of sin and woe, the answer comes, "*Not here.*" From the higher seat of Michael, the archangel warrior, "who standeth for thy people," and from Gabriel and the countless hosts in that glorious, wider realm of light and life eternal, the reply is, "*We are not able;*" and earth, with despairing wail, cries, "*Not here! not here!*"

Well might the holy apostle say of that awfully sublime scene, as unfolded to him in that apocalyptic vision, "And *I wept much.*" And then "the Lamb came forth and took the book out of the right-hand of him that sat upon the throne," and all those firstborn sons of glory "fell down and worshiped before the *Lamb, and sung a new song.*" Nor is it strange that John ceased to weep, and joined in the anthem which celebrates the redemption of humanity. Men and angels sing this song in unison. In the biblical doctrine of the *Trinity in Unity the possibility of redemption is laid. A tripersonality* in unity of nature is indispensable. "Lo, *I* come to do *thy* will, O God!" "If *I* go, I will send the *Comforter* to you," "and he shall *reprove* the world," etc.

The second Person in the adorable Trinity, who was in the beginning with God, and was God, the Son whose throne is forever and ever, whom all the angels are commanded to worship, who created all things for himself, and was before all things, who is God over all, and blessed forever, was incarnated, born of the Virgin—very God and truly man—being begotten of the Holy Ghost, came forth from the bosom of the Father as Mediator between God and man. Such he was preëminently qualified to be, perfectly meeting all the demands of the divine law and the necessities of man. He, and he only, in all God's universe, was able to save man, and, in saving a lost and ruined race, glorify God. This process required *atonement, regeneration,* and the *resurrection* from the dead. Without an atonement there could be no pardon; "and without shedding of blood is no remission of sin." The penalty of sin is death, temporal or natural, moral or spiritual, and, by consequence, eternal. Whether we consider the object against whom it is committed, the far-reaching consequences of unrestrained and unpunished transgression, we must feel that *satisfaction* must be made, or the penalty be inflicted. Justice, truth, and even divine goodness, required it to maintain order essential to the welfare of the universe and the glory of God. To subserve this great purpose the Son of God, in the person of Jesus Christ, comes forth. As God incarnate, he stands as a fit Mediator, being equally allied to both parties. In his human nature, of " soul and body subsisting," he places on the altar of sacrifice *his all*—his mind and will to obey, his body to be tortured, and to die—" his soul as an offering for sin"—until, wrung to the height of distress, he exclaims, " Now is my soul troubled—what shall I say?" " Thy will be done." " It is finished," and " gave up the ghost." The mysterious union of his divine with his human nature, which constituted his personality as Jesus Christ our Lord, and imparted to this " oblation of himself" a moral and legal worth and merit, is, and ever will be, without a parallel. The character of the Sufferer, the nature and intensity of his sufferings, his voluntary sacrifice of life upon which death had no original claim, the acceptance of the substitution of the Advocate for the criminal by the Father, as shown by the voice from heaven as he hung on the cross, his resurrection from the tomb, his triumphant ascension, and his installation as High-priest of humanity, demonstrate both the fitness of his claim and his recognition as Redeemer and Mediator. He had the power and the right to lay down his life and to take it again. And he did it. It was a voluntary, vicarious, and piacular offering for the sins of the world. It originated in the love of God, satisfied justice, and while it showed his hatred of sin, it sustained all the righteous ends of his government by the conditions of salvation;

it so gloriously illustrated his character of God, as Father and Governor of the world, as to give the highest incentive to true piety and the sternest rebuke to sin.

In tracing the outlines of the redemptory scheme, and defining the parts borne by the respective divine persons in accomplishing it, let us bear in mind that the *resurrection of the body* is, in the order of time, the final great act in the triumph of Christ over natural evil. At death the soul passes into paradise—Abraham's bosom. The body returns "to earth as it was;" but "*all* that are in the graves shall hear his voice, and shall come forth; they that have done good, unto the resurrection of life; and they that have done evil, unto the resurrection of damnation" (John v. 28, 29). And when the last echo of that "voice" shall have returned, changing the living and awakening the dead—when every grave shall have yielded its prisoner, the ocean given up its slumberers, and the countless myriads of humanity of all climes and ages shall have come forth,

> From world to luminous world afar,
> As the universe spreads its flaming walls,

assembled by the resistless call of God, shall stand for trial in the universal judgment at the bar of God; then, having finished his Mediatorial commission, will the Son receive, by acclamation, his promised throne, and proceed to execute supreme judicial power. The scenes that follow will be retributive, the results unchangeable and eternal. The drama of probationary existence will be closed forever.

"They that were ready" entered with the bridegroom into the marriage-supper of the Lamb, and the door be shut; and those not ready, driven to the prison of the damned, and that door too be closed forever and ever.

Inseparably associated in this system with the works and offices of Christ is the doctrine of the *third* Person in the adorable Trinity — the Holy Spirit. All those scriptural arguments which so clearly prove the personality and divinity of the Son, apply to establish the same claims to him; and but for him, and his coöperation with the Father and the Son, the great scheme would fail. The moral depravity of our race, our infirmities and heart-troubles, would render the efforts of the Father and the Son abortive without his regenerative, strengthening, and comforting agency. The new birth and *holiness* are as needful as pardon. "Ye must be born again — born of the Spirit." "Without holiness no man shall see the Lord." And these are the works of the Holy Spirit. Like to the Father, and the Son, he is in the Scriptures called God (Acts v. 3). Divine attributes and acts are ascribed to him (Heb. ix. 14; Ps. cxxxix. 7; John xiv. 20; 1 Cor. ii. 10, 11). He is worshiped as God (Matt. xxviii. 9). His name is associated with the names of Father and Son in baptism, and a special degree of guilt and punishment are denounced to sins against him. He "proceedeth from the Father and the Son — is of one substance, majesty, and glory, with the Father and the Son, very and eternal God."

Having attempted to show the insufficiency of mere theism, and of every form and modification of skepticism, to afford substantial comfort to hearts troubled by doubts, fears, and trials, and, on the other hand, the abundant provision presented in the gospel scheme for all our wants by the gracious co-operation of the Godhead, as manifested through our Lord Jesus Christ, let us inquire how we can avail ourselves of the benefits of this provisionary plan. The *answer is*, "*Believe also in Me.*"

The entire plan of salvation is conditional. What the Redeemer *only* could do, he has done for us. His death was the condition upon which " we were reconciled to God." The benefits of his vicarious sufferings extend to the *race* he represents. The curse, or condemnation for original sin, is lifted from it by Him who " was made a curse for us;" and the free gift is come upon all to justification to life, insomuch that all the race who are *incapable* of complying with the laws of Christ are unconditionally saved from condemnation. But those who can understand their obligations, and the reasons for obedience, are placed on a different foundation. Their salvation is conditional. They must accept the provision made and tendered them, or they cannot be saved. Who but Christ has the right to prescribe this condition? He has done it, and it is *faith in him*.

This is a most wise and gracious prerequisite. It recognizes our faculties and all our wants, and is adapted to our condition. It says to sinful and troubled man, Lift your eye to the Redeemer. He is not only faultless in himself, but, standing in the relation he sustains to God and man in the economy of redemption, his character is surpassingly interesting. Faith and philosophy, reason and revelation, point alike to him as the visible representative of the Godhead, and the sympathizing friend of humanity. His is the bright excellence which has disarmed hostility, on which so many millions have dwelt with unmingled love and veneration — an excellence which no fiction or history besides furnishes us — in whom power and wisdom are subordinated to perfect love. It is the picture of one gentle toward the infirmities and follies of man — patient with his waywardness, lovingly forgetful of his wrongs — of one who "never broke the bruised reed," who came to soothe and bind up the troubled heart, to give deliverance to the captive, to welcome penitence to his feet, and to offer to the weary rest. In a word, it is a picture whose whole life was one long yearning of sympathy with the sorrows of humanity, whose death expiated the sin of the world, and whose resurrection and mediation reöpened the long-closed gate of paradise to the troubled in heart. To Him, then, let the weary and heavy-laden bring their burden of sin, doubt, and grief, and lay them at the foot of the cross. Let all who believe in God and tremble, believe also in Him to whose divinity heaven, earth, and hell, bore testimony. Are they ignorant, he is their wisdom; are they condemned, he is their justification; are they depraved, he is their sanctification; are they blind, impotent, friendless, and wretched, he is an ever-present and all-sufficient Saviour. All this assuredly he is to them that *believe* in him. Faith in him honors the Father who sent him, the Holy Spirit who testified of him. *It is his due.* To discredit the Son is to give the lie direct to God, who declared him to be his Son to angels, who worship him, and to millions of the wisest and best men, living and dead, who trusted him. A humble, penitential faith in Christ, and an implicit trust in him as our Redeemer, is the condition of forgiveness—the only one adapted to our state and practicable to us—the only one which protects the divine government by leading to loving obedience to God, practical charity to men, insures the victory "that overcometh the world," and provides for all our wants here and hereafter. *This is our remedy.* We have no other—we need no other. "Earth hath no sorrow that Heaven cannot heal."

XVI.

LESSONS FROM THE BAPTISM OF JESUS BY JOHN THE BAPTIST.

BY THE REV. H. C. SETTLE, D.D.,
Louisville Conference.

"Suffer it to be so now, for thus it becometh us to fulfill all righteousness." Matt. iii. 15.

The earthly life of Jesus was a model life. At twelve years of age he was thoughtful and studious. His life-work was well defined even then, and earnestly and wisely he engaged in the preparation for it. He was about thirty years old when he spake the words of the text, but still unprepared to enter upon his ministry. Eighteen years have passed away since he spake those strange words to his troubled parents: "Wist ye not that I must be about my Father's business?" And he has not yet presumed to feel that his time for work has come. Although Jesus began a preparation for work earlier in life than do most children, he was also longer engaged in that preparatory course, and entered upon the responsibilities of public life at a later period than do most men. If the life of Jesus be God's ideal of a correct human life, may not the length of time spent in preparation for work be an important feature in this model life? May not Heaven be teaching us this truth—not the number of years given to work, but the nature of it, and the spirit of engagement in it, and the manner of its performance, are the subjects of interest to Heaven?

The importance of this lesson can scarcely be overestimated. The great fault of our times is haste. Our people are indeed a fast people. Young men, certainly not more highly gifted than Jesus, have finished their education, graduated, mastered professions, and entered upon public life, and assumed the responsibilities of important offices, before they have attained the age of Jesus, at which he stood in the presence of John the Baptist, modestly but earnestly asking baptism at his hands. Girls eighteen years of age enter, without fear, upon the delicate duties and weighty responsibilities of womanhood.

It is probable that this contrast between human lives, as we see them, and Heaven's ideal life, as realized in Jesus, explains the fact that his life, commencing without promise, was successful, grand, and beneficent; while multitudes, beginning with promise, end in failure.

Hasty commencement of work, assuming responsibility before thorough preparation to bear it has been made, will go far toward a satisfactory explanation of the demoralization of our times. To work well in any department of life, something more than information is required. There is a difference and a distance between knowledge and wisdom; and some time must elapse between the acquirement of knowledge and the acquirement, or development rather, of ability to wisely and thoroughly use what we have. The child is physically a man in miniature. He never will have an additional sense, nor an additional member. Muscles and sinews are all in place, but who would think of putting a man's burden upon a child's shoulders? He has all that is necessary to man's work save the development of muscle and sinew. Until that development is brought about by preparatory exercise he cannot do a man's work. And woe to him if he seriously and persistently attempt it! and bitter disappointment to those who expect it of him!

There are intellectual sinews and muscles, and there are sinews and muscles to the moral man. To bear responsibilities, to meet the obligations of a public life, to carry the burdens and resist the strains that try all who work among men, something more is needed than that which our parents and teachers can give us—something more than can be acquired in any way. Knowledge of men, knowledge of self, knowledge of God, all are important; but these must do in us, intellectually and morally, what food and exercise are doing for the boy physically; and, intellectually and morally, we must become what the boy, at last, becomes physically, ere we are fitted for life, and prepared to "quit us like men." Three years of a man's work is worth far more to the world than many years' work of a child. Three years of work wisely done is better than fifteen years of unwise work. This thought is so important as to justify a repetition. The world is more benefited by three years' earnest work of a wise man than it can possibly be by the life-time of one who goes from school into life confident that the professors have furnished all that is necessary for the march and the battle.

If there ever was a life and work which justified haste, it was the life and work of Jesus. In moments of careless thinking we have wished that he could have lived longer, or commenced his public ministry sooner. But the time of his work was inconsiderable in contrast with the time of preparation for it. The world can better do without you, young man, for years to come, than it could spare Jesus all the eighteen or twenty years he spent in obscure preparation. And the world will be the better, and you the happier, if you will lay to heart this lesson from the model life, and think upon the important duties and weighty responsibilities you are expected to meet and discharge, and be not rash in assuming them, but, like Jesus, prepare for them, that you may do your work, and exclaim, at the close of your life, with satisfaction akin to his, " It is finished."

Let us now come to the study of the words of the text in search of other lessons from this model life. "Suffer it to be so now." This is the language of one who "*is to increase*," addressed to one who "*is to decrease*." To John, who has just now said of Jesus, " He that cometh after me is mightier than I, whose shoes I am not worthy to bear"—to John, who thus recognizes himself as unworthy to be even the servant of Jesus, does Jesus say, "*Suffer* it to be so now." These are strange words. "Suffer"—

what is its meaning? Used in this way, its meaning is this, according to the dictionaries: Allow, permit, do not forbid, do not hinder. But there is another meaning in this word thus used by Jesus, the Model-man, emerging from his obscurity and about entering upon his public career, which is to end not upon the cross of shame, but upon the throne of universal empire. In this word is recognition of John's position and authority. Here, at the very threshold of his wonderful life, Jesus gives us a lesson of subordination.

The speaker is the Son of God, fully conscious of his relationship, and of his consequent inherent superiority to John, and of the greater glory of the work he will soon begin; for all this John has declared, or intimated, and Jesus has admitted; nevertheless, he says to John, "Suffer it to be so now." In official position John is superior now to Jesus, the Son of man. And Jesus recognizes this fact, and would not have John forget it, or ignore it. Subordination, therefore, is the lesson taught us in this portion of the text.

Insubordination appears in the fatal transaction of Eden, and through all the sighing ages since it has been the leading evil spirit whose wings have eclipsed the light, and by whom individuals, and families, and States, and nations, have been led into dissatisfaction, and rebellion, and grief. The discipline of the family and school cannot create the spirit of subordination. Ordinarily, recognition of parental and collegiate authority is constrained. Though outwardly the boy may be submissive, yet inwardly he chafes, and is longing for the time when he shall be his own man—independent of all restraint. It is not a willing, cheerful recognition of authority, and submission to it, that exists, and are manifested by the masses of young people; hence the departure in after-life from old land-marks—hence the erratic thoughts, the erratic speeches, and the libertine-lives of many who, in early youth, seemed observant of the proprieties. The Apostle Paul declares that the carnal mind is not subject to law of God, neither indeed can be. Now, it appears evident that, if we will not recognize the authority of God, and cheerfully submit to do and to be what he wills, there certainly can be no authority which we will recognize, and no law that we will obey, but as we are compelled. But, though this is true, and men, natural men, still aspire to be as gods, that they may be a law unto themselves, no man is prepared to work among men and for men, wisely and efficiently, until he has learned subordination. We think, therefore, it was not without design that the first revelation Jesus gives us of the spirit of his mind, when he emerges from the eighteen years of obscurity spent in preparation for his life's work, is in this recognition of the superiority of John's present position, and his deference to him, expressed in the words, "Suffer it to be so now." They may be thus paraphrased without violence to the truth in outward fact or inner thought of Jesus: Suffer it to be so now. It may be true that thy work is nearly done, and mine is about to commence. Thou wilt decrease, I shall increase. Thou mayst be but my herald, my messenger going before me; but I am a Jew, thou art a prophet, teaching and baptizing the Jews. Thy work is not finished, thine office is not yet passed away. My work is not begun, I have not yet entered into my office. I recognize thee in thy official capacity, and, as one of the people—for as yet I am officially nothing more—I come to thee for baptism. Suffer it to be so—recognize thy position, magnify thy office, and baptize me.

This important lesson of the text escapes the observation of some, it is to be feared, because they do not regard that which Jesus was seeking at the hands of John as the baptism administered to the masses of the Jewish people, but an induction ceremonially into the high-priesthood. It is modestly suggested that there is no hint of any such thing in any part of the ministry of John, nor in any part of the conversation between him and Jesus. There may be some coincidences, some analogies, between the ceremonial induction into the priesthood, under the Jewish economy, and the baptism of Jesus, and the descent of the Holy Ghost upon him afterward. But these, at best, fancied resemblances should not lead us to forget that it was to John the Baptist that Jesus came. John claimed no such office as would qualify him to induct any one into the priestly office. His work was clearly defined. Jesus revealed to him no new work that was expected at his hands. That, therefore, which was asked of John was baptism—nothing more—and it must have been the baptism John had been administering to other Jews. But one may ask, What need had Jesus of John's baptism? In reply it may be asked, What need had he of circumcision? what need of any of the ritual and sacrificial service of the temple? This, however, would be trifling. It is repeating about Jesus what so many ask about themselves: What need have I of this ordinance? What good will this sacrament do me? Cannot I neglect this privilege, or pass by this unpleasant duty, without damage? O how common, and yet how strange, this error! The question is not of personal need, nor of personal benefit to be derived from any observance; but the question, all-important and fateful, is of duty. John at Jordan fell into this common error. He had cried, Prepare ye the way of the Lord, and make his paths straight. He had gathered Jerusalem and all Judea to his preaching, and had baptized multitudes, turning away, we suppose, no applicant for baptism. Now there stands before him a Jew who has been strict to observe all the requirements of the law. This Jew comes to him recognizing his official position, and asking baptism, but John answers, You do not need to be baptized of me. True, I have baptized all others who have applied, but I will not baptize you, for I need rather to be baptized of you. To which Jesus replies, It may seem strange that I should ask, and improper for you to grant me, baptism; but I am a Jew, and if it were your duty to administer it to other Jews, and it was their duty to ask it, then is it my duty to be baptized, and your duty to baptize me. It becomes us thus to fulfill all righteousness. I have been obedient in all else, and would not fail in this. This is all that remains of the religious rites made binding by God upon those who would be prepared for that kingdom which you have been declaring to be at hand. Paul, in Hebrews v., recognizes and declares this feature in the life of Christ. He says: "Christ glorified not himself to be made a high-priest. Though he were a Son, yet learned he obedience."

The baptism of Jesus by John is then an example to us—not an example of baptism, not a model of place or mode, but an example of subordination, and that strict obedience which flows from it.

Whatever the ordinance of God, we should not think ourselves exempt from its observance on any consideration. Whatever the requirement of the Church, we should comply with it, not raising the question of personal need, nor asking about expediency. It is always proper to do what Heaven requires when we can, and it becomes us to leave no duty unperformed, no privilege unenjoyed. Nothing of Church-duty was neglected by Jesus. And this last extraordinary demand upon the people of God, preparatory to the revelation of the Messiah, he wished to meet. Whether he knew that his baptism would be followed by the descent of the Holy Ghost, and the public recognition and declaration of himself by the Father, is a question with which we now have nothing to do. We know that it was no thought of this which prompted him to press his claim for baptism. He did not say to John, "If you baptize me, the Spirit will descend upon me, and the Father will reveal my true nature and work"—not that, but simply this: "Thus it becometh us to fulfill all righteousness."

Let this be to us sufficient inducement to obey all law, to use all means of grace. It becometh us thus to fulfill all righteousness. Duty is a word lost, we fear, to many; or if the word be retained, its force, and meaning, and application, are lost; else many of the excuses with which they attempt to salve wounded consciences would appear to them worse than frivolous, exceedingly sinful. Pleasure hath no rightful place in opposition to duty. Appearance hath no right to absolve from duty. Loss or gain has naught to do in the question of duty. Suppose we do not feel like doing some particular Church-work—is that work, therefore, any the less important, or any the less binding upon us? Suppose it is not pleasant—does it cease to be duty when it becomes unpleasant? Suppose it appear to be unnecessary and unprofitable, as some argue the baptism of innocent babes to be—is it, therefore, not binding upon you? Scripture and reason unite in answer: With duty made plain in statute or ordinance, or temple regulation, or extraordinarily, as was the case in John's baptism, appearance of needlessness and unprofitableness has naught to do with the decision of obedience or disobedience. How did it appear for John to baptize Jesus—baptize unto repentance one who was without sin, and his superior in every sense save official position? It matters not. Appearances, worldly questions of propriety, and human questions of profit, must give way before duty. It is John's duty to baptize, it is the people's duty to be baptized by him; and Jesus, as the Son of man, and the Son of David, stands in his lot with the people before John for baptism.

Let us not turn hurriedly away from this lesson of subordination and obedience. Here is the opening of a model life—here is the beginning of a revelation of God's ideal of a perfect man, who is to master all things, and govern all things, because he is worthy. But he can never rule others who has not learned to govern himself, and he can never know how to govern who has not been governed.

"Let every soul be subject to the higher powers," an inspired injunction, was illustrated and enforced throughout the life of Jesus. His parents complied with the law, notwithstanding the peculiarity of his conception and the wonders attending his birth, and presented him for circumcision; he was subject unto his parents; at twelve years of age he sought instruction from the teachers appointed by the Church; he strictly observed all the requirements of the law of God, and all the regulations of temple service, and he recognized John in his office, and received baptism at his hands.

Subordination in all the relations of life was thus taught by him in rendering unto Cæsar the things that were Cæsar's, and unto God the things that were God's.

The third lesson we find in the baptism of Jesus is one of encouragement.

It has already been said that questions of expediency have no rightful place in the decision to do or not to do duty. "It becometh us thus to fulfill all righteousness" will be sufficient to the true man—sufficient in the face of inexpediency or of uselessness, yea, even of impropriety, as it was with John and Jesus. But this is so not without reason. Duty may seem to be unnecessary and unprofitable, but it is not so. He that goeth forth bearing precious seed, though he may go weeping, perplexed, bewildered, and saddened by the seeming loss of time, and labor, and treasure—going forth because he is bidden to go—shall surely return; yea, come with rejoicing, bringing his sheaves with him. Duty is never inexpedient, never unnecessary, never unprofitable. A man's work may be better than he supposes it to be. This may be made stronger and fuller: every man's work, done from sense of duty, is more important than it appears to him, and far more fruitful in good results to himself and others than he imagines when he enters upon it and continues in it.

Pharaoh's daughter knew not the work she was doing when she rescued the Hebrew babe, and provided for its protection and instruction. His mother knew not the work she was doing for her people and the world when she trained Moses to fear God and obey his word. The instructors of Luther knew not the work they were doing for the enlightenment and blessing of the Church and the world. John knew not what he was doing when he baptized Jesus. His objection was based upon his Jewish hope of a Messiah who would reign an earthly king, and deliver his people from political bondage. The opening heavens, the divine voice, the words spoken, the descent of the Holy Ghost upon Jesus, were all unexpected revelations, following not successively merely, but as consequences of his obedience to duty, which had seemed unnecessary and unprofitable. Not until then did he know, and probably not otherwise could he have ever known, that Jesus is the Lamb of God which taketh away the sin of the world.

Father, mother, teacher, minister of the gospel, class-leader, steward, officer and teacher in the Sunday-school, to you may come the words, "Suffer it to be so now." What is required of you in your place may be unpleasant, or difficult, or may seem to be unnecessary to be done, or vain and fruitless in your hands. Are you in your place? Then do your work; do it despite discouragements; do it in the face of failure and defeat; do it though your reason may whisper it is useless and profitless. Fulfill all righteousness, however difficult the task or disagreeable the duty; if a subordinate, submit; if a superior, exercise authority and execute discipline. Let nothing turn you from duty. It was in discharge of duty, by fulfilling all righteousness, that Joseph passed through the hands of envious brethren, through the pit, through the prison, to the second place in Egypt, and became the blessing of the world. It was in the line of duty that the wise men of the east saw the herald-star in the midnight skies, and found the "Desire of all nations." It was in the place and performance of duty—on the plains watching their flocks—that the shepherds received the angelic announcement of the birth of

Jesus. It was Simeon, a just and devout man, waiting in the temple of his God for the consolation of Israel, who received the infant Jesus into his arms and rejoiced. To them who, from a sense of duty, left all to follow Christ, was it given to behold the goings forth of his divinity in miracle-working power. It was to them who were called to the privilege, and availed themselves of it, that Jesus showed his glory in the mount.

It was Stephen, falling and dying under a shower of stones, hurled upon him because of his allegiance to duty, who saw heaven open and Jesus sitting on the right-hand of God. It was John, banished to Patmos because of his devotion to duty, who had presented to his enraptured spirit grand apocalyptic visions. And Jesus hath formulated the whole, and made this cheering truth universal in its application: "If any man"—that brings you, reader, old or young, wise or simple, great or humble, within the circle of glory upon which we have been looking— "If any man will do his will"—is willing to do his will—"he shall know of the doctrine whether it be of God."

The revelation made to John at Jordan is not singular—his experience was not peculiar to himself. The heavens open, the Spirit descends, and God reveals Jesus to all his dutiful servants. "The secret of the Lord is with them that fear him." Within the soul of him who "fulfills all righteousness" the words of God are heard: "This is my Son." And that soul rejoices to behold the Lamb of God which taketh away the sin of the world.

XVII.

FUTURE REWARDS AND PUNISHMENTS.

BY BISHOP KAVANAUGH.

"And these shall go away into everlasting punishment, but the righteous into life eternal." Matt. xxv. 46.

Our subject presents us with the solemn and final issues of our entire race, which are made to turn upon the character acquired in a probationary relationship of the creature to the Creator—as one has expressed it, "The great day of dread decision and despair," in regard to one class; and it may be added with respect to the other class, a day when hope meets its consummation, and bliss its perfection and eternity.

This great subject is introduced and delineated in a pretty extended discourse of our Saviour, in the twenty-fourth and twenty-fifth chapters of Matthew. In the twenty-fourth chapter he describes the then coming destruction of Jerusalem in terms so strong and high as to intimate the destruction of the world. In allusion to the destruction of the temple, and of Jerusalem, the disciples had asked, "Tell us when shall these things be? and what shall be the sign of thy coming, and of the end of the world?" He answers the last of these questions, concerning the end of the world, in the twenty-fifth chapter. This he describes, 1. By the parable of

THE REV. BISHOP H. H. KAVANAUGH, D.D.,
Of the Methodist Episcopal Church, South.

the ten virgins; 2. By the parable of the talents; and, 3. Without a parable he describes the coming of the Son of man: "When the Son of man shall come in his glory, and all the holy angels with him, then shall he sit upon the throne of his glory; and before him shall be gathered all nations; and he shall separate them one from another, as a shepherd divideth his sheep from the goats; and he shall set the sheep on his right-hand, but the goats on the left. Then shall the King say unto them on his right-hand, Come, ye blessed of my Father, inherit the kingdom prepared for you from the foundation of the world." Then follow the reasons for this glorious invitation: "For I was a hungered, and ye gave me meat; I was thirsty, and ye gave me drink; I was a stranger, and ye took me in; naked, and ye clothed me; I was sick, and ye visited me; I was in prison, and ye came unto me." The modest righteous, not remembering to have seen their Saviour in all this variety of condition, shall inquire, When saw we thee thus conditioned, and ministered unto thee? "And the King shall answer, and say unto them, Verily I say unto you, Inasmuch as ye have done it unto one of the least of these my brethren, ye have done it unto me. Then shall he also say unto them on the left-hand, Depart from me, ye cursed, into everlasting fire, prepared for the devil and his angels. For I was a hungered, and ye gave me no meat; I was thirsty, and ye gave me no drink; I was a stranger, and ye took me not in; naked, and ye clothed me not. Then shall they also answer him, saying, Lord, when saw we thee a hungered, or athirst, or a stranger, or naked, or sick, or in prison, and did not minister unto thee? Then shall he answer them, saying, Verily I say unto you, Inasmuch as ye did it not to one of the least of these, ye did it not to me." Then comes the language of the text, "And these shall go away into everlasting punishment, but the righteous into life eternal."

Thus coming to the language of the text, we proceed to the discussion of the points suggested by the language it contains.

I. The characteristics of the subjects under the judgment process.

1. The points to be established by the facts of the case.—The grand point on which the decision turns is, Have you loved the King now on the judgment-seat? The evidence taken in the case are the works done by the parties. In Matt. xii. 36, 37, we read, "But I say unto you, That every idle word that men shall speak, they shall give account thereof in the day of judgment. For by thy words thou shalt be justified, and by thy words thou shalt be condemned."

The *justification* presented in this passage, and in others that will be adduced, is taken in a second sense in the work of our salvation. Where the question of *pardon* is concerned, *faith* is the only and indispensable condition of justification — as unbelief is the ground of condemnation — damnation to the unbeliever; because, while faith accepts and appropriates the great provisions of salvation in the gospel of the grace of God, *unbelief* rejects all the love, blood, suffering, and glorious, godlike work of triumphs over sin, death, and devils, and cuts off all the possibilities of salvation; for St. Paul informs us, in Heb. xi. 6, "Without faith it is impossible to please him."

The justification we now have under consideration is the evidence offered in works of the genuineness of our Christian pretensions—the reality of our faith and love. It is affirmed that faith *works* by love, and purifies the heart. On this subject James (ii. 14–18) speaks with force and point: "What doth it profit, my brethren, though a man say he hath faith, and have not works? can faith save him? If a brother or sister be naked, and destitute of daily food, and one of you say unto them, Depart in peace, be ye warmed and filled; notwithstanding ye give them not those things which are needful to the body, what doth it profit? Even so faith, if it hath not works, is dead, being alone. Yea, a man may say, Thou hast faith, and I have works: show me thy faith without thy works, and I will show thee my faith by my works." This is a forcible way of putting the question, as it is impossible to show faith without adequate evidence, and we can see faith only through works. The apostle proceeds: "But wilt thou know, O vain man, that faith without works is dead?" He then adduces, as a fine illustration, the case of Abraham in the offering of his son: "Was not Abraham our father justified by works, when he had offered Isaac his son upon the altar? Seest thou how faith wrought with his works, and by works was faith made perfect?"

14*

Abraham was justified by faith when, despite the circumstances, he believed that Isaac would be born, and that specific act of his faith was counted to him for righteousness in the sense of pardon. It is generally estimated that it was twenty-four or twenty-five years afterward when he was called upon to sacrifice Isaac as a burnt-offering on the altar. Abraham's faith was still living, and he gave a sublime illustration of it when, without hesitation or remonstrance, he proceeded to the awful work; and though the promise of God concerning the promised seed was involved, in whom the hopes of the world were placed, yet he asks no questions, suggests no incongruities, makes no pauses on the path of duty, though he thought of the covenanted seed, and appreciated the blessings for the world contained in him; for his faith, reposing in the veracity and power of God, believed that though he should burn Isaac to ashes, he would raise him up, and fully redeem all that was in that broad promise, that proposed the highest blessings for all nations, and all the families, to the end of the world. Here was splendid work, but it was faith that made it perfect—faith wrought with the work.

These quotations show the doctrine of justification before men in this life, and before God at the day of judgment, not by the *merit*, but by the *evidence*, of good works. I may add that an obedient life is evidence to ourselves. 1 John v. 2, 3: "By this we know that we love the children of God, when we love God and keep his commandments. For this is the love of God, that we keep his commandments; and his commandments are not grievous."

Then, at the day of judgment, there is nothing said about repentance, faith, pardon, regeneration, adoption, sanctification, orthodoxy, or heterodoxy, but of such conduct as shall *prove* that we love God. To love God, or not to love God, then, decides the destiny of those before the final Judge.

Since this principle of love to God holds so controlling a position in the destiny of our race, let us look into the nature and character of the principle. The Saviour says of it, as exercised toward God and man, according to the standards he specifies, that on it hang all the law and the prophets. The Apostle Paul says, " The end of the commandment is charity out of a pure heart, and of a good conscience, and of faith unfeigned." Again he says, " It worketh no ill to his neighbor; therefore love is the fulfilling of the law." Again, "Owe no man any thing, but to love one another; for he that loveth another hath fulfilled the law."

The moral quality of an act lies in the intention. Love cannot intend harm to its object, and hence it regulates all the aims of the mind. Hence, in 1 Cor. xiii. 4–8, the apostle says, " Charity suffereth long, and is kind; charity envieth not; charity vaunteth not itself, is not puffed up. Doth not behave itself unseemly, seeketh not her own, is not easily provoked, thinketh no evil; rejoiceth not in iniquity, but rejoiceth in the truth; beareth all things, believeth all things, hopeth all things, endureth all things. Charity never faileth." In another Epistle the apostle, after exhorting to the observance of some important duties, adds, "And above all these things put on charity, which is the bond of perfectness." This principle springs from God, belongs to holy angels, is imparted by the Holy Ghost to regenerated men, maintains the harmony of heaven, prompts all holy spirits to the adoration and praise of God. It is a principle of loyalty to the Sovereign of the universe, and therefore must forever be maintained. It is a principle that God must approve, and bless forever.

> This is the grace must live and sing
> When faith and hope shall cease,
> Must sound from every joyful string
> Through the sweet groves of bliss.

It is joyful to think of heaven, "where all the soul is love"—where every spirit is filled and fired with a joyful consciousness of a free and full fellowship with God, with the angels that kept their first estate, and with the spirits of just men made perfect—where God is known to be love, and where all heaven is filled with the blessings which love imparts, forever flowing from the infinitude of God. It is enough to make the adoring minds of heaven burst with the thunder of eternal praise, saying, "Alleluia! for the Lord God omnipotent reigneth!"

> Love is the fairest flower that blows,
> Its beauties never die;
> On earth among the saints it grows,
> And ripens in the sky.

So much for that great principle, the proof of having which is required at the last great day.

II. Our second point for consideration is the character and duration of the punishment and the reward proposed in the text.

The text uses the words "everlasting punishment" and "life eternal." The Greek Testament uses the same word for the duration of punishment and reward, hence the one is as long as the other.

God, by all the force of motive, has labored to prevent sin, and hence his legislation has moved upon the deepest feelings and the most enduring interests of mankind. To keep Adam in a state of blessedness and life, God gave him an Eden-home, abundantly furnished, as it is stated in Gen ii. 8, 9: "And the Lord God planted a garden eastward in Eden; and there he put the man whom he had formed. And out of the ground made the Lord God to grow every tree that is pleasant to the sight, and good for food; the tree of life also in the midst of the garden, and the tree of knowledge of good and evil." Thus furnished, and also blest with the visits and association of his infinite Maker, he had all the elements of physical and mental happiness. A holy and good God must design this happy condition. The point of danger in the man was the fact that he was made a free moral agent. He had intelligence enough to perceive his relations and feel his obligations. To enforce these obligations, his Maker gave him a positive law and a moral faculty to feel its force, and the power of the will to determine for or against his duties; and, to keep him to his obligations, he fixed a fearful penalty to the transgression of the law. The death-penalty was the greatest barrier that could be raised against allurement or temptation. To intensify the death-penalty, the Lord has called our attention to what he has set before us in Deut. xxx. 19, 20: "I call heaven and earth to record this day against you, that I have set before you life and death, blessing and cursing; therefore choose life, that both thou and thy seed may live; that thou mayest love the Lord thy God, and that thou mayest obey his voice, and that thou mayest cleave unto him; for he is thy life, and the length of thy days."

The appalling penalty of *death* and *cursing* does God interpose to keep us from sinning. And the whole book of God keeps this fearful warning before us, saying, "The soul that sinneth it shall die." "The wages of sin is death." And in the fervor of his love to us he follows us on our way to death, crying out, "As I live, saith the Lord, I have no pleasure in the death of the wicked, but that the wicked turn from his way and live. Turn ye, turn ye from your evil ways, for why will ye die, O house of Israel?"

To escape this penalty, and avoid a hell, the Universalists generally try so to interpret the language of the New Testament as to destroy the common idea entertained of hell, by criticisms on the original words which have been translated hell in our English version of the Scriptures.

I have lately read, with much satisfaction and edification, a work of Bishop S. M. Merrill, D.D., of the Methodist Episcopal Church, on "The New Testament Idea of Hell." I shall avail myself of some of his critical remarks on those Bible-terms:

The Old Testament word *Sheôl* is used with some latitude of meaning and application. It, however, always relates to the state of the dead, unless used in a metaphorical sense of something in this world; but sometimes it expresses the state of the body, and at other times of the soul. **It does not express** duration. It means, in general, the unseen world—the state of departed souls. It is not the decisive word in this discussion, **and its use will occupy** but little of our attention.

Tartarus occurs **but once** in the Scriptures, and will require **but** brief consideration. **It is** found in 2 Pet. ii. **4:** "For if **God** spared not the angels that sinned, but cast them down **to** hell [Tartarus], and delivered them into chains of darkness, to be reserved unto judgment," etc. It is the prison of the fallen angels.

Hades is a more important word. It occurs eleven times in the New Testament, and is translated "hell" ten times, and "grave" once. It **is the** Greek equivalent for the Hebrew *Sheôl*. **When a** passage is quoted in the New Testament from the Old, containing *Sheôl*, it is rendered *Hades*. There is no disagreement among scholars as to the meaning of *Hades*. Some difference **of application may** be found, but, upon the whole, **there is substantial agreement. This fact** renders our task **comparatively easy, so far as the word** is concerned. It means the unseen world, the place of departed souls, and expresses nothing as to their character or condition. It always relates to the soul in a disembodied state, and never to the body; **so that** it should never be rendered grave. There are other Greek words **that** express the receptacle of the dead body, such as are rendered grave, tomb, sepulcher, etc., but this word has no such meaning, and admits of nothing material. Hence, its true and only application is to the state of the dead between death and the resurrection. This point is to be emphasized in this treatise.

Gehenna is the next word. It occurs in the New Testament **twelve times, and with a single exception (James iii. 6,** where it is used metaphorically) it occurs in the discourse of our Lord alone. It related **to the** Jews primarily, and would only be understood by them. Here, also, there is substantial agreement among scholars. The origin and meaning of the word are not in dispute. It is composed of two Hebrew words which together mean the valley of Hinnom. This was a place in the valley south of Jerusalem, once the seat of idolatrous worship, where stood the image of Moloch, where the Canaanites, and afterward the Israelites, in their backslidden state, performed the cruel rites that distinguished the worship of that monstrous idol. King Josiah destroyed this worship, and polluted the place, so that it became the receptacle of the filth of the city. In the Old Testament it was also called *Tophet*, in allusion to the beating of drums that was kept up during the worship of Moloch. The name of this place became the synonym of all that was opposed to God, and hateful to his people, and very naturally came into use to express the Jewish idea of the punishment of the enemies of God after death. In this condition of things, and in this sense, our Saviour used *Gehenna*, with reference to the ultimate punishment of the wicked. Its use comes nearer to the meaning which the popular sentiment attached to the English word hell than does any other of the terms so translated, and yet it is a proper name—the name of a place well known—and should have been transferred, and not translated. The discussion of this word has reference not to its origin, history, or meaning, but to its application. The questions raised are as to whether the Saviour used it literally or figuratively, and whether he designed it to apply to punishment in this world or the next world.

It is certain, from the above scrutiny of these words, as made by the Bishop, that the Saviour used the term *Gehenna* in a figurative sense, applying it to future punishment; but he sums up a review of his criticism of these words in the following manner:

Here, then, is the arrangement to be observed: Sheôl is translated by *Hades;* and *Hades* being the New Testament word, we take it in the truest sense as applying to the invisible world, the state of the dead between death and the resurrection, and never to any thing beyond the resurrection. *Tartarus* is another word for the same thing, with only the difference that it is the prison of the fallen angels this side of the judgment. It is, therefore, substantially the same as *Hades*, and may be considered as a part of *Hades*. In other words, *Hades* covers the entire ground this side of the resurrection. Gehenna applies to nothing till *Hades* is past. It relates to the period beyond the resurrection and the judgment—the final state. This is the true distinction, and it is certainly plain, and easily comprehended, and quite as easily demonstrated.

This well-stated position of Bishop Merrill brings the intermediate state impressively before us, and inclines us to look after our condition during so protracted a period. Fortunately for us, it appears pretty clear that, though it may not be our final state, nor, as Christians, the best state we have in prospect, yet we think that there is a very glorious heaven, as well as a fearful state of punishment, in the intermediate state.

The Saviour called that Paradise in which he and the penitent thief were that day to meet. Paul, when taken up into the third heaven, calls the place Paradise, and, from his account of it, it is an overwhelmingly glorious place; for when he writes about it, fourteen years after its occurrence, he had not settled the question "whether he was in the body or out of the body." So intensely charmed was he by the grand disclosures of the place, both to sight and hearing, he "heard unspeakable words," and the translators make him say, "not lawful for a man to utter." The marginal reading is, "not *possible* for a man to utter;" and with the marginal reading the commentators generally concur. It was above what human language has the power of expressing. Then what a glorious destiny awaits the child of God, even in the intermediate state! In the view of this, the apostle is well sustained when he says that, "For to me to live is Christ, and to die is gain. For I am in a strait betwixt two, having a desire to depart, and to be with Christ, which is far better." Phil. i. 21, 23. And again, 2 Cor. v. 1-4: "For we know that, if our earthly house of this tabernacle were dissolved, we have a building of God, a house not made with hands, eternal in the heavens. For in this we groan, earnestly desiring to be clothed upon with our house which is from heaven; if so be that being clothed we shall not be found naked. For we that are in this tabernacle do groan, being burdened; not for that we would be unclothed, but clothed upon, that mortality might be swallowed up of life."

These declarations clearly indicate that when the earthly house—the body of man—is laid aside, the soul maintains its consciousness; and the language suggests that the soul passes into some sort of spiritual incasement, that it might be clothed upon, and not be naked. And this cluster of passages farther indicate a heavenly locality so rich in its resources as to be called "The Paradise of God." These passages conduct us to the conclusion that in the intermediate state and in the bosom of Abraham there is a large comfort.

In this intermediate state there is also a terrible amount of suffering. In the parable of the rich man and the beggar, as given in Luke xvi. 22-25, it is stated: "And it came to pass that the beggar died, and was carried by the angels into Abraham's bosom; the rich man also died, and was buried; and in hell he lifted up his eyes, being in torments, and seeth Abraham afar off, and Lazarus in his bosom. And he cried and said, Father Abraham, have mercy on me, and send Lazarus, that he may dip the tip of his finger in water, and cool my tongue; for I am tormented in this flame. But Abraham said, Son, remember that thou in thy life-time receivedst thy good things, and likewise Lazarus evil things; but now he is comforted, and thou art tormented." Here are two individuals that pass into the intermediate state, and one is *comforted*, and the other *tormented*. The comfort of Lazarus was such as Paradise could afford, which doubtless was of a very great character; and were he to describe the case, he would likely find the language of the apostle important to his task. The rich man confesses himself tormented in a flame, and begs a drop of water to cool his tongue. This suffering is aggravated by the fact that he obtains no relief, and is reminded that in his life-time he had his good things and Lazarus his evil things—he is now tormented, and Lazarus comforted. His farther information is sadly discouraging. The Saviour adds: "And beside all this, between us and you there is a great gulf fixed; so that they which would pass from hence to you cannot, neither can they pass to us that would come from thence."

This intermediate state, then, has place and condition. The condition is "comfort and punishment, or torment." The places are divided by an "impassable gulf." A poor prospect for the exchange of places. The language may be figurative or literal — in either case I think the sense is not changed.

The rich man, despairing for himself, then makes a feeling and affecting appeal to Abraham in behalf of his five brothers yet at his father's house, and says, "I pray thee therefore, father, that thou wouldest send him to my father's house; for I have five brethren; that he may testify unto them, lest they also come into this place of torment." How affecting that the lost in perdition should be entreating for those who are neglecting their opportunities! And how solemn and impressive is the answer of Abraham! "Abraham saith unto him, They have Moses and the prophets; let them hear them. And he said, Nay, father Abraham; but if one went unto them from the dead, they will repent." O let the living hear this voice from the dead, and repent! But how true it is, as Abraham affirms: "And he said unto him, If they hear not Moses and the prophets, neither will they be persuaded, though one rose from the dead."

To the doctrine of future and eternal punishment Universalists have offered various systems of escape. They have hell-redemption — no hell at all — God saving from his great mercy — his love in the exercise of his sovereignty, making every man holy and happy. If it shall appear that for their sinfulness some men or persons are finally lost, when all the methods of salvation are exhausted, or done away, then the doctrine of universal salvation is not true.

Except the doctrine of a final restoration from hell-torments, every other system of Universalism proposes the salvation of the sinner this side of the resurrection of the dead and of the final judgment. To settle the question clearly, we must follow up the sinner to the final close of the case, and see what his destiny is. Well, when the resurrection occurs, the judgment ensues, as we have already seen in the twenty-fifth chapter of Matthew. There are the sheep and the goats—the righteous and the wicked. —all nations—all that are in their graves—the just and the unjust. The decisive sentence is pronounced in strong, clear, and well-defined terms. And it is the last thing done on that fearful occasion. There is nothing else, affecting the human family, said or done to secure salvation. The solemn and fearful doom of the wicked is to a lake of fire and brimstone, prepared for the devil and his angels. Let Universalists, or any others, find a deliverance from this awful doom, which is styled the second death, and they will teach the world more than they ever learned before.

Some startled minds shrink from this awful sentence, and affirm that they cannot believe this of a good and merciful God; but they should remember that, in a wicked and persistent abuse of their free agency, they forced our merciful, loving, and gracious God, to the reluctant necessity of pronouncing this fearful doom upon them. God, in his goodness, had " wooed, blessed, and chastised them, and still they were rebels amidst the thunders of his throne." It is stated in Prov. i. 24–30: "Because I have called, and ye refused; I have stretched out my hand, and no man regarded; but ye have set at naught all my counsel, and would none of my reproof; I also will laugh at your calamity; I will mock when your fear cometh; when your fear cometh as desolation, and your destruction cometh as a whirlwind; when distress and anguish cometh upon you. Then shall they call upon me, but I will not answer; they shall seek me early, but they shall not find me; for that they hated knowledge, and did not choose the fear of the Lord; they would none of my counsel; they despised all my reproof."

Here is a stubborn fight against all the efforts of the God of goodness and love, and, never yielding, he "will laugh at your calamity, and mock when your fear cometh." All this time thou "treasurest up to thyself wrath against the day of wrath, and revelation of the righteous judgment of God, who will render to every man according to his deeds." Rom. ii. 5. Under such persistent rebellion against all these efforts to save the rebel, what could God do, as the Governor of the race, but execute the penalty of his violated law? No wonder that in the resurrection we should find such characters described in the language of the Prophet Daniel (xii. 2): "And many of them that sleep in the dust of the earth shall awake, some to everlasting life, and some to shame and everlasting contempt." Here is the resurrection, and all the time of the soul-saving process of the Universalist (except that of the hell-redemptionist) is past, and souls standing before you, risen to *shame* and everlasting *contempt*. What an awful resurrection this! To shame! Shame is one of the most unmanning passions that ever comes over the soul of a man. It recognizes a deep sense of degrading personal guilt. The person stands self-condemned, and perhaps it is the loyal angels of glory, and the spirits of just men made perfect, that pour upon this quailing spirit of guilt the contempt due to the rejecter of the salvation prepared at so great a price, and offered as a gift of God through Jesus Christ our Lord. Shame in one's self, and a burning contempt from all that is wise, and good, and pure, with the everlasting appended to it, is a fearful damnation, from which may God save the poor sinner!

In view of the awful condition of the sinner doomed to so dreadful a punishment, I have started in my mind the inquiry: "May there not be a second probation in which the sinner may return to God, receive pardon, and enter into rest?" But I know nothing in the Scriptures to authorize such a hope, or prospect. The Bible idea is, the judgment turns upon the deeds done in the body, on the testimony of the works we have performed in time; and the case is finally settled here, and on this ground. The sentence here rendered settles the case for eternity. "As the tree falls so must it lie." We are told in Rev. xxii. 10–12: "The time is at hand. He that is unjust, let him be unjust still; and he which is filthy, let him be filthy still; and he that is righteous, let him be righteous still; and he that is holy, let him be holy still. And, behold, I come quickly; and my reward is with me, to give every man according as his work shall be."

Bishop Merrill says, "Death stereotypes character; the purgatorial probation of Romanism is a myth; prayer for the dead is a cheat."

The idea of a second probation is rather discouraged by the fact that sinners with whom God has great forbearance and long-suffering grow harder, more indifferent to religion, become settled in habits of neglect, also a habit of indulgence in sin which they persuade themselves that they cannot break, and by neglect of duty on one hand, and hardening in sin on the other, they become vessels fitted to destruction; and thus may so provoke the wrath of God that he may swear in his wrath that they shall not enter into his rest.

To overcome this indisposition to obedience to God they have him to exert his almighty power to make them holy, that they may be happy. It is incongruous, in the very nature of the case, that God should make a free moral agent, and then control him as though he had no such agency. Again, if God be so disregardful of free moral agency, why did he not interpose his almighty power to prevent the occurrence of sin? To have prevented the occurrence of sin would have saved a world of woe in this world, and also the deeper sorrows of the world to come, on the part of transgressors. It would have saved himself the sacrifice of his Son—his life of humiliation, suffering, and death, to save the involved; but such a procedure would contradict every rational idea of a moral government, consisting of law, motive, persuasion, threats, and penalties—the will of the agent—rewards and punishments—praise and blame—in a word, the whole system of things that now exist, in fact, by divine arrangement.

God, having established this system of moral government, based on the freedom of man, and the righteous requisitions of his holy law, had to save us according to this system of things, or not at all. And of one thing I feel fully assured, that at the day of judgment (if never before) it will appear that God has done all that he could do, consistently with his moral government and the freedom of the human will, to save every human being; for he is "no respecter of persons." What knowledge did we need that he has not revealed? What law did we require that he has not enacted? What warning did our condition demand that he has not given? What grace did our guilt require, in order to obtain pardon and salvation, that he has not presented to us in his Son Jesus Christ? What light do we need that his word does not afford? What power do we want that his Spirit cannot bestow? Does not this provision for our every necessity show us that God cannot be blamed for the unhappy destiny of any human being?

We will conclude these remarks with some review and reflections on the results of character noticed in the text.

The characters alluded to in the expression, "these," is well defined in the context, and has

15

been noticed so far as to need only a remark or two. This final punishment is called the second death. It is a final separation from God, the fountain of all life, and the source of all blessing. And then to endure "the vengeance of eternal fire," in the "lake of fire and brimstone, where they shall be tormented, day and night, forever and ever!" It is an appalling punishment, which is announced to men as a motive to keep them out of it, and a vindication of divine justice should the sinner force him to put him in it.

The issues of a righteous life, according to the text, is "life eternal." Life, whether considered as vegetable, animal, or spiritual, is a most mysterious existence, and, with sentient beings, a thing greatly enjoyed. To have a consciousness of being, of enjoyment, of satisfaction, a realization of the thousand things that minister to our enjoyment in the present state of things; and then the higher and more extended hopes that we are allowed to cherish in regard to the future—to take in the sweep of the plans and purposes of God concerning us, which culminates in a final exemption from every disturbing element that might intermeddle with our joys! Then comes the broad benediction of our Father and God, springing from the fervor of his infinite love to his spotless child, washed in the blood of the Lamb—pure as wool—white as snow—glowing in his likeness and image, who assures us that our life is eternal. "Our inheritance is incorruptible, undefiled, and fadeth not away." He has gotten up for the good man a whole eternity of heaven, with all that can make a heaven complete, produced by infinite wisdom, power, and goodness, with all the gracious designs that the love of an infinite Being would suggest. And then we have an immortality of being to take in the boundless prospect, with no drawbacks, such as disease and death, failure of property and means, to check the eternal advancement, or curtail the boundlessness of prospect. This glorious amplitude of arrangement looks like the doing of a God who can with infinite ease accomplish it all, and in doing so gratify his fatherly feeling as well as the cravings of his own intellectual and immortal child.

Will you accept these chances of eternal well-being? Will you strive to escape the torments to which sin exposes you, and aspire to the sublime privileges to which your Father and God calls his immortal offspring?

XVIII.

CHRIST AND HIS WORK.

BY THE REV. A. A. LIPSCOMB, D.D., LL.D.,
Vanderbilt University.

"Wist ye not that I must be about my Father's business?" Luke ii. 49.

"I have finished the work which thou gavest me to do." John xvii. 4.

EACH of the four evangelists was so intent on giving his own personal view of the Lord Jesus Christ as unconsciously to make his narrative one of a fourfold biography. Our final impression of the Man Divine is not taken from what St. Matthew, St. Mark, St. Luke, or St. John, individually records, but from that unity of character in which their representations coalesce — a unity altogether independent of a set purpose on their part. The unity is complete because the individuality is perfect. These writers knew that they were inspired by the Holy Ghost; yet this inspiration, proceeding from the source of eternal wisdom, penetrated their minds deeper than they understood. So it is, indeed, with all our higher knowledge. It illuminates, and it darkens. It excites and restrains. It reveals our strength, that we may be more sensible of our weakness. Like the light of day, it ascends from the night of the east, and sinks down into the night of the west. Not strange is it, then, that these inspired evangelists were wiser than they knew. After all, the conscious man is only a fragment of the unconscious man; and it is in the latter, alike in the supernatural and the natural, that the Holy Spirit chiefly works.

Imagine such a genius as Michael Angelo conceiving the plan of the dome over St. Peter's. Sectional drawings are made and given to his workmen. Each of these workmen executes his allotted part. Ignorant of the general design, he keeps attention fixed on his special task, and performs it all the better since it alone engages his thought. The different portions are afterward brought together. Each takes its predesigned place, and when the whole has been completed, a thoughtful spectator sees how division of labor rests on division of mind, and how division of mind depends on the unity of a presiding mind, supreme over all the details. Thus it was with these evangelists. Four they were, four very unlike men, four with tastes and habits of thinking wide apart. And yet they were one. Beneath their active consciousness lay the secret unity of unconsciousness, known only to the Holy Ghost, and controlled by him in fulfillment of his purpose. Instance the two texts we propose to discuss. One-third of a century, perhaps more, lay between the times when they were written. The intervening period was violent, revolutionary, and destructive. A scattered nation, an extinct hierarchy, the ashes of Jerusalem and her temple, separated the era of St. Luke from that of St. John. Very different also were the two writers. St. Luke had the eye of a scientific observer. Keen perception and calm meditation were singularly blended in his intellect. He saw things twice—once without, then within—analyzed his impressions, estimated his facts, after poising them, by the principles they contained, and gave nothing to his pen which had not been accurately considered. On the other hand, St. John was the most instinctive of thinkers. The inner eye in him was large and lustrous. Had he not lain on the bosom of Jesus, and heard the throb of eternity in the beatings of his heart? And how else could he think save in rapt contemplation, his faculties forgetting their distinctions, and coöperating in rare oneness under the mastery of that sublime theme which was as habitual to his thoughts as breath to the lungs? Despite of this dissimilarity, St. Luke and St. John afford us a unitary view of Christ's work. Picture it to yourselves: Yonder in the temple is the little boy. A wonder he is, and yet perfectly simple, natural, appreciable, in his wonderfulness. And there in the upper chamber at Jerusalem is the mature man, some thirty-three years of age, as men reckon years. What is the uppermost idea in the boy's mind? "My Father's business." And what is the opening thought in that prayer which had been reserved as the closing grandeur of his divine ministry? "I have finished the work which thou gavest me to do." The consciousness of an infinite work is the same; the utterance in the gentle accents of the child and the firm emphasis of the man is essentially the same;

so that the circle, which had drawn its unbroken line around his native land, and inclosed in its majestic curve every possible act of beneficent service, closes its line at the point whence it started. Notice—

I. *Christ's early consciousness of his divine work.*

The story, as narrated by St. Luke with such touching simplicity, need not be repeated. Like a marvelous apparition, he is found in the temple, "sitting in the midst of the doctors, both hearing them, and asking them questions." Long afterward the people "were astonished at his doctrine," but even now "all that heard him were astonished at his understanding and answers." Our first glimpse of him is as a learner, and the impression he makes is remarkable. Observe, however, it is not in contact with the learned doctors, but in connection with his mother, that the depth of his wisdom is most apparent. Nothing that he said to the doctors is reported. Yet he could hardly have spoken any thing to them so wonderful as the words addressed to his mother. The surprise of Mary, that he should have lingered behind in the temple, contrasts strikingly enough with his half-concealed astonishment that she should not understand the reason of his conduct. Did you not know "that I must be about my Father's business?" To realize our true relation to God as our Father is always, under all circumstances, the supreme act of human intelligence; and this the holy child Jesus evinces in the reply to his earthly mother. There in that famous hall, there in the presence of priests and teachers, he will let her know gently and earnestly what his true Sonship is, and what his "business" in the world. Who taught him that? How knew he it? The order of Nature is reversed —the child teaches the mother. The order of Nature is reversed again—elderly men, life-long students, celebrated instructors, the Hillels, the Simeons, the Gamaliels, of the day, are "astonished," and the child-pupil is calm, meek, unamazed. The order of Nature reversed, did we say? Rather let us say, an expansion of Nature in that Temple of Transfiguration. Was Nature ever so natural, so beautiful, so resplendent, in the stage of childhood? Many scores of times has genius painted and sculptured childhood. Oftener still has imagination signalized its power by giving its image in poetry and prose. Fiction has delighted in its exquisite ideal. Yet here in the third Gospel is the solitary picture, once sketched, never anticipated by a precedent, never followed by an imitation.

It is worthy of the closest study. No human invention has ever been competent to create such an idea, such a form, such a scene. At an age when boyhood is fully open to all the accesses of the material universe; at an age when it is the creature of fresh and eager senses, and lives only or chiefly in the stir of the blood and the flush of sensation; at an age which, if it has thoughts of God, it catches them as soft gleams from maternal eyes, or has them throbbing in its pulses while asleep and dreaming on the maternal breast; at this age, when even the most exceptional boyhood, though favored with spiritual influence, never associates it with God as the "business" of life, we find the boy Jesus giving utterance to the sublime consciousness of a divine Sonship and a divine duty. Yet, if we recall the Annunciation of Gabriel to the Elect Virgin, and the language of Simeon and Anna, instead of startling us, it is thoroughly congruous with what we have been taught to expect. Too many wonders are here in close and bright array for any one to assume preëminence of augustness. When we look at the nightly heavens, radiant from the dim line of the horizon to the splendor of the zenith, it is the oneness of the magnificent scenery that makes the thought of God so welcome and so powerful. We see it all, and it satisfies the imagination. The wholeness is the grandeur. Precisely in this way a devout mind is affected in contemplating the life of the Lord Jesus. Childhood, youth, and mature age; sorrow and joy; silence and speech; home and homelessness; love and hatred; the friendship that honored and the betrayal that cruelly wronged him; his birth and death—what a mysterious force of affinity binds them together! A typical example of this is presented in the incident connected with the text. Had "the child Jesus tarried behind in Jerusalem?" The act is prophetic. Years hence he will have to detach himself from his mother, and the quiet associations of Nazareth, that he may reappear in that same temple, and assert its sanctity as the house of his Father. Had his mother sought him "sorrowing?" Twenty years subsequent to this occurrence she left her home "sorrowing," hastened to him after his final rupture with the Pharisees, and, on reaching the scene of his ministry, desired an interview with him. But his words were, "Who are my mother and my brethren?" Each time, yea, many a time besides, Simeon's declaration came true: "A sword shall pierce through thy own soul also." Even in the outset of his career, did not his loving and "sorrowing" mother learn the same lesson at the wedding in Cana? The place, the circumstances, the action, the words, of "the child Jesus" on the occasion in the temple were not only prophetic, but symbolic of his destiny. "I must;" "Father;" "business," or "work"—how frequently was this first utterance of his repeated!

Let us be careful, however, that we do not misunderstand this matter. "The child Jesus" was a real child—a divine child, indeed—and yet thoroughly human, and all the more so because divine. It was this sense of the human in him that spoke the great words of the text. So far from denying the motherhood of the Virgin Mary, he admits and honors it to the full, and his surprise is that his earthly mother fails to recognize his heavenly Father. Hence, the unqualified admission of his childhood as to its nature and limitations must be felt before the profound wisdom of his language can be appreciated. It is not, then, the consciousness of *a* child that speaks, but the consciousness of "*the* child Jesus." St. Luke is careful to guard this point. Mistakes here were not only possible, but very probable, as we see in the apocryphal gospels; and, therefore, the wise evangelist informs us that "Jesus increased in wisdom and stature," no distinction being allowed between his conformity to physical laws and to intellectual laws. Such a consciousness, though existing under the conditions of childhood, was entirely adequate to express the thought and feeling contained in the text. The firmament could not be reflected in the ocean unless it were pictured in a drop of dew, for the ocean is only an immense globule of water. The consciousness of Jesus as a child was perfect as the consciousness of one only twelve years of age, and accordingly just as perfect for that period of life in him as it was when he entered on his public ministry. Here in this small room a tiny lamp is burning; yonder in that hall a large lamp is blazing; the degree of illumination varies, and yet in both instances there is light sufficient. The tiny lamp does its work just as well, and answers its purpose just as completely, as the large lamp. So with Christ's consciousness as a child. Time, meditation, experience, all the various constituents of human growth, would enlarge and intensify that consciousness because they would expand and deepen his human nature. But these means of development would add nothing, and could add nothing, to the fact of the consciousness itself, nor by any accretion vary the essential quality of the consciousness peculiar to him as the Son of God. Nothing that he ever said was more like him than the words, "Wist ye not that I must be about my Father's business?" Observe—

II. *Eighteen years followed of preparation for his divine work.*

Over these years a veil of obscurity is drawn. Beyond the facts that he lived at Nazareth, was "subject" unto his parents, "increased in wisdom and stature, and in favor with God and man," wrought at the trade of a carpenter, and attended the synagogue on Sabbath, we know nothing. "Great is the mystery of godliness;" and it was fit and proper, suited to the laws of the human intellect and to the conditions of Christ's own development, that "God manifest in the flesh" should not make a sudden and premature display of his glory. On Christ's account as Son of man, on man's account as a fallen and imperfect being who must be put in a position to learn before he can be instructed, this period of solitude was ordained. Had not Christ been more than a man, it is quite probable that we should have had his continuous history. A mere teacher, exemplar, benefactor, could hardly have made his position tenable in the absence of a continuously open career. For us likewise this seclusion was necessary. We have in our souls a sense of solitude, a deep and mighty sense of isolation and loneliness, and it has to be educated by Providence and the Holy Spirit to fulfill its high purpose. To be "made like unto his brethren," Christ's biography for these eighteen years was written on his heart alone. Aside from this, who can prize the worth or realize the beauty of another's character unless there be some hiddenness? If facts teach, hints and suggestions quicken and excite; yea, they often inspire the mind's best efforts, and lead to its grandest achievements. Now, as it respects this season of Christ's obscurity, how very happily has inspiration consulted the profound needs of our mental nature! The darkness is not unrelieved. Gleams of light direct our thoughts. "Hail, holy Light, offspring of Heaven first-born, . . . bright effluence of bright essence increate!" for by it we see Jesus submitting to the terms of earthly existence, taking on himself in advance the burdens and sorrows of human kind, dignifying common toil, sanctifying the home of humble life, and illustrating in his own history the content and quiet satisfactions of an honest and cheerful poverty. Surely, among the many lessons he came to teach the world, this was not the least of those so much needed.

This period of eighteen years was a period of constant and diligent preparation for his great work. The wise thinker must precede the wise worker—this is Nature's law, and Providence sees to its stern enforcement. Experience is worth little in active life if no basis has been previously laid; and the knowledge of the world, and of the world's affairs, especially the knowledge of human nature, is piecemeal and fragmentary where one has not studied his own soul in privacy—the supreme blessing of youth and early manhood. Christ was in no haste to begin his public ministry. For thousands of years he had delayed his incarnation by waiting for "the fullness of time," and now he would repeat that same principle of his divine economy, and gather "the fullness" into his humanity before he manifested his glory. How much of the work afterward done in Jerusalem and Galilee was virtually accomplished in the retirement of Nazareth it is easy to conjecture. In every parable, in every miracle, in every discussion with wily Pharisees, every time he was tested by casuistical questions, whenever he had to confront danger and face imminent peril, he was not only beforehand with the occasion, but beforehand with himself; every nerve trained, every muscle obedient, every faculty disciplined; so that he was incapable of irritation, and of spasmodic impulse, and of sudden surprise, and never other than ready for whatever might need his sympathy or deserve his rebuke. The "fullness of time" was in all his hours, and with it the "fullness" of wisdom, love, power, and majesty.

It is with this period we connect his culture. It was self-culture in an eminent degree. Of education, in the rabbinical sense of the term, he had little or none. Likely enough he may have attended the school of the synagogue, but he was never a pupil of the rabbis. No doubt his mother taught his boyhood. One accustomed to analyze thought can easily detect the unmistakable impress of womanly mind, both in the contents of his ideas and the peculiar mode of their expression. That depth of sentiment lying beneath every principle he unfolded was due to his mother, and could not have been acquired, the natural laws of mind being assumed as dominant, except in very early life, and under circumstances of unusual impressionableness. Next to maternal influence, we trace the effect of Moses, David, and Isaiah, on his intellect. In the culture of his profound sense of law — that realization of law which is infinitely higher than mere deference to rules, and which produces habits of thinking, feeling, acting, even when apparently most spontaneous, by the secret virtue of obedience to lofty conceptions—Christ was evidently the pupil of Moses. His very heart was closely akin to the great lawgiver. Imagine with what personal emphasis he uttered the words, "Had ye believed Moses, ye would have believed me, for he wrote of me." In fact, the main controversy of his life was on the dishonor of Moses by the oral law. If he vindicated the Sabbath against superstitious observance, if he reclaimed for marriage its original sanctity, if he protected family relationships against the corban—in brief, wherever he touched the sordid, hypocritical, vindictive spirit of the ruling portion of the Pharisaic sect, it was in defense of Moses, whose seat these fanatics had usurped, and under cover of whose authority their mad zealotry was driving the nation into the abyss of ruin.

Like his ancestor David, he loved Nature, and delighted in its communion. This was a marked trait in his character. If it emerged in his intellect, and through it in his parables and discourses, it was because of its deeper hold upon his heart. He did not like cities. The freedom, the simplicity, the buoyancy of rural life, were ever welcome to him, and, like all reflective minds, he courted the companionship of the fields, the mountain, the flowering meadow, the terraced hillsides, the orchards of the olive, and the winding aisles of the graceful palms. Far more than Solomon, or any Jew of a later day, he reproduced and perfected David's mode of regarding the physical universe, looking on it as a transparency, through which the infinite glory shone in the gorgeousness of the day and the brilliancy of the night. Poetry had always found its emblems here, but the psalmist saw in these things the ordained symbols, far more expressive than figurative signs, of truths which addressed sentiments in man other than those belonging to the imagination and its distinct order of emotions. Christ carried this habit of viewing Nature, and of presenting its illustrations in parables, much beyond David. Yet David, in this, was one of his teachers. And how favorable was Nazareth for this form of self-development! The hill, rising between four and five hundred feet in the rear of the town, afforded a view of a landscape as wonderful in extent as in the diversity and interest of its objects. Toward the west, some twenty miles distant, Carmel lifted its wooded head over the white sands of the Mediterranean shore. Northward were the uplands of Galilee. Hill rose above hill, mountain over mountain, till Hermon, ten thousand feet above the sea-level, bounded the magnificent panorama with its crowning sublimity of snow. On the east, Tabor was visible, with its summit of oak and terebinth. The famous Plain of Esdraelon lay southward, and beyond it the broken surface of Samaria. Safed, "the city set upon a hill," at an elevation of nearly three thousand feet, was within reach of the eye. Great roads, extending in various directions over the country, were the highways of caravans and the busy thoroughfares of a swarming population. Greeks, Romans, Phenicians, Arabians, Samaritans, Jews, were in daily transit from point to point where trade had concentrated. Yet, with all this activity of life near by, Nazareth was sheltered within its inclosure of hills, as a cove safe from a stormy sea. Here it was, then, that Christ's human soul grew into fuller light and larger freedom under the quickenings of King David's more kingly Psalms. But, at the same time, his own consciousness gave him an insight into their meanings the royal psalmist never saw. Therein, too, he saw himself revealed as none but an inspired poet, and he a monarch, could portray him. The inmost sentiment of his nature as Son of man, which held in itself alone the keenest capacity of suffering in its relations to his family and countrymen, was found only in these Psalms; and what an infinite import the contact of his own mind gave to them!

And was he not to be a suffering Messiah; "despised and rejected of men;" to be "stricken, smitten of God, and afflicted;" to be "a man of sorrows, and acquainted with grief;" to be led "as a lamb to the slaughter;" to be "bruised" and "put to grief," and to make his "grave with the wicked and with the rich in his death?" Deeper than all else in his soul lay that instinct of sorrow, by means of which he was to render the highest obedience to law, and through it to infinite justice. Who was the prophet of this atoning grief, of its multiplied agony, of its sacrificial death, but Isaiah? Think of the prophet's large and generous views, of his glowing sympathy with the Gentiles, of his quick and tender humanity, of his indignation at wrong, of his exposure of the sins and crimes of his nation, of his sublimity, of the easy access of pathos to his patriotic heart, and you can form some conception of how Isaiah must have impressed the opening mind of Christ. Returning to Nazareth after the opening of his ministry, how natural it was that he should preach to his townsmen from the passage Isaiah lxi., and declare to them the fulfillment that day, in that synagogue, in their presence, of those memorable words uttered seven hundred years before!

Most of all, during these eighteen years, was the growth of Christ's consciousness enlarged and intensified by communion with his Father. No incitement needed he for contemplation, for prayer and praise, for the awe solemnized by grandeur, and for the holy joy kindled by the glories of infinite love. These were in him ever. Yet he was "made under the law"—the law requiring growth by experience—the law of "perfect through suffering." "Holy, harmless, and undefiled," he needed no grace to conquer sin or fortify him against evil propensities. Such a nature, however, as his was far less at home in this world than we are. The contrast between him and the condition in which he placed himself amid poverty, adverse criticism, false views of his motives and purposes, and whatsoever else was included in "the form of a servant," was infinitely greater than any contrariety we know in our existence, or can imagine. To adjust himself to the state of things about him was a constant and grievous trial—not a trial in the sense of probation, nor a trial that involved the risk of failure, but one of that higher discipline which consisted in adapting himself to the work he had undertaken. It was because he was perfect, "separate from sinners, and made higher than the heavens," that such a peculiar training of himself was required. Nor was it more necessary at any period of his life than in those years of seclusion. Impulses, natural and innocent, had to be kept in check. His goodness had to be veiled. A young villager, the sole possessor of an infinite secret, he had to be reticent. The virtues in him, superior incomparably to any religious excellence in Nazareth, could make no manifestation proper to his divinity. Instincts, high and holy instincts, had to be restrained. Too early a bloom in that Asiatic spring might have invited the frost of blight and death. Self-denial, such as only a perfect man could practice, nay, such as only the Son of man could exercise, was a constant and urgent duty. For all these varied tasks, for submission to daily toil in the workshop, for the long concealment of his self-recognition as the Son of God, what communion with his Father was needed! With whom else was the fellowship of his soul possible? Only one outlet to his pent-up heart existed—intercourse with his Father. Consider—

III. *The spirit of Christ's work.*

It was a spirit of profound reverence for law. Not only did he evince this with regard to the law of eternal right, but toward every form of law with which his position brought him in contact. John the Baptist had an insight into the holiness of Christ when, in remonstrance against baptizing him, he said, "I have need to be baptized of thee; *and comest thou to me?*" But the Lord Jesus will take his place among the multitude John is baptizing, conform to the rite of a preparatory economy, and so "fulfill all righteousness." Nothing could be as to outward aspect more remote from his baptism in the Jordan than his payment of the tax by the coin from a fish. Here as before, "suffer it to be so." The same condescension is exhibited; and while claiming immunity from the temple-tax on the ground of his divine Sonship, he instructs St. Peter to pay the demand; yet, at the instant, he works a miracle to show that, while he obeys law, he is Lord over all laws.

Sovereignty over law and submission to law are two facts that Christ never allowed to be separated in his personal history. Men must have in him a person to adore as well as an example to imitate. Disjoin the imitation from the adoration, take the former alone, admit its perfect beauty, and then tell us what is there in it peculiar as to the principle involved. To be of any avail, imitation must rest on authority. This was Christ's method, and accordingly he conjoined in his acts sovereignty and submission.

Take two illustrations. Notice his obedience to the laws of the human body. He was never sick, never an invalid, never so much exhausted that food and rest did not promptly restore his strength. Probably he was the healthiest man that ever lived.

Three years of extraordinary labor, three years of most exhaustive duties, three years during which he combined the offices of Healer, Teacher, Preacher, Benefactor, Founder and Administrator of a new economy of providence and grace, left him unimpaired, so that he came to the last night in the garden fresh and strong. Hours of the night could be spent in prayer with no loss of energy for the next day's tasks. This was due, we apprehend, to the wisdom and fidelity with which he obeyed the laws of physical manhood. Remarkable as was the care of his body, how the wonder increases when we see that he could at any moment set aside the laws of the body, vanish from a turbulent crowd, or tread the thin crests of a billowy sea! Here, as subjecting himself to physical laws in their closest connection with our nature, he permits no interest of benevolence, no pressure of sympathy, to lessen his working force. And here, in the same domain of life, he suspends those laws when occasion demands. Subject and Sovereign! In the one he will be imitated, in the other adored.

Turn from this to his obedience of the law of prudence in his public ministry. There was danger, very serious danger, that others would bring on a conflict between him and the Roman government. Friends were often injudicious. His own family tried to press him into an open and formal inauguration of his Messiahship. On the other hand, his enemies, with adroit malignity, sought to put him in an attitude of hostility to the political authority. Rome never had so turbulent a race as the Jews to govern, and in Christ's day Rome's suspicions were more easily aroused than at any previous time. Christ, at every step, was liable to be mistaken for an insurrectionist. Fortunately enough, the "*Sicarii*" had not yet been introduced from Rome, the reign of the dagger had not begun, and "blood-money," common so soon afterward, was not now known. Nevertheless, Jerusalem was in the prelude to this condition, and already the air was tremulous with the coming tempest. Under such circumstances, how acutely perplexing was Christ's position! Not a miracle could be wrought, not a parable spoken, not a kindness shown to a poor outcast, not a quotation drawn from the Jewish Scriptures, not a visit made to the temple, not a Sabbath passed in a synagogue, not a benediction pronounced on little children, not a tear shed over the grave of a friend, that was not misunderstood, perverted, turned against him. Can it surprise you that he so often imposed secrecy on the beneficiaries of his mercy, laid gratitude under the stern injunction of silence, and even sealed the lips of the apostles, his chosen witnesses? Had the glory of the transfiguration to be remanded to the night, out of whose bosom it had flashed in unwonted splendor? Why make the first clear announcement of his Messiahship to a fallen woman, and she a Samaritan? The answer to all such questions is found in the fact that Christ had to observe the utmost prudence while his work was unfinished. Men need an example like this of strict conformity to the law of prudence. The want of prudence is the next evil to the want of conscience, and it became Him who was made "under" this "law" to set us an example of the blessedness abiding in that obedience which renders it honor. But here too he is a sovereign. When the hour comes to withdraw self-protection, he resigns himself to his enemies. "I lay down my life." "No man taketh it from me, but I lay it down of myself." So that in this instance, as before, we have an exemplar to follow, and the eternal Son of God to worship.

Furthermore, the spirit of his work was the spirit of infinite love. It was not a love that grew out of tastes and imaginative emotions. It was not a love that consulted fluctuating interests and momentary gratifications. It was not a love that exists because of reciprocation, for "his own received him not." Not an element of luxury, of romance, of self-regard, such as we find so generally in human affection, belonged to it. Son of man was he, and the love was therefore tenderly human. Son of God in an exclusive sense was he, and hence the love was divine. The two natures, although perfectly distinct, were as perfectly united; and they formed one Person, who, out of his infinite fullness, the fullness that "filleth all in all," gave complete expression to the interblended attributes of humanity and divinity not only in wisdom and power, but preëminently in love. The grandeur of that love was in its self-origination, its self-inspiration, its self-direction. It knew no will but the Father's will. It desired no glory save the Father's glory. Toward man it sought his earthly welfare in harmony with providential laws, while securing his spiritual and eternal well-being in reconciliation with God and conformity to his character.

Intelligent love—how rare it is in its higher forms! Christ was wise in every act of affection. Martha and Mary, dear to him as friends, sent for him when Lazarus was ill, but he loved them too much to gratify their longing for his presence. The tenderness was postponed till it could become a miracle. *Discriminating love*—how seldom seen! Christ showed his regard for St. Peter and St. John very differently. So, too, he touched the hearts of the two publicans, Matthew and Zaccheus, in unlike ways. But in every case his sympathy assumed the expression adapted to the object. *Teaching love*, that labors to instruct the ignorant, and binds itself down to the wearisome monotony of helping the dull, the obtuse, the froward—are not men agreed that it is beautiful? Christ's immediate pupils, after three years' instruction, forsook him and fled. Were the Teacher's love and faithfulness of no avail? If the pupils failed to understand, they failed not to remember, and, in a short time, out of those memories came Christianity, destined to reproduce for myriads the words and images of the Divine Master. *Misrepresented love*—does it not find its patience sorely taxed? To have its motives impugned, its integrity slandered, its generosity vilified, its patriotism stigmatized as treachery, its philanthropy hated as Satanic—all these Christ had to bear. Despite of ingratitude, annoyance, vexation, persecution, his acts of benevolence surpassed detail; so that frequently we have no record except in language like this: "He healed many that were sick of divers diseases, and cast out many devils." Again, it was *atoning love.* If Christ's love differed from all other love in the variety and extent of its earthly offices, so that, while being human, it was human in an extraordinary degree, we must seek the cause and reason of this in something beyond the merely human. There is no foundation in our ordinary nature for such a superstructure as the Gospels present of the teachings, deeds, and self-denial of the Lord Jesus. View him as only a man, and you cannot account for his manhood. He was "meek and lowly." Meekness and lowliness are human; Christ's meekness and lowliness were human; but the meekness of his character, and the lowliness of his outward condition, as the sign of his lowly spirit, were impossible on any known laws of earthly combination. Men have been poor, but not as Christ was poor. When he gave the measure of his poverty, he did not compare it with that of Lazarus at Dives's gate: "Foxes have holes, and the birds of the air have nests, but the Son of man hath not where to lay his head." Moreover, poverty and meekness are not natural allies. Still less are they able to say, "Learn of me." Moses was the meekest of men, and he gave up Pharaoh's palace and its "pleasures," yet he never taught these virtues to the Israelites because they were traits of his personal character. On the contrary, Jesus made them fundamental to the Christian life. "Blessed are the poor in spirit," opens the beatitudes as the day opens in a low line of brightness along the horizon. Did Christ teach these qualities as matters of mere law and ethics? Nay; but as qualities personal to himself, and communicated from himself to his disciples. Most of Christ's ministry consisted in revealing his nature, character, and offices, and he left it to his apostles to preach the Christianity which was in him before it assumed form in doctrines, duties, and sacraments. And hence, we urge, that Christ's wisdom and goodness, while thoroughly human, were yet human with a spirit and in a way inexplicable by any facts of mere humanity. He was a man. He was a perfect man. Farther than this, he was the ideal man, not son of a man, but "Son of man," humanity begetting him (so to speak) in her ancient womb as the first and last product of her supreme capacity. As such, he was a man of love. But the man, the perfect man, the ideal man, was not the atoning man. The atoning Son of man was the divine man. And so here, as before, we have something to admire and imitate, but infinitely more to honor, to reverence, and to adore.

Such a love could only consummate *its self-denial in self-sacrifice.* Eighteen years at Nazareth, three years of public ministry—these were his years of self-denial. It is the self-denial which unites the two periods. Otherwise, they have no official relation, no peculiar connection, and, indeed, are contradictory. Christ's work was mainly done before entering on it publicly; and it was done by that calm, steady, and thorough-going culture which had its root, trunk, branches, foliage, fruit, in patient and persistent self-denial at Nazareth. No word describing a locality has such significance in the New Testament as Nazareth, Calvary excepted. Recall the scene in the orchard of olives on the last night. "Whom seek ye? They answered him, *Jesus of Nazareth.* Jesus saith unto them, *I am he.*" Recall the conversion of Saul of Tarsus. "Saul, Saul, why persecutest thou me? And I answered, Who art thou, Lord? And he said unto me, I am *Jesus of Nazareth*, whom thou persecutest." When he, in his public career, so often "charged them that they should tell no man" who he was, it was Nazareth and its seclusion over again. Concealment of what is lofty, elevated, glorious; concealment of majestic power, and of those attributes which endow intellect with rarest grace and loveliness, is an exceptional form of self-denial. This is what Jesus of Nazareth practiced in Capernaum and Jerusalem, and never so signally as before Caiaphas, Herod, and Pilate. Yet it was only one of the manifold forms which it assumed. Is not reputation the last thing that men, good and true men, ever think of foregoing? Christ "made himself of no reputation." The friendship, services, devotion of his friends to him, so often mixed with those infirmities which have a certain touch of beautiful weakness in them, Jesus restrained. Neither in his friends nor in himself would he be other than one who had "emptied" himself of the glory belonging to his nature. Immediate success he might have had. The thousands he healed, comforted, and cheered, might have been gathered as a retinue about him.

Little children would have flocked in his path and sung the ancient hosannas of Israel in his praise. But these were all denied. The diet of his daily life was the simplest hospitality of very plain people; and when he would work his two great miracles for the benefit of multitudes, a few loaves and fishes were all that could be commanded. Now, these things, taken in themselves, may be viewed by some as commonplace matters; but in Jesus Christ they had an infinite significance. With other men, they are the accidents, or the incidents, of human relations. With him, they were the laws of his being, inward and spiritual forces, expressions of his soul, just as words were the utterance of his thoughts, or acts of healing the manifestation of his sympathies. Yet why all this? The self-denial is unique. Nothing like it was ever seen before. What can it mean? On its own ground, and for its own sake, it cannot be justified. In its mere physical results of diseases healed, and temporal blessings bestowed, it cannot be vindicated. As an example only, the means employed are out of all proportion to the apparent end. Was the alabaster-box of a precious life to be at last rudely broken, its contents poured on the ground, and its fragrance scattered to the winds of the desert and the sea?

Thanks to God, there was no "waste!" The wondrous childhood of Jesus, the next eighteen years, the three years following, went forward in oneness of spirit and aim to their ordained consummation on the cross. Why he had humbled himself, and taken the form of a servant; why he had repeated so far as possible the original act of humiliation, and descended to circumstances of poverty, homelessness, isolation, and dependence; why he was man in such a true sense, and yet in a sense so exceptional; why he dwelt apart from the world in a loneliness experienced by no other, the solitude broken by none save the Father, but, notwithstanding, touched life at every point—this is all plain enough when we see him accept the cross, on which, "by the grace of God," he "should taste death for every man." In the immortal issues of that sacrificial altar self-denial, such as he had exhibited in manifoldness of shape, and in life-long intensity of degree, has its explanation and supreme warrant in the final act of self-sacrifice. The human was there to suffer visibly and palpably, and likewise intellectually and morally, his body nailed to the cross, his "soul an offering for sin." The Godhead was there to impart dignity and merit by its infinitude, so that the sacrifice should be as divinely glorious as it was humanly perfect. Various terms present the relations and aspects of Christ's death. Not one of them can be spared. Whether, then, it is spoken of as vicarious, expiatory, propitiatory, or in whatever images and illustrations, make sure for yourselves of this one paramount idea, that the death of the Lord Jesus Christ, Son of man, Son of God, was a death of reconciliation—the reconciliation of God to man, and of man to God. "Through the eternal Spirit" he "offered himself without spot to God." The offering was sacrificial in every thing to which the word "sacrifice" can be applied. It was perfect and entire, wanting nothing. Justice could ask no more than he rendered to its majestic claims, and the transcendent epoch in the annals of its sovereignty occurred when he died on the cross. Law had never beheld its image so mirrored in beauty, so irradiated in truth, so magnified in holiness. Grace had now free course, and its freedom was the possible freedom of Adam's enslaved race. It could institute a new scheme of Providence. Its reign was proclaimed universal. Angels were arrayed in its service, and commissioned to be "ministering spirits" to the "heirs of salvation." All things in heaven and on earth were made one. Rising with instant swiftness from sea and land, the "great cloud of witnesses" filled the ample spaces of the firmament, and beyond the darkening winds lay in their moveless folds over a redeemed world. Side by side in the administrations of love should henceforth be found the cottages "where poor men dwell," and the sainthood in "Cæsar's household;" side by side the lowly huts of sorrow and the palaces of joy and renown; side by side the dynasties of the world's worthiest and best, though here unrecognized; and the thrones, principalities, dominions of heavenly hierarchies, enriched in their first estate, and made happier by accessions of glory from the coronation splendors of Him who had returned as their Head and Lord.

Blessed be God for such a Christ! for a Christ who "learned obedience," that we might not only understand the law as transferred from "tables of stone" to his heart, but see how to obey by the light of his divine example! for a Christ whose righteousness is reckoned as ours when we believe and enter thereby into the fellowship of his sufferings and death! for a Christ whose perfection of merit covers our infirmities no less than our sins, redeems us from the insignificance and wretchedness which plunge us deeper into the abysses of evil, and completes the motives to holiness by making us "joint-heirs" with him in the glories of his kingdom! Only through him have we the true sense of sin, so much more profound and self-revealing than the superficial sense of sins. Evil has ingrained itself nowhere in our nature so thoroughly as in the capacity to believe, and hence unbelief **is the stronghold of depravity.** Christ taught the faith of the heart, and thereby secured its ascendency among the principles of human action. The heart had lost its rightful place in man. Conscience still uttered its witness, though faint, in behalf of truth and goodness; but the heart had been dethroned from its seat, its influence sacrificed to the intellect of the senses, and its authority crushed beneath the tyranny of Satan. Christ restored the heart's supremacy. Follow his footsteps day by day, and whither is he treading? Always in some pathway leading to human affection. One hour he is gaining access to a father's heart, as in the instance of the ruler (Matt. ix. 18); then to a mother's heart, as in the cases of the widow of Nain and the Syrophenician woman; again to a sister's heart, as in the example of the bereaved Martha and Mary; and oftentimes to hearts barred against society, as Levi's and Zaccheus's, or to those in whom it lay buried beneath the ashes of despair—outcasts, lepers, demoniacs—to whom gentle tones and tender acts were alien and forgotten things. In all these beneficent deeds he was seeking the soul of the sinner. Bread from heaven was in those Galilean baskets that were filled on the mountain-side when the multitudes feasted on his bounty. Bread from Galilean baskets still supplies the world. The spiritual Physician, the spiritual Benefactor and Friend, appeared in the earthly Healer and Helper. So that we never hear such words as *Behold the Philanthropist, the Humanitarian, the Reformer!* but those other and infinitely greater words, "*Behold the Lamb of God, which taketh away the sin of the world!*"

Thus it is that we are "complete in him." Late in life, St. Paul's absorbing idea was the "plenitude" in Christ, Image of the Invisible God, First-born of creation, eternal Word, only Potentate, only Mediator. Though not obscured in the earlier Epistles to the Corinthians and Romans, it is set forth in the Epistles to the Philippians and Ephesians in a manner signally resplendent. Nor is this surprising. A great river like the Amazon, as it approaches its mouth, feels the strong waves of the ocean pressing up into its channel, and mingling the mighty tide with its own waters. Overhead the sky is changed. No longer in its bosom lie the shadows of forests and mountains, but instead thereof the tranquil heavens reflect their beauty. So it was that the Apostle of the Gentiles, feeling "the powers of the world to come," expanded in the conception and realization of Christ's fullness. Natural age is a foretokening of death—Christian age a prophecy of immortality; and how much it was like "Paul the aged" to anticipate the near future in outbursts of rapture!

Such a Christ! What a dreadful mystery it is that any man should be willing to live and die unsaved by him! It is to the heaven of his presence to which his followers are exalted, but it is to the hell "prepared for the devil and his angels" that his enemies are banished. The everlasting anguish of remorse will be not merely the loss of the soul, but, greater still, the loss of Christ. "Depart from *Me!*" This, ah! this is the woe of exile!

Such a Christ! The idea of human nature, which found its first embodiment in Adam, is now perfected in the ideal revealed in him. "What lack I yet?" asked the young man. Wealth, virtue, beauty of character—these he had; but he lacked Christ. And of what avail were all his possessions? Manhood now has a value immeasurable. Its capacity to suffer and enjoy has been largely enhanced. Its destiny for good or evil has been vastly augmented. If we view this matter rightly, it is a glorious thing to be a man. Long time the one-hundredth Psalm waited the fulfillment of its joy. Only a few elect spirits entered into the meaning of the words, "It is he that hath made us, and not we ourselves. . . Enter into his gates with thanksgiving, and into his courts with praise." Long time men understood not that human nature was a ground of "thanksgiving" and "praise." Alas! many are in our midst who hear no melody in this sublime hymn of gratitude. But wherever Christ Jesus is accepted, loved, and served, there the soul rejoices in the blessedness of humanity, and looks forward exultingly to the day when it shall utter its thankfulness in the song, "Unto him that loved us, and washed us from our sins in his own blood, and hath made us kings and priests unto God and his Father, to him be glory and dominion forever and ever. Amen."

THE REV. O. P. FITZGERALD, D.D.,
Of the Pacific Conference.

XIX.
THE GREAT AWAKENING.
BY THE REV. O. P. FITZGERALD, D.D.,
Editor of the "Christian Advocate."

"And from the days of John the Baptist until now the kingdom of heaven suffereth violence, and the violent taketh it by force." Matt. xi. 12.

JOHN THE BAPTIST was the agent, under God, of the greatest religious awakening ever known. Let us consider—

I. THE CHARACTERISTIC FEATURES OF THIS AWAKENING.

The general conditions were favorable. The national mind was in a state of excited expectancy. The people were looking for the Messiah—not the meek and lowly Jesus, but a mighty prince of the line of David, who would unfurl the conquered banner of Israel, lift it aloft, and call her sons to follow it to victory.

The hour had come, and the man appeared. *In those days came John the Baptist, preaching in the wilderness of Judea, and saying, Repent ye, for the kingdom of heaven is at hand. . . . Bring forth fruits meet for repentance.* This was the stern and fiery message of the man of God. It went home to the hearts of the people, and soon was witnessed the sublime spectacle of a whole nation awakened, repenting, and seeking baptism at his hands.

The great movement went forward. John, fearing not the face of man, preached repentance and restitution to the wicked Herod, and was thrown into prison. He had done his work. No! his work was not fully done, nor his ministry ended, until he had sealed the truth with his blood. His last sermon was preached in the tyrant's palace, when his trunkless head, with glazed eyes and lips that were mute, was presented to Herod and his partner in sin, and woke a Sinai of terror in their guilty souls. John's ministry would have been incomplete without its tragic ending. I greatly misjudge him if death by martyrdom was not the very thing that suited his heroic nature. John was in every respect adapted to his work. The agent employed by God is adequate to the task in hand, whether it be to nurse a little flock in the wilderness, or to shake a kingdom. There is no provision for doubt or danger of failure in any enterprise sanctioned by the authority and backed by the power of the Highest. The minister of the gospel, fortified and inspired by this conviction, feeling assured that God has called him to do a special work, enters upon it with a serene confidence utterly inexplicable to the world. The handful of Protestant missionaries among the hundreds of millions of heathen in the vast Chinese empire are as hopeful of ultimate success as the great lights of the pulpit in the capitals of evangelical Christendom. They have the promise of God, and know that the infinite resources of the Almighty One guarantee its fulfillment. This is the hiding-place of ministerial power. They who lack this inwrought persuasion of the divine presence and help become the Jonahs that shirk, the Demases that go back, and the Judases that betray. With the divine afflatus upon him, and the word of the Lord as a fire in his bones, John neither doubted nor delayed.

The people were expectant and receptive. They were looking for the birth of some great event. This is an important fact in this connection. Almost any thing is better than apathy and dull stagnation. Where there is no expectation there shall be no achievement. The Jewish people had passed through such a phase of experience. Their religion had lost its vitality. Their national life had been crushed under the iron heel of Rome. They had sunk into the gloom of sullen despair, relieved by an occasional flicker of the dying lamp of their nationality. Their teachers and guides, the scribes and Pharisees, were corrupt, and the masses of the people were no better than their leaders. A few still read the Scriptures, studied the prophecies, maintained their faith in God, and were looking for the redemption of Israel. But a change had come over the spirit of the people—a mighty reaction. The prophecies concerning the Messiah were remembered and repeated; the patriotism of the nation, dormant under the stern and cruel repression of Roman policy, awoke to new life—and multitudes were looking for some new manifestation of the power of God. The feeling deepened, the excitement increased. With some, it was a correct understanding of the Scriptures that kindled expectation; with others, doubtless, it was simply sympathetic feeling that swept them on with the tide of popular excitement. There is in all communities a large class of persons who float with the current. Happy is it for them when, as in this instance, the current flows in the right direction! As men's sympathies so often lead them hellward, why not allow their sympathies to lead them heavenward? Every instinct and susceptibility of human nature may be made to work for, not against, the salvation of the soul. When a great movement sets the right way, move with it. Take the flood-tide. Know the day of your visitation, and make the most of it. Do not be afraid of excitement. The excitements of the world draw our loved ones from the altars of the Church into the paths of sin, and down to hell, and it requires a counteracting excitement to bring them to Jesus. There is nothing to fear from excitement if God be in it in the power of his truth and the demonstration of the Holy Ghost.

The special circumstances were favorable to the concentration of thought upon the subject of religion. It was a happy inspiration in John that led him to call the people out of the cities and towns into the country. The country is the place for concentrated and earnest thought. The voices of Nature " soothe the throbbing passions into peace," her sights charm and tranquilize the soul, and it is thus made more receptive of truth and grace. When a man begins to think earnestly, he will soon begin to feel deeply. The trouble with many is that they will not think;

they smother thought on the solemn and momentous questions of religion. The consequence is, that their lives are as purposeless and unstable as their ideas are vague. *I thought on my ways, and turned my feet unto thy testimonies*, was the testimony of a man who had sounded all the depths of religious experience. Ponder the paths of your feet. Get away from the crowded haunts of men; recover your individuality; "re-collect" yourself, as the old German divines express it. Stop and think now, lest too late you wake to thoughts of despair.

Under the mighty impulse that stirred their hearts, the people broke through all conventionalities. An earnest man was preaching the kingdom of God with strange boldness and power. Called of God, he had waited for no other credentials, but began at once to proclaim his message. Here was a new thing under the sun. Like cobwebs before a tornado, conventionalities were swept away by the breath of the Lord. Ecclesiastical and social barriers were broken through; temporizing regard for popularity and profit was laid aside. The people pressed into the kingdom of heaven; they took it by the force of an earnestness that could not be resisted. Know ye that the kingdom of heaven can be entered in no other way. But to how many are the petty conventionalities of life impassable obstacles in the way of their salvation! The traditions of family prejudice, the *dicta* of a circle of triflers, the sneer of a skeptic, or the laugh of a fool—these bar the way, and nothing but the holy violence of genuine earnestness will be able to break through them.

He that loveth mother or father, or houses or lands, more than Me, is not worthy of Me. That is to say, all family ties, all social surroundings, all temporal advantages, must be held in subordination to the claims of God and the paramount interests of the immortal soul. There is no salvation promised or possible to temporizing and compromising. All must be given up for Christ.

The people, in their earnestness, got ahead of their religious teachers. Their instructors and guides were asleep. They would neither enter the kingdom of heaven, nor permit others to enter in if they could prevent it. It was impossible for a self-seeking, conceited, ambitious hierarchy, to accept the gospel of repentance and restitution. This was substantially affirmed of them in the scorching reproach of Jesus: *How can ye believe which seek honor one of another, and seek not the honor that cometh from God only?* As much as was in their power they obstructed the way to the kingdom of heaven. So the common people had to push by them or over them—and this they did. Even the publicans and harlots pressed into the kingdom of heaven before them. This is the earnestness that succeeds. When the salvation of the soul is at stake, let nothing hinder you, let nobody get in your way. Do not wait to be coaxed, or led, or propped, or lifted by human agency. Lay hold of the hope set before you in the strength of a fixed determination, with reliance upon God, knowing that the excellency of the power that saves is his. Human agency is not to be despised or rejected. It pleases God to employ men in saving one another. But, after all, it is not by might, nor by power, but by my Spirit, saith the Lord. The honest, earnest soul will find the kingdom of heaven —to such it is always at hand.

The people, in their earnestness, did not shrink from a little discomfort. They left their pleasant city homes, and went out to hear the great preacher who used such plainness of speech, and who demanded an obedience so rigid. They did not prize their ease above their salvation. Laziness and luxury destroy their thousands. He who prefers to spend the precious hours of the holy Sabbath-day in novel-reading, or to sleep them away in luxurious unconsciousness, rather than undergo the exertion of an hour's serious thought, repels all gracious influence, and forfeits every promise made to the earnest seeker after God. He who shrinks from the penitential pain resulting from self-examination and true self-knowledge is far from the kingdom of heaven. The philosophy of the success of camp-meetings, and other special agencies of like character, may here be found. The very effort necessary to make use of such agencies detaches the people from their settled habits, lifts them out of the ruts into which they had sunk, and prepares them for new departures and better lives. Old truths are invested with a fresh interest when presented under new conditions. The crowds that hung upon the lips of John on the sacred banks of the Jordan, under the broad, blue sky, amid the capaciousness and freedom of Nature, were affected very differently from what would have been the case had the same truths been spoken amid the cramped conventionalities and traditionary routine of a synagogue in the city.

John's preaching.—That strange, wild man, with his lion heart and tongue of fire, preaching repentance and announcing the coming kingdom of heaven, touched the conscience of the nation, and there was a mighty stir in that mass of formalism, bigotry, and hypocrisy. There was a national revival of religion on that basis. There is no other basis for a real revival. The preaching that does not reach the conscience falls short of its true aim, which is the conversion of souls. Paul, Peter, and all the apostles, preached to the consciences of their hearers. The sermon that cost Stephen his life, and hastened his ascent to meet his Lord in the heavens, was such an indictment of his audience, such a searching of their evil consciences, that when they heard they were cut to the heart, and by the power of truth were brought to a moral crisis where they must yield to the messenger of God, or silence his fearless voice by murder. Our Lord himself addressed the consciences of his hearers with a directness and pungency that left no room for evasion or escape. Preaching directed to the sensibilities, the imagination, and to the logical faculty, has its place. The moral nature of man is a unit, and every part of it is moved upon by the gospel, and molded, guided, and developed, in the process of salvation. But for purposes of real awakening and conversion, the conscience must be laid hold of by that truth which is a discerner of the thoughts and intents of the heart. The will, the rudder that directs the course and destiny of the soul, never turns to God until an enlightened and awakened conscience rouses it to action. John Wesley was in respect to this truth a second John the Baptist. The great religious movement inaugurated by him was in its beginning simply an awakening of the conscience of a sleeping, backslidden people. The superficiality and feebleness of religious life in our Churches today is doubtless largely due to the fact that this feature is less prominent in our pulpits than in the days of our fathers. The humanitarian philosophy that attracts applauding crowds to the ministry of men who have the gift of genius, but not of the Holy Spirit; the salvation-made-easy methods of a class of modern teachers who reduce the whole process of the regeneration of a soul to the assent of the mind to a syllogism; the substitution of external ceremonies for the internal work, the soul-awakening and soul-subduing power of the Holy Ghost; the tendency observable in so many who are set for the defense of the faith to come down from their vantage-ground and fight the battles of the Lord with the carnal weapons employed by their adversaries—are not these the main causes of the weakness of the Church and the growing infidelity of the age? In every pulpit in the land is needed a John the Baptist to proclaim the law of God as with the thunder and flame of Sinai, that a righteous and holy God may be reënthroned in the consciences, the hearts, and the lives, of a favored but thankless and sinful people. God of our fathers, call, commission, anoint, and send forth men after thine own heart for this mighty work!

Such were the characteristics of the great revival under the ministry of John the Baptist. It was under these conditions and in this spirit that the people pressed their way into the kingdom of heaven, taking it, as the text tells us, by violence. It remains briefly to speak of—

II. THE FRUITS OF THIS AWAKENING.

An interesting inquiry presents itself: What was the blessing obtained by the subjects and beneficiaries of this great revival? It seems enough to say that the kingdom of heaven is ever the same in its essential elements—the same in its Author, the same in its principles, and essentially the same in its methods. The people pressed into the kingdom of heaven as it was then presented to them. They laid hold of the hope set before them. And it was a tangible thing to them, something they knew they possessed, and in the possession of which they rejoiced. Our Lord himself testified to this fact, saying: *He [John] was a burning and a shining light; and ye were willing for a season to rejoice in his light.* It matters not that many of them failed at the last, stumbling at the cross, rejecting the crucified Jesus. John did his appointed work. He prepared the way of the Lord. By him Peter, and James, and John, and the other disciples, were made ready for the moment when the One greater than he should say to them, Come, follow Me. The "great multitude" of Jews that believed had received the baptism, and realized their first impulse toward the kingdom of heaven, from the Forerunner, whose light was as that of the glad dawn between the star-illumined night of the law and the prophets and the full-orbed glory of the risen Sun of righteousness.

After the crucifixion, the ascension, and the Pentecost, there was a fuller development of the kingdom of heaven; but, let it be repeated, there was no essential change in its operative agencies, its principles, or its methods. The kingdom of heaven is at all times that revelation of the truth, and that manifestation of the grace, of God that satisfies the inquiring mind and the receptive heart.

We may then ask, What is the kingdom of heaven now? And we are not left in any doubt: *The kingdom of heaven is righteousness, peace, and joy, in the Holy Ghost.* (See Rom. xiv. 17.)

1. *Righteousness.*—The righteousness of the kingdom of heaven is the righteousness of pardon and of purity, of justification and regeneration. Being justified by faith, and born of the Spirit, the kingdom of heaven is set up within the believing soul. Its reception is conditioned on nothing but the faith of the heart and the obedience of the will. Blessed be God, nothing can prevent the entrance of the willing soul into this kingdom of heaven! Its door was opened wide by the hand that was nailed to the cross for sinners, and none may shut it against him who heeds the voice of Jesus saying, Come!

2. *Peace.*—Peace follows pardon. This peace is the believer's consciousness of the favor of God by the witness of the Holy Spirit. *The Spirit itself*

beareth witness with our spirit that we are the children of God. The fruit of the Spirit is peace. He who is a stranger to this peace is a stranger to the kingdom of heaven. Whoso possesses it has the secret of the Lord. Perfect trust brings perfect peace. The kingdom of heaven! The words are deep in their meaning, and carry a whole heaven of suggestion to him who knows by experience. It is the land of Beulah this side the river of death, where the sun shineth night and day, and where pilgrims may rest and rejoice safely, their King having brought them to his banqueting-house, where his banner over them is love. The kingdom of heaven! It is the blossom here of the flower whose fruit is eternal life, the possession by the believer initially of that which is to constitute the essential elements of his eternal felicity when, freed from the disabilities and limitations of earth, he shall join the glorified millions on the mount of God.

3. *Joy.*—Peace deepens into joy in the soul in which the kingdom of heaven has been set up. It is the consciousness of the love of God shed abroad in the heart by the Holy Ghost, which is given unto all true believers. It is the assurance of faith, the joy of an assured hope. We are the sons of God now, but it doth not appear what we shall be. The kingdom of heaven, which begins in grace here, shall culminate in the glory that excelleth hereafter. The sure word of promise is ours, and we rejoice in hope. We hope for that we see not except with the eye of faith, and with patience we wait for it. We can afford to wait, and rejoice while we are waiting,

for the philosophy of our faith is this: that as God is true to every blessed promise that has reference to the kingdom of heaven now, so he will also fulfill every promise that has reference to the better life to come. He gives grace now, he will give glory then.

Seek now this kingdom of heaven. Whosoever will may take it now. All things are ready. Take it by the force of an earnest purpose; take it in the strength of the Lord; take it by the exercise of a courage that defies all opposing influences, and a faith that claims what God offers so freely to give.

The "now" of the text is not an echo, but the voice of the living Jesus. The door of the kingdom of heaven was not shut when John's faithful voice was silenced, but only opened wider, that every penitent, earnest, yearning soul, may press into it, and possess its righteousness, peace, and joy, forever.

XX.

LIFE LOST AND FOUND.

BY THE REV. JOHN C. GRANBERY, D.D.,
Vanderbilt University.

"He that findeth his life shall lose it; and he that loseth his life for my sake shall find it." Matt. x. 39.

A MAN sits at night-fall in his own chamber with bowed head and troubled face. What is the matter? "I have lost a whole day," is his sad reply. No small loss is this to one who knows the value of time. It is irreparable. Where shall he search for the lost hours? The shadow goes not back upon the dial. Time is ever giving to eternity past, and never recovers. Time is ever borrowing from eternity to come, but our days are numbered, and soon they will all have been told, and not one can be added—this makes them precious.

"I have lost a day!" How shall he be consoled? But hear the cry of this despairing wretch: "My life is lost!" The lost life, neither in whole nor in part, can be restored.

Many spend life without learning its true worth. They never taste its sweetest flavor. They never use its mystic power. Life is to them like a rough gem in the hands of a rustic ignorant of its preciousness: he has it, and yet he has it not; for it is no better in his eyes than a common pebble, and it does him no service. Life is to them like a rare medicinal herb in the garden of a man who confounds it with useless weeds; he understands not its healing virtue, and is not advantaged by its possession. Life is to them like a magnetic needle to a traveler who knows not its relation to the polar star, and therefore finds in it no guidance; it is to him a dull mineral, or, at most, a pretty toy.

In an English graveyard is this epitaph: "What I kept, I lost; what I spent, I had; what I gave, I have." Confederate money furnishes a good illustration: What you kept proved an utter loss; what you spent, you enjoyed at the time; what you gave to the relief of need and the cause of Christ, you still have in the testimony of conscience, the knowledge of good done, and the blessing of God. The same principle applies to all worldly treasure, for it possesses value only during a limited period.

Who loses his life? He that findeth it, says the text. "Whosoever will save his life," we read in Mark—that is, whosoever *wills* to save it. "He that loveth his life" is John's statement of the Master's words. Who finds his life? "He that loseth his life for my sake shall find it;" "Whosoever shall lose his life for my sake and the gospel's the same shall save it;" "He that hateth his life in this world shall keep it unto life eternal." Let us study this paradox.

I. It is true of life in its literal sense.

He who supremely loves and seeks life loses this blessing. In the excess of his zeal he overshoots the mark. He is in perpetual terror lest it be lost.

17

He fears the assassin. He fears fatal accident. He fears the epidemic. Sick, he fears that he will grow worse and die. Strong, he fears that he will be stricken down by a sudden attack. He fears in the storm, on the rail, on the sea. He is ever haunted and hunted by this grim specter, Death. The uncertainty of life is to him a torment, and there is no means by which it can be assured even for an hour. The absolute certainty that it is wasting, and will in a few years be gone, is another torment; for he loves nothing except this life, and he shudders and shrinks back at the cold, dark, desolate prospect of the grave. Does he not lose his life? If his fears do not actually extinguish like a blast the vital flame, do not hurry him to the hated tomb, they do prevent the use and pleasure of life. He resembles Damocles, who sat at the sumptuous feast with a keen appetite, until his eye caught the glittering, suspended sword, and then for terror he could not taste a morsel. The undue intensity of the love of life keeps the skeleton ever present to his imagination. Neither day nor night can calm that fluttering heart. He dies a hundred deaths. He can say, but in a very different sense from Paul, "I die daily; I have the sentence of death in myself." The apostle was peaceful and confident amid the thick-flying darts of death, and in bodily weakness and pain; this man is pale with fright in health and apparent safety.

The Christian may be said to lose his life in the act of consecration. He becomes a free-will offering, a living sacrifice. He parts with life in giving it to the Lord. He is not his own; his life is the property of another. He claims not the right to control it; he seeks to please and serve not self, but Christ; he is self-devoted. He lives not, nor does he die, unto himself, but unto the Lord. To Christ, therefore, he leaves the question when and how he shall die. He takes, indeed, all proper precautions against danger; he uses all prudent means to prolong life; this he does as a faithful servant in the interest of the Master. But he would not protract life save as the Lord wills, and for his glory.

This man, my brethren, belongs to the noble army of martyrs. In the first centuries of Christianity some disciples coveted the martyr's crown. They were eager to die for the honor of the gospel. They shrank not from torture and a violent end. They longed to be wrapped in a robe of flame, that their names might be enrolled on the honorable list of martyrs, and that they might be exalted to the high rank which martyrs receive from their Lord. There was too much of self in this ambition, and it was not wise. If he wills that we tarry, why should we be in haste to depart? Christ looks upon the heart, and we have already died for his sake who are willing to die when it shall please him. It was formerly the usage that ministers on joining an Annual Conference, if willing to serve in a foreign land, should place their names on a separate list; they were not yet missionaries in fact, but they were in spirit, and might be sent to any part of the globe. So ought each of us to place his name on the roll of Christ's servants as fully consecrated, ready for any service, ready for any length of life, ready for any hour and mode of death. There is sometimes in an army a picked body, a forlorn hope, men who are willing to be sent on the most desperate enterprise, to be placed in the forefront of danger. The soldiers of the cross should not court peril for its own sake, but not one of them should refuse to encounter the severest at the command of the Captain.

The man who thus loses his life by self-surrender shall find it. God is able to bring him safely out of the thick of the battle. We forget that "unto God the Lord belong the issues" (the escapes) "from death." Life is among the promises to his servants, and an untimely death one of the threatenings against transgressors. Safety is nowhere found except beneath his sheltering wing. Abigail understood this truth. She had a strong faith which prevailed against appearances. Saul sat on the throne, and hated David with a deadly hate. David was a fugitive, hiding in wilderness and mountain. Yet Abigail said to him: "The Lord will certainly make my lord a sure house; because my lord fighteth the battles of the Lord, and evil hath not been found in thee all thy days. Yet a man is risen to pursue thee, and to seek thy soul; but the soul of my lord shall be bound in the bundle of life with the Lord thy God; and the souls of thine enemies, them shall he sling out, as out of the middle of a sling." Perhaps you are thinking that this was under the old dispensation, when the divine promises referred more to temporal blessings than under our spiritual economy. But listen to Peter as he repeats the words of the psalmist: "For he that will love life, and see good days, let him refrain his tongue from evil, and his lips that they speak no guile; let him eschew evil, and do good; let him seek peace, and pursue it." I doubt not that God ofttimes spreads his shield around his servants in the hour of danger, because they have not hesitated to risk life in his service. They are kept alive in the time of famine; they are delivered from the snare of the fowler, and from the noisome pestilence. "With long life will I satisfy him, and show him my salvation."

The consecrated man truly enjoys so much of life as it pleases God to give him. His is a charmed life. I do not say that he is not mortal, that his life is secure against disease, accident, and murder; but he wears a charm against anxiety and alarm. Fear has not a weapon in all her armory that can harm him. Death stands in his path, and brandishes a resistless dart; but he does not quit the way of duty, nor slacken his pace, nor tremble and grow pale: his strong enemy is defeated. The intensest anxiety cannot preserve life, and may cut it short; but the servant of Christ can derive from life the greatest profit, because saved from tormenting fear. Calm and confident, he makes the best use of all his hours, and commits to Providence the question how long he shall live and labor. He walks amid dangers, and fears not.

II. The paradox is true of all those blessings which make life happy and desirable. He who seeks them as his chief end suffers their loss; he who sacrifices them for Christ thereby gains them.

Even life in its narrowest sense is often lost in the

eagerness to gain the world. Men toil beyond their strength for mammon and honor, or expose themselves to voluntary danger, and meet a premature end. They are immoderate in pleasure and fashion, and their race is soon run. They live fast: the candle is soon consumed to make a bright blaze. Many men and women put themselves in an early grave by over-devotion to the world.

If they do not shorten life, they reduce the stock of earthly goods by the very means employed for their increase. Avarice, grasping after more, drops from her hands what she already held. Ambition, eager to climb some towering height, grows dizzy, heeds not the slippery rocks, and is dashed against the rocks below. Vanity, ever listening for praise, and boastful, provokes contempt and ridicule. Pride, casting away with scorn all friendly support, trips and falls, and there are none to help him to his feet again. Greed is punished by satiety; pleasure, too long pursued, produces exhaustion and *ennui;* the edge of appetite is dulled, and the choicest luxuries cannot whet it; gluttony becomes gout, and drink mania; the craving grows stronger, but the capacity of enjoyment lessens, and the worst of the wine is at the last of the feast; life indeed has lost its wine, and has become mere dregs, if not wormwood and gall.

Besides, we should take into account the retributive providence of God. World-worship and self-worship are idolatrous, and all idolatry is accursed of God. Often he breaks to pieces the idol. This may be a mercy as well as a judgment: peradventure, when the idolized object is removed, we will seek the Creator, and give him our hearts. But often men lose the world without gaining the soul. Haman thought only of self and the glory of the world; he would have poured forth the blood of the whole Jewish captivity as a libation to his wounded pride; but just Providence thwarted his revenge, and hung him on the gallows he had built for a better man—wealth, honor, family, and life, all destroyed in a day.

When the man of the world loses his portion, he is deeply grieved and disconsolate, for it is his all, and his heart was so set upon it. "He that *loveth* his life shall lose it." He is like Jacob mourning over Joseph, his favorite son. He is desperate as Micah when he cried with a loud voice after the children of Dan, who had stolen his ephod, and teraphim, and graven image, "Ye have taken away my gods which I made, and what have I more?" The gloss is worn off from life, and it appears a dull and worthless thing. The sparkle and the sharpness are vanished from the bowl, and it is henceforth flat and insipid. The remainder of his days are spent in complaining of the injustice or caprice of fortune, in grieving over riches that have flown to return no more; honors that have withered never to rebloom; youth, and health, and flow of spirits, that have given place to the depression, querulousness, and infirmities of sickness and old age; joys which like torches are consumed, and leave an uncheered gloom to deepen into the despair and horror of the grave.

The believer, in consecrating life to Christ, consecrates also whatever is accessory to life. Life, with all its incidents, he puts into the hands of the Master. Not only how long he shall live, but his lot and the mode of his service, are matters not self-elected, but surrendered to Christ, whose he is, and whom he serves. He thus loses, places out of his own choice and control, the good things of life; and in the loss he finds. He gets back what he has given up, and he gets it back with a heightened value. The true use and enjoyment of the world are possible only on condition of entire devotedness to Christ.

We must glance at the attitude of the Christian toward the good things of earth—I mean riches, honor, friendship, domestic happiness, health, and like comforts. In the strong language of the Master, he is required to forsake, and even hate, them all for his sake. But he has explained the sense in which this renunciation and hatred are to be understood. "He that loveth father or mother more than me is not worthy of me; and he that loveth son or daughter more than me is not worthy of me." The hatred is, therefore, a relative term—they are to be hated in comparison with Christ. They are not the principal thing. They are not supremely loved. They are not sought as the prime end of life. They are counted loss for the excellency of the knowledge of Christ Jesus our Lord. The disciple has virtually forsaken them in the fixed purpose to do so, rather than let them hinder him in the service of Christ, and in his willingness that they be taken away at God's pleasure. But these things are promised to the faithful servant, and therefore he does not cease to prize and desire them, if they can be enjoyed consistently with duty.

This is true of riches. "The blessing of the Lord, it maketh rich, and he addeth no sorrow with it."

It is true of esteem and friendship. "A good name is rather to be chosen than great riches, and loving favor rather than silver and gold." "When a man's ways please the Lord, he maketh even his enemies to be at peace with him."

It is true of promotion. "I will set him on high, because he hath known my name." "Length of days is in her right-hand, and in her left-hand riches and honor."

It is true of the endearments of home. "Whoso findeth a wife, findeth a good thing, and obtaineth favor of the Lord." "A prudent wife is from the Lord." "Lo, children are an heritage of the Lord." "Thy children shall be like olive-plants round about thy table."

Now these things are doubly blessed to the faithful man. They give him the greater pleasure because his heart is not set on them—because they are not his sole, nor his chief, portion. For, instead of insatiate craving, he has a thankful and contented mind; he enjoys what it pleases Providence to furnish. Instead of anxieties lest what he has be lost, he is peaceful and fearless. Every worldly possession is precarious and perishing. The apprehension of its near destruction, and the assurance that after a few years it will be no more, embitter the present use to him who loves it with supreme affection. But the Christian depends not on these things for his happiness, and can innocently enjoy them while they last without being cast down by their insecurity.

Moreover, his enjoyment is not poisoned by remorse. It is heightened by a good conscience. Whatever he possesses he has acquired in an honest and honorable manner. He puts it to a pure and proper use. He holds it in subordination to God, as a loan or trust from him. This gives to every treasure an enhanced value, and to every enjoyment a keener relish. Let us apply these general truths to certain details of life.

Take two soldiers at the close of a day of deadly struggle. Each is alive and unhurt. But one, supremely and selfishly loving life, skulked and ran: the other hated life, in comparison with duty, and seemed ready to throw it away as a vile thing; it would have been vile in his eyes if bought by cowardice and desertion of his post. Which of the twain has the happier feeling, the richer enjoyment of life and health, when the battle is over? Or take two members of the same family, when the house is visited by a fearful contagious disease: one flees for safety; the other watches day and night by the bed of the sick, not loving life so as to interfere with this task of duty and affection. One saves life by flight, the other is preserved amid dangers. Who is the happier?

See this man, who is not a money-lover, not covetous, nor penurious; he has wronged no man, defrauded no man; he has taken no short cuts to fortune by impure, crafty, harsh means; he has not withheld bread from the hungry, nor gold from the Lord's treasury. He has been diligent and prudent in business, and at the same time faithful to God, and full of good deeds; and he has prospered. Now that riches have increased, he sets not his heart on them; he knows that they are uncertain and untrustworthy; he is willing that God who gave shall take away, and meanwhile he is rich in good works, ready to distribute. Does he not enjoy wealth far more than the avaricious?

See this man who is not selfishly ambitious. He has not been a worshiper of fame, a seeker of place and praise. He has striven to serve Christ, the Church, and humanity, with a pure motive, in forgetfulness of self. But others have discovered and recognized his worth, and said, "Friend, go up higher." They have felt their need of his talents and integrity, and, like the ointment which Mary poured on the feet of Jesus, the fragrance of his virtues and charity has spread abroad; what he did with a single eye for Christ's sake has come back to him in the shape of esteem, confidence, and an enviable reputation. Modestly he wears the honors he did not seek, but does not make of them an idol —does not consider them essential to his happiness. Has he not a fuller enjoyment than the most successful aspirant after office, rank, and fame? Joseph risks every thing rather than sin against God, and God raises him to power and dignity only less than royal, and by him dispenses greater than royal bounty. Was not his a richer satisfaction than if he had gained the same height by crime?

See this man in the bosom of his own family, and among friends. He has never sought favor at the expense of duty. He does not love wife and children more than Christ. Not even to please them, not even to enjoy their dear society, would he relax principle, or neglect the service of his Lord. He loves them in the Lord. He seeks not self, but them, in his daily course; and they love him with a depth and intensity proportionate to his generous worth; and he enjoys their happiness and affection in the degree of his own pure love. But he loves and cherishes them in the spirit of consecration to the Master, and commits them, as he does himself, to the gentle care of his faithful Saviour. Is he not the happier husband, father, friend, because of this spirit? Isaac, child of love and promise, is offered and restored; but henceforth he has a higher value, he is a greater blessing, because the father had not withheld his loved son.

III. The paradox is fulfilled even in those cases in which the devotee of worldly good not only seeks but *finds* it; the finding proves to be **not profit, but loss**; and in those cases in which life and its comforts are not only risked, but *lost*, for Christ, the loss proves to be gain.

Excessive love of the world unfits for its proper use and enjoyment. The miser is a notable instance. He is possessed with a demon of avarice—an insane and insatiate greed of gold. Does he enjoy his wealth? He begrudges every penny spent on himself or his family. He hates to pay his taxes and debts. He is in the fire of torment through dread that all he has will be lost. He is never satisfied, but his hungry heart ever cries out, "Give! give!" He finds and loses at the same moment, and in the same process. Avarice may gather and hoard, but cannot enjoy; half-starved, it keeps the manna until it rots.

A like misery is the curse of inordinate ambition. The man of ambition, in seeking honor, is uneasy and fearful of failure. As soon as the summit is gained, he trembles lest he be cast down; or, in restless aspiration after something higher, he loses the joy of the triumph already achieved.

The selfish man, if vain and athirst for flattery, vexes himself when praise is withheld or faint, or by the suspicion that it is insincere; and every slight or censure is like a poisoned arrow in his sensitive soul, or like a wound in itself trifling, when the blood is bad, for it festers, and cannot be healed. The selfish man longs for esteem, confidence, and love; but if he be able, despite his unworthiness, to draw forth such sentiments, he can have little gratification, because we must love with a pure and generous heart in order to enjoy the happiness of being loved; the feeling must be mutual. The selfish man is willful, head-strong, jealous, envious; and thus he makes his own rough road to travel by day, and his own bed of thorns on which to lie down at night; for he ever provokes, or else imagines, opposition. If there be no substantial cause for jealousy,

> Trifles light as air
> Are, to the jealous, confirmations strong
> As proofs of holy writ.

And however prosperous and exalted he may be, he will find some rival of whom to be jealous, or some superior whom to envy.

Let me cite a few examples: See King Ahab in all his pride and affluence. Is he the happiest person in all the kingdom? There is many a maiden dowerless who sings merrily at her task, early and late; there is many a peasant in rented cottage who owns no foot of land, but goes forth with light heart and quiet countenance to his daily toil for humble hire; but this king is heavy and displeased, and shuts himself up in his house and chamber, and lies abed, and turns his face to the wall, and will not taste food. What has happened? He is not sick; none of his children have died; no enemy makes war against him. But Naboth, one of his subjects, has a vineyard near the palace which Ahab fancies as a garden of herbs for himself, and offers to buy it, or to give a better vineyard for it; and Naboth refuses to part with this land, which has come down from his fathers. Did not Ahab, in his coveting and willfulness, lose all benefit of his wealth and royalty?

See the first prince of Assyria, the favorite of Ahasuerus. We will look into his heart, not when the color fled his cheeks and strength his joints, and, all his pride and insolence crushed, he fell at the feet of Esther to beg his life; not when he was dragged forth to the gallows he had made for Mordecai; but when he stood proudly erect, a pillar of state bearing up the weight of an empire, when he was in the midst of his untold wealth, and many children, and peerless honors. Shall I call him a wretch? Shall I declare him more miserable than his own servants, than even the despised and downtrodden Jews? I will let him tell the tale himself. I bid you listen when, in a moment of confidence, his overcharged heart uttered itself to a council of his friends, and of Zeresh his wife: "And Haman told them of the glory of his riches, and the multitude of his children, and all the things wherein the king had promoted him, and how he had advanced him above the princes and servants of the king." Eloquent description! Fortunate man! Do they listen with real envy, through pretended sympathy? or is he too great for their envy? and are they content to catch a few drops of happiness that overflow his cup, and to shine in his favor as he shines in the light of the royal countenance? But he has not told all. His honors are not stale. The charm of novelty, the happy surprise of fresh favors, still remains. He is mounting, and his foot is well-nigh on the top-round of a subject's possible attainment. He has not one competitor. "Haman said, moreover, Yea, Esther the queen did let no man come in with the king unto the banquet that she had prepared but myself; and to-morrow am I invited unto her also with the king." Now hear the conclusion of this glowing description of Haman's glory: "Yet all this availeth me nothing, so long as I see Mordecai the Jew sitting at the king's gate." He goes, by the advice of his wife, to ask the immediate and ignominious death of Mordecai, as a sweet morsel to appease the gnawing hunger of his proud heart, that made vain and empty all, all the glory of his state.

> With light tread stole he on his evil way,
> With light tread Vengeance stole on after him.
> Unseen, she stands already dark behind him—
> But one step more—he shudders in her grasp!

Yet life was wretched, its profit and pleasure lost, before he met his doom on the gallows; no gifts of fortune could avail him aught, because he had a selfish, haughty, greedy, cruel heart.

Life is really lost when saved at the expense of conscience, honor, character—of those principles which are too precious and sacred to be bartered away for any price. Satan said, "All that a man hath will he give for his life." But life, though weighted and glittering with all earthly jewels, is a dear bargain when purchased with guilt and shame; it will prove, like the fabled apples, beautiful and inviting to the eye, but rottenness within. Macbeth listened to the "juggling fiends" who cried, "All hail! thou shalt be king hereafter," and, by the murder of his friend, guest, and king, seized the "golden round," and crowned his own brow. But what value had his crown when he exclaimed,

> I have lived long enough; my way of life
> Is fallen into the sear, the yellow leaf.
> And that which should accompany old age,
> As honor, love, obedience, troops of friends,
> I must not look to have; but, in their stead,
> Curses, not loud, but deep, mouth-honor, breath,
> Which the poor heart would fain deny, but dare not.

Herodias indulged a guilty love for Herod, or an ambition to be his wife, and she forsook her own husband, his brother. She attains what she sought—Herod's fondness, a share in his wealth, the flattery of the courtiers, all the gayeties and splendor of his position. But is she happy in this criminal course? There is one eating ulcer in her heart—an evil conscience—that keeps her uneasy with fear that Herod will cast her off; that excites a deadly, implacable rancor and hatred against John the Baptist, who rebuked the sin. She rests not until the head of the prophet is brought to her in a charger by that beautiful and graceful dancer, Salome—those lips forever silenced which had declared her shame. But does she rest now? Did her crime need an outward voice to proclaim and denounce it? Did not conscience speak within—conscience, whose lips could not be sealed by the knife of the executioner? Did the fresh sin of a good man's blood soothe her troubled breast?

Take another case—Judas Iscariot. Money was life in his estimation, for he had a covetous soul, and was a thief. He sold his Lord, and the silver coins were counted, and paid into his hands. He wins and loses—loses far more than he won. What shall he do with the money? The rust, the canker of the innocent blood upon the silver, eats into his flesh like fire. He is self-consumed by remorse. He dashes down the wages of his treachery, and hangs himself, losing at once riches and life.

To-day men live who, in the too eager craving for life, or for life's treasures and joys, have saved life when endangered, have saved property, have acquired wealth, office, rank, the brave show and glitter of the world, by fleeing from duty, by the compromise of principle, by the violation of truth, justice, honor; they have lost self-respect, and the respect of their fellows; they have offended God, and put into the hand of Conscience a scourge; life is robbed of all peace and comfort, and becomes a burden; they loved it too well, they were too hot and hasty to preserve it, and they have gained only a loss and a grievance.

Life is lost also when its opportunities for noble self-culture and useful deed slip away unimproved. Youth passes, and all its facilities for the education of the heart, for the acquisition of true wisdom and of pure and generous habits, are neglected and despised. That soul is bare and barren ground, or a wilderness of weeds, which should be a beautiful and fruitful garden unto the Lord. Manhood advances to the fullness of strength, and declines to old age; but no pains have been taken to cultivate the spiritual nature, and enjoy the hallowed delights of fellowship with God. Means are plentifully furnished by Providence for works of piety and usefulness—the whole world, from his own doors to the most savage wilds, calls aloud for help; but he heeds not the call; he squanders the hours and all his resources in idleness, intemperance, extravagance, or selfish pursuits. At length life's limit is reached, and he looks back with vain and bitter regret, saying, "My life is lost, lost, lost. It has been a long one. I had many advantages to make it happy, exalted, and beneficent. Some may call it fortunate. I have had my pleasures, friendships, success. But what profit is there in it all? I have thrown away my soul. I have not used my privileges. I have not finished the work which God gave me to do. Life has not been adorned with good deeds; and when I sleep, no holy influence shall survive my body to bless the world. Nothing of solid and permanent worth has been accomplished. The very blessings of life have drawn away my mind from its real purpose, its highest aims. I have found only to lose."

He who not only surrenders, but actually loses, in Christ's cause the good things of this world, finds life in a nobler sense, and is far more than compensated. In the language of our Lord, he receives a hundred-fold now in this time. For the true life, my brethren, does not consist in, does not depend on, the outward, capricious condition—on the measure of riches, reputation, and honor—not even on the health of the body—not even on the lives of our household. The true life is of the soul, of the conscience, of the higher and immortal affections, of spiritual desires and capacities. This is the life of God in us, our life in God, our life hidden with Christ in God. "To me to live is Christ."

O my brethren, never is the question so inappropriate, never is the reproof so unjust, "Wherefore all this waste?" as when Avarice asks it in reference to the service and costly gifts poured forth freely for Christ's sake!

You have taken precious time away from your

business, and spent it in doing Christ's work, looking after his poor and afflicted brethren, or studying and toiling for the advancement of his kingdom. Is it time lost? Are you not rewarded in the approval of conscience, in the knowledge of usefulness, in the testimony of Christ's love, in the expansion and refinement of your own nature?

You have given money to the cause of God, or refused money because of a scruple of conscience. I do not promise that it will be returned in silver and gold; but is it lost? It will come back, and with a manifold increase, in the luxury of doing good, in the peace of a good conscience, in the thought that you have testified your love to Christ, in the spirit of unselfish benevolence you have cherished.

You have left for a season family and home, and gone on a wearisome journey for the sake of Christ and souls. But were you not repaid in the assurance of his presence and smile? Though your household lacked your care, and perhaps you could not hear for weeks how they fared, and could not have hasted to their side if they had fallen ill, yet was there not a profounder peace, a better security, in intrusting them to the Master you served?

Health, reputation, friendship, may be sacrificed for Jesus; but a joy infinitely sweeter and deeper is derived from the loss, because his love exceeds them all. Whatever we give up in his name is restored in patience, resignation, fortitude, courage, faith, hope, charity, a closer clinging to Christ, a stronger conviction of the value and substantial truth of eternal things.

IV. That life is lost which makes no preparation for the endless hereafter; and though life be actually lost for the sake of the gospel, it is kept unto eternal life.

How will you think of it, friend, on your dying-bed? I grant you a long and prosperous career on earth; but it is finished. I grant you great riches here; but you have not laid up any treasure above. I grant you the honor which comes from men; but no crown of fadeless glory awaits you yonder. I grant you a merry and joyous lot; but you anticipate no delight in the eternal future. Every arrow in the quiver is spent. Each day was a diamond of greater value than all the crown-jewels of earth; but the store is exhausted—these gems have dropped into the bottomless sea of the past. The oil of life's lamp is consumed, and its bowl is shattered. What remains? Too late to think of that now. Hope, that would have allured you to a better land, and thrown upon the future a radiance more intense by contrast with the deepening darkness of life's close, has left you, reluctant to leave, but slighted, scorned, driven away—has left you, never to return—has left you, and will not hear, however loud you call; and eternity has for you no promise, no light, no treasure. You will be flung, a miserable wreck, upon the coasts of the eternal hereafter, when you might have entered with swoln sails the haven of heavenly happiness.

The believer, in dying, does not lose, but finds, life. He loses the wants, pains, infirmities, sorrows, of life; he gains rest, joy, honor, plenty. He puts off the mortal; he puts on immortality. He dies as the grub dies into the butterfly; as the seed dies into the beautiful flower, and the grain into the fruitful stalk; as the night dies into the day, and the winter into the quickening spring; as faith dies into sight, and hope into full fruition. He now finds all that he ever lost for Christ. The moth-and-rust-eaten riches he gave up are here in the form of incorruptible treasures. The honors, withering as the grass of the field, which he forsook, are here in the form of a crown of imperishable glory. The friendships he sacrificed rather than violate duty, which might have been a solace and support a few years below, are here in the form of the family of God, never to be parted. The labors he performed for Christ are here in their testimony in his favor, and in the reward his Lord bestows. The hours spent for Christ come trooping to bear record to his fidelity and useful deeds, and Jesus will not fail to say, "Well done!"

The life he lost for Christ's sake is here, but, it must be confessed, can scarcely be recognized as the same. We have never witnessed rejuvenescence, but we may imagine the reverse of the change by which a young man grows old; yet this will not suffice to illustrate the change from a mortal to an immortal life. We have seen the weak and wasted invalid who could not move a limb, or speak a word, raised to health and strength again; but this cannot compare with dropping corruption and being clothed with incorruption. The transfiguration of our Lord may represent it to us. Our life here shall be transfigured, glorified—the same, yet how different! The same—for if we have not the true life of God and heaven in us now, we cannot enjoy it hereafter: there must be the germ, the principle, of love and holiness; yet different, for the decrepitude, the soil, the dullness, the burden, the sorrows, the temptations, of life shall have forever vanished, and the soul be disencumbered, enlarged, invigorated, exalted, glorified.

> Here would we end our quest:
> Alone are found in Thee
> The life of perfect love, the rest
> Of immortality.

THE END.

www.ingramcontent.com/pod-product-compliance
Lightning Source LLC
Chambersburg PA
CBHW020541300426
44111CB00008B/751